Seattle Public Sculptors

Seattle Public Sculptors

Twelve Makers of Monuments,
Memorials and Statuary,
1909–1962

Fred F. Poyner IV

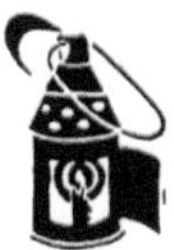

McFarland & Company, Inc., Publishers
Jefferson, North Carolina

Library of Congress Cataloguing-in-Publication Data

Names: Poyner, Fred F., IV, 1969–
Title: Seattle public sculptors : twelve makers of monuments, memorials
    and statuary, 1909–1962 / Fred F. Poyner IV.
Description: Jefferson, North Carolina : McFarland & Company, Inc.,
    Publishers, 2017. | Includes bibliographical references and index.
Identifiers: LCCN 2017014030 | ISBN 9781476666501 (softcover :
    acid free paper) ∞
Subjects: LCSH: Sculptors—Washington (State)—Seattle—Biography. |
    Public sculpture—Washington (State)—Seattle. | Seattle (Wash.)—
    Biography.
Classification: LCC NB235.S43 P69 2017 | DDC 730.92/2797772—dc23
LC record available at https://lccn.loc.gov/2017014030

British Library cataloguing data are available

ISBN (print) 978-1-4766-6650-1
ISBN (ebook) 978-1-4766-2866-0

Front cover: *top* Chief Seattle, at Fifth Avenue and Denny Way, 1936
(Seattle Municipal Archives); *bottom* clay model for the World War I
memorial statue, 1922 (Webster & Stevens, Photographers. Museum
of History & Industry, Seattle); sculptors' tools © 2017 iStock

———

Printed in the United States of America

McFarland & Company, Inc., Publishers
    Box 611, Jefferson, North Carolina 28640
        www.mcfarlandpub.com

For Annie and Gavin

Table of Contents

Acknowledgments

Several primary sources provided invaluable insights for this book. I would like to give special thanks to Miro FitzGerald, daughter of James FitzGerald, Nina Ward, daughter of the sculptor Alice Robertson Carr (de Creeft), and William Carr for sharing their family histories and photographs. Equally helpful were David Plummer's research on the life and work of his nephew, John Carl Ely, and the information collected by Mary Henry and Olaf Kvamme from Margaret Guilford-Kardell, Finn Frolich's niece.

My appreciation also goes to Alan Stein at HistoryLink for his help with identifying specific buildings on the UW campus that predated the Olmsted Plan for the A-Y-P Exposition of 1909 as background for Lorado Taft's monumental George Washington statue. Alan's book, co-authored with Paula Becker, is by far the authority publication on the history of the Exposition. Nicolette Bromberg at the University of Washington Libraries Special Collections provided assistance with reviewing many of the original Exposition blueprints produced by the architects Howard & Galloway.

Both Dr. Christine Leander's work on the August Werner statue design of Leif Erikson and the files from the Port of Seattle detailing the relocation of the statue in partnership with the Leif Erikson International Foundation complimented expansive archival materials about the sculptor held by Pacific Lutheran University, the University of Washington and the Nordic Heritage Museum in Seattle. My appreciation goes out as well to both Mari-Ann Kind Jackson and Katherine Beck for their insights into the life of August Werner.

Jon Frembling at the Amon Carter Museum of American Art deserves special thanks for his patience with my endless queries to him about sculptor casting orders documented in the partial records of the Roman Bronze Works foundry's archive (some destroyed in a fire at the Works in 1921), and to Jack Conklin, who provided both insight into the statue and copies of original lecture notes from Thomas Newman, the son of sculptor Allen Newman.

The following individuals and institutions have my appreciation for assistance with access to their manuscript and photography collections: Cara Setsu Bertram and Katherine Nichols at the University Archives, University of Illinois at Urbana–Champaign; Anne Frantilla, Julie Irick and Julie Kerssen at the Seattle Municipal Archives; Ann Ferguson and Joe Bopp, Seattle Public Library; Carolyn Marr and Kathleen Knies, Museum of History & Industry (MOHAI); Eileen Price and Ashley Mead at the Washington State Historical Society in Tacoma; Synthia Santos, Lewis Army Museum; John Hennes, Queen Anne High School Alumni Association; Benjamin Levy and Judy Sourakli at the Henry Art Gallery; Ken House, National Archives in Seattle; and Natalie Russell at the Huntington Library in San Marino, California.

I would offer acknowledgment to several individuals for their contributions made during the research process: art historian Peter Hassrick concerning Frederick Remington; curator Gwen Whiting, for her feedback on August Werner and Alice Robertson Carr (de Creeft); Chris Dysart, for his photography efforts; Paul Dorpat, for his photograph of the John McGraw statue; David Towne, for his personal recollections about the Harding memorial; and Craig Holstein, for his assistance with the history of the Lake Washington Floating Bridge.

Also, my best wishes to Marie McCaffrey at HistoryLink, for her friendship and advocacy as a fellow historian and moral support offered during the writing process.

Finally, I would thank my family for their patience, love and support during the countless hours I have spent on this historical account of Seattle's public sculptures, the origins of these artworks and the people who made them possible.

Introduction

At the dawn of the twentieth century, Seattle was transformed into a vital metropolis of the West Coast, primed by the discovery of gold in the far north, new transportation infrastructure, expanded commerce by land and sea, and a wealth of natural resources such as timber, coal and fish. The city was a terminus for many people who came out west, some to seek their fortunes in the goldfields of Alaska, others to begin anew with the promise of starting mercantile businesses or applying trade skills in the mills, foundries, shipyards, or a hundred other occupations in demand.

Artists and their families had also come to the Pacific Northwest. Some were drawn by the prospect of teaching fine arts at the University of Washington, an institution whose time had arrived in many respects to support such a curriculum. Others had arrived years before, and earned distinction as "Territorial Pioneers" predating Washington's admission into the Union in 1889. Yet others came to Seattle via longer routes and from cities already steeped in the arts: New York, Chicago, Paris and Rome. Of these men and women arose a distinct group that offered the city and its citizenry a multi-faceted gift.

For the first time in over a half century of its existence, the city was ready for its first public sculpture. These first statues, monuments, plaques and reliefs together heralded the start of another major event in the city's history, with the coming of the Alaska-Yukon-Pacific Exposition of 1909 at the new campus of the University of Washington.

The work accomplished by these sculptors during Seattle's "Golden Age" of public sculpture (1905–1915) was primarily to preserve history through figurative portraits of famous individuals—most regional, others national or even international—while helping to embody the positive characteristics and traits of these figures, their lives and accomplishments, into a visible medium for all to see.

These sculptors were primarily American in nationality, although not exclusively so; and in any case, the majority was either trained in European art academies or had a global perspective where their profession of sculpture was concerned. Realism in anatomy and detail were the rule, tempered with elements symbolic, allegorical or inspired by classical models from antiquity. Added to this mix were a wide variety of influences unique to each sculptor, ranging from identity derived from Nordic ideals, to passion for Northwest Native American culture and its legacy of regional art.

A second period or "Silver Age" of public sculpture is observed during the 1920s to 1945 in Seattle. Themes specific to war, memorials to the dead, reconciliation with the fallen on both sides of a conflict predominate the public sculpture added to the city's landscape during this time period. In a few cases, we see the first hints of something different—something distinctly *modern*—begin to emerge from the sculptors' works. This book, however, has chosen to focus on statues and other public sculpture inspired and driven to form by historical figures, and their sculptors' vision to this end.

Regional prosperity flourished with the end of World War II and the rise of the aerospace industry from the ashes. Also out of these ashes emerged another sculptor, one whose sculpture was inspired by the water and woods of the Pacific Northwest. His coming heralded a new vision of what public sculpture could be for a city.

The 1950s heralded other changes underway in Seattle and its public sculpture. Chief among these was the idea that the development of public spaces with new community centers, facilities, parks and fountains could serve as memorials and tributes, rather than seeing these take form as statuary and monuments dedicated to lone individuals or memorable historical events. As this shift in thinking about what could constitute a public sculpture took hold in the public's collective consciousness, existing monuments were reexamined in a new light. Some were relegated to out-of-the-way corners of the city. Others were eventually buried entirely.

In 1962, Seattle again restructured its public landscape for the common good, with a plea towards the future. The World's Fair or Century 21 Exposition remodeled the lower Queen Anne neighborhood into a civic center with the Armory Building of 1939 at its core. This "second coming" of an international Exposition to the city marked the continuation of Seattle's re-investment of community space for the common good, while serving as a platform for debate over the addition of new sculptures proposed and the value of these as significant (or not) to the city.

Twelve sculptors in all are examined. A multitude of sculpture works are as well, though finite in scope and background as to how each came to bear a place in the public eye.

1

Lorado Taft (1860–1936)

Amongst the sculptors who contributed public sculptures to Seattle in the 20th century, Lorado Taft has the distinction of being the first to produce a lasting monument for the city. The subject was no less than the namesake of the state: a statue of George Washington for the University of Washington campus.

For Taft, the opportunity to bring a new monumental statue to Seattle began four years prior to the Alaska-Yukon-Pacific (A-Y-P) Exposition, as the result of an effort conceived by a local civic-minded community group in 1905. The commission that followed marked the beginning of a "Golden Age" of public sculpture that resulted in a wealth of new historical portrait busts, statues, reliefs, medallions and plaques spread throughout the city. In this regard, Taft was the first sculptor of this era to make such a lasting contribution.

This initial effort to bring a new statue to the city had some of the same hallmarks shared by later public sculpture projects done by other sculptors for Seattle. The subjects selected for representation were historical figures of national or local prominence and importance. Sculptures were monumental in scale and incorporated water elements that promoted or enhanced their appearance as far as public fixtures (such as the melding of the artwork as part of a fountain). These works were either planned for display as part of an official event (the A-Y-P Exposition) or the sculptor had some association or professional involvement with the Exposition's organizers. Lastly, financial support of these public sculptures was achieved through the leadership of civic groups, state and city funding, public donations, or some combination of the three sources.

Unlike other sculptors such as James Wehn (a local Seattle sculptor), Finn Frolich and Max Nielsen (who both came out to Seattle to work on the A-Y-P Exposition of 1909), Taft was not from Seattle nor did he ever relocate to the city. His studio was in Chicago, and the sculptor was notable for having achieved a great deal of success in life by the time the Seattle commission came his way.

In the case of Taft's statue, the impetus for this work originated with the Rainier Chapter of the Daughters of the American Revolution (D.A.R.) of Seattle. The idea was first discussed amongst the chapter group members at their meeting held on March 27, 1905, led by Mrs. Eliza Ferry Leary.

Just a week later, the group met again and held a business meeting at the home of Mrs. Julia Hardenbergh, with further discussion centered on "the proposed erection of a full length statue of George Washington for the University grounds ... [to be] unveiled by the local chapter, February 22, 1906."[1]

The chapter's vision of having such a statue ready for unveiling in less than a year was ambitious, to say the least. Over the next few months, the group enlisted the aid of Professor Edmond S. Meany, who was an advocate of public statuary of a historical nature and well-known to the D.A.R. as an authority on the history of the Pacific Northwest.

Meany had already been instrumental in the development of the new campus for the University of Washington. His input into the planning for the campus contributed to the University Board of Regents' enlistment of the Olmsted Brothers as the landscape architects hired in 1903 to prepare a new design for a general campus plan. Meany was soon named secretary of the newly formed committee for the statue project. It was a wise move on the part of the D.A.R. members and brought the vision of a George Washington statue one step closer to reality.

A month after the initial D.A.R. planning meeting, Meany made the public announcement that the statue committee was not yet ready to receive prospective designs for consideration. The experienced historian well understood the challenges of public projects, and offered a more realistic timeframe going forward while encapsulating the need for excellence in such an undertaking:

> The work when completed must be one of the finest statues of Washington in existence. Haste is not at all necessary. In order to make sure of the best method of selecting a sculptor and then of passing on his designs, or of conducting a competition, if that plan should be adopted, the committee is now corresponding with the best-known sculptors of the world.[2]

Good to his word, Meany began corresponding with the top sculptors of his day. In all, six were consulted: Augustus Saint-Gaudens, Daniel Chester French, Frederick MacMonnies, Karl T. Bitter, William Ordway Partridge, and Lorado Taft. Throughout the spring and summer months of 1905, Meany sought advice and insights from these renown artisans on a prospective sculpture of the nation's first president. Should the sculptor for the project be chosen by a national competition? What terms would attract the best talent? And what would be the cost of such a sculpture, especially considering factors such as bronze casting and display of the work? Meany closed his first letter to Taft with a final question: "how is your own time and inclination for such an undertaking?"[3]

On the issue of cost, the Rainier Chapter members had already arrived at an initial estimate of $30,000 for a monumental statue and granite pedestal for the display. As the chairman of the statue committee, Ferry Leary led the chapter's efforts in the difficult challenge of raising money to pay for the project. The group made appeals both statewide and on the national level to solicit funds from other members, with the assertion "a statue on the shores of Puget Sound will prove a continual reminder that this Republic, from ocean to ocean, loves to honor the chief patriot of the revolution."[4] Despite the heartfelt language, few members outside of Seattle responded to the call for assistance.

Meanwhile, the correspondence between Meany and Taft had become an intimate exchange where the George Washington statue was concerned. The sculptor had been invited by the University lecture bureau to come to the University in the fall as a guest speaker on the subject of sculpture. The timing for Taft's visit in October was perfect as far as the George Washington statue. Here was a sculptor, coming to the University with his tools and modeling clay, ready to offer a personal demonstration in modeling technique. Taft undoubtedly saw the opportunity his visit presented and thus seized the moment.

By October 1905, Taft was well on his way to securing the commission for the new statue. Meany's opinion in such matters counted for much, and his impression of Taft as an experienced sculptor carried significant weight with the Rainier Chapter members. To this end, Meany arranged for a luncheon to be held at one of the member's homes with the sculptor.

Taft gave his first University lecture on November 1, 1905, to an assembled audience that same evening at Christiansen's Arcade Hall on campus titled "The Work of a Sculptor." In his remarks, the sculptor expressed a vision of growth in the arts across the nation, and that the West in particular "has in it the making of many artists, the natural surroundings being conductive to such productions."[5]

The visit proved to be a productive one for Taft. Earlier that same day, he met with Eliza Ferry Leary, Meany and other members of the statue committee at a reception hosted by the University President, Dr. Thomas Kane and his wife. To the assembled group, the sculptor laid out his conceptual plan for a statue in detail. It would be fine in quality, large in scale, and would portray Washington in his historical role as a colonial general. Furthermore, Taft envisioned the statue fourteen feet tall and mounted high on a pedestal (twenty feet) with the figure "probably on horseback."[6] He confirmed that the medium for the final version of the artwork would be cast in bronze, with a revised estimated cost of $25,000 to complete. This estimate included a granite pedestal, which Taft suggested could be easily provided by Pond and Pond, an architectural firm based in his home city of Chicago.

The sculptor had even picked out a site on the University's campus for the placement of the statue. Accompanied by Meany, Kane, Ferry Leary, and three other members of the statue committee, Taft led the group to the spot where he recommended the Washington figure should be placed. His selected location was a prominent one and took into account the layout of several existing University buildings as seen in the oval-style plan developed for the campus in 1898 by A.H. Fuller. Near the top, northern edge of the campus central oval roadway was Lewis Hall, constructed in 1896 as a men's dormitory. Taft envisioned his statue one hundred yards in front of Lewis Hall, on a line between Lewis Hall and Denny Hall, which had served as the University's administration building since 1895. On the subject of statue placement, the sculptor was deliberate: "You do not want your statue of Washington to be an accident … it must not be easily passed by…. I believe the site suggested will prove to be an ideal location…"[7]

Compelling as he was as a sculptor, Taft departed the city without a clear mandate from the D.A.R. as the sculptor selected for the Washington statue. Instead, as way of further demonstration of his knowledge and skill, Taft left with a promise to send the statue committee a conceptual design so that they could judge for themselves if he was a suitable choice for the commission.

The formality of submitting a design was likely one of necessary assurance on the sculptor's part, in order to finally gain the full confidence of the D.A.R. sponsors. The correspondence between Taft and Meany beginning in 1905 proved that a close association had developed between the two men, with a shared interest in seeing the project come to fruition as well as a mutual respect for their respective professions. Taft replied favorably to Meany on April 9, 1906, expressing his willingness to enter into a nationwide competition with a design of Washington that promised to be rich in details both figurative and symbolic. With Meany's support, Taft needed only to present his model for the Washington statue for review.

In addition to his earlier visit to the University as a recognized authority on the subject of sculpture and his professional connection to Meany as an advisor, Taft had several other attributes that made him stand out as the preferred choice for the George Washington statue commission. While not on the West Coast, his Midway Studios in Chicago did offer well established connections with stone masons, architects and foundries that all specialized in pedestals, monument design, and bronze casting, respectively. At this time, Seattle offered few options for the first two needs; and none in the way of foundries that were equipped for fine art casting work by sculptors, local or otherwise. Taft's studio also boasted a space large enough to accommodate the modeling and plaster casting of several monumental, large-scale sculpture groups and statuary at any given time, as well as a number of assistants who could work on commissions in progress.

Taft's reputation as a sculptor was already well established by the time he was approached by Meany. At the age of twenty, he had traveled to Paris where he studied sculpture for five years, with three years of this time spent at the École nationale supérieure des Beaux-Arts. His subsequent return to the Chicago, Illinois, in 1886 coincided with his first hands-on commission when he assisted a Belgian sculptor to repair a series of sculpture casts for the art gallery at the University of Illinois.

He was equally accomplished in the academic and writing fields. His return to the states marked the start of a teaching career in sculpture at the Art Institute of Chicago, a position he would hold until 1929. Only two years before discussion began about the Washington statue for the University of Washington campus, Taft had successfully published his *The History of American Sculpture*, acknowledged today as the first authoritarian treatise on the subject released in America.

The sculptor notably achieved national recognition in sculpture with three medals earned in American expositions: a Designers' Medal at the Chicago Exposition of 1893; a Silver Medal at the Buffalo Exposition of 1901; and a Gold Medal at the St. Louis Exposition of 1904.

More to the nature of the figure requested by the D.A.R., Taft was accomplished as a sculptor at representing historical personages of the nation in a neoclassical, yet uniquely American sculptural style. In this regard, he was not very different from other sculptors who were originally contacted by Meany with August Saint-Gaudens (along with Taft) counted chief among these. Taft held to the ideal that public sculpture could perpetuate American history and ideals symbolically, through statues, fountains and memorials made by a new generation of American sculptors.

By 1905, Taft had already modeled public statuary for two major commissions in the United States. The first of these was the LaFayette fountain sculpture in marble, placed at the Tippecanoe County Courthouse in Lafayette, Indiana (1887); the second commission was for a bronze statue of Vice-President Schuyler Colfax, Jr., placed at University Park in Indianapolis, Indiana (1887).

In October 1906, Taft mailed a watercolor sketch to Professor Meany and the other D.A.R. statue committee members that showed his first designs for both the George Washington statue and its pedestal. These were judged acceptable by Meany and the other members of the statue commission, although some members expressed doubts about the need for an elaborate pedestal such as the one envisioned by Taft. It foreshadowed a controversy over the statue's placement that would last for years.

On November 22, 1906, Meany sent official word to Taft that he was selected as the project's sculptor. In his letter, Meany stressed that the decision had been affected by Taft's willingness (at Meany's earlier request) to reduce his studio fees by $2,500 for the cost of the statue alone, which lowered its total price to $10,500.

The first public photograph of the clay maquette appeared on the front page of the February 25, 1907, edition of the *Seattle Daily Times* along with promise of a full-scale version to come in 1909:

> With hands crossed on the hilt of the sword that led the way to victory for the Revolutionary army he looks across a country greater than ever seemed possible to those sturdy men whom he gathered around him in the dark hours of the winter before his triumph over Cornwallis at Yorktown. Clad in the simple uniform he wore, the folds of his heavy cloak reaching almost to the ground ... the head bare, the face in thoughtful repose, the whole impression of the model is one of majestic and forceful dignity that shows the sculptor has thoroughly mastered his subject.[8]

From the design Taft had submitted for consideration, the figure of Washington was clearly presented as a victor, hero of the American people, and military General in posture, dress and physicality that captured both the personae of the man and his portrait. The sculptor titled the statue *The Universal Washington* and defined the figure's pose as one "looking into the future of this great section of country."[9] An alternate title for the statue—*Alloway Washington*—had also been attributed by the sculptor as a reference to part of an ode by Charles R. Alloway in honor of the first President. The sculptor was struck by the words "his bruised arms he thought were hung up through all Eternity ... he thought now to live a life of real serenity" and took from this passage inspiration to create his preliminary sketch of the Washington statue.[10]

Following the D.A.R. statue committee's acceptance of the design, the sculptor next created an enlarged plaster cast model. Pleased with the effort, Taft briefly displayed the model as part of a group exhibition held by the Chicago Society of Artists at the Art Institute of Chicago in 1909, where he taught coursework on the subject of sculpture.

While Taft worked in his studio to complete the models, a major development was shaping the future of the city and the University with the idea of an exposition to promote the cultural, historical and economic ties of the Pacific region with the Alaska and Yukon Territories. This Alaska-Yukon-Pacific Exposition had grown from a concept advocated by local citizens, into a new plan put forward by the Olmsted Brothers to transform the University of Washington grounds with new buildings, exhibitions and landscaping.

Meany himself was at the center of the A-Y-P planning, and indeed, spent the first two months of 1907 traveling around the country to meet with representatives of the eastern states to garner financial support and participation in the Exposition. It was during this same trip that he visited Taft in the sculptor's Chicago studio to see firsthand the statue model done in clay.

The A-Y-P Exposition changed everything for the statue committee in Seattle, which had been working to secure funding for the project for the past two years without much success. Now the group decided that in order to raise funds it would enlist the support of schoolchildren from across the state. The effort was scheduled to begin on February 22, in observance of George Washington's Birthday with participation pledged initially only by the Spokane school district east of the Cascades. The Seattle School Board at first objected to the collections, citing a rule prohibiting collections made within city schools.

Schools in King County eventually were allowed to make contributions with individual amounts ranging from one to five cents per child. As a result, by February 1909, the D.A.R. managed to raise approximately $5,500 to put towards the statue project. But it was still not enough.

The solution to the statue's funding problem was found in the A-Y-P Exposition. Great progress had already been made in 1907 for the Exposition, so the addition of the statue was a natural fit as part of the larger scale plan to transform the University of Washington.

On May 17, 1907, the Exposition plan that had been commissioned the previous year was submitted by the Olmsted Brothers and approved by the University of Washington's Board of Regents. The plan was unique in that it incorporated designs for buildings and walkways that would be retained, after the exposition closed in October 1909. Not only was this a practical approach to saving many of the architectural elements as part of the future campus, it also helped to persuade the 1907 State Legislature to fund the Exposition effort to the tune of $1 million. Of this sum, "$600,000 would fund construction of three permanent buildings ... an auditorium (Meany Hall) ... a facility for chemistry and pharmacy laboratories (Architecture Hall) ... and a College of Engineering Building."[11] The funds for the State's appropriation were raised from the sale of Lake Washington and Lake Union shore lands over the next two years.

Lacking funds to complete the statue project, the D.A.R.'s statue committee petitioned the State Legislature for financial assistance. Previous, unsuccessful efforts to solicit public funds had highlighted that this would be the first statue of Washington "erected west of the Mississippi ... the intention is to unveil it during the Alaska-Yukon-Pacific Exposition."[12]

The new effort with the Legislature proved successful. The Session of 1909 approved House Concurrent Resolution No. 9, which authorized an appropriation of $14,500 to aid the Daughters on the project. The State's support was further made with the understanding that the statue would be used for display during the A-Y-P Exposition period and subsequently become the property of the University of Washington. The statue committee had requested that the appropriation also be used to cover the cost of the statue's pedestal, but owing to the "condition of the University grounds" a site for the permanent placement of the statue was not chosen, so only $8,010 was spent to cast the statue into bronze and pay Taft for his work.[13]

In the Olmsted campus plan map published on November 5, 1906, no specific statue of George Washington was identified on the University grounds. Instead, it presented a band stand as a primary attraction on Alaska Avenue, just inside the main exposition entrance gate. In the final plan map of 1909 approved by the Exposition's supervising architects, Howard & Galloway, the George Washington statue was identified as "number 66" on the grounds map and shown placed in the center of Puget Plaza as a greeting to visitors entering from the main entrance that fronted Fifteenth Avenue and East 40th Street.

Gone was Taft's earlier idea to have the statue placed in front of Lewis Hall, along with the notion of presenting Washington on horseback. These would prove to be minor adaptations for the project, compared to the latter ramifications of the pedestal not being funded.

The official photographer for the A-Y-P Exposition, Frank Nowell, captured the installation of the bronze statue shortly before the official opening of the Exposition on June 1, 1909. The Nowell photograph shows the statue hoisted by an array of ropes wrapped around the figure to lift it into place. A worker is shown standing on top of the pedestal, both hands placed on the front of Washington's chest to help position the statue as it was raised by a wooden derrick. The statue was placed in the center of Puget Plaza and faced towards the west, corresponding to its location on the A-Y-P Exposition map.

While the pedestal based upon Taft's original design was provided to the statue committee, the one on which the statue now rested was constructed of wood, not granite. Also, in the weeks leading up to the start of the Exposition, tests using wood frame and cloth scale models of both the fourteen-foot statue and a pedestal twenty-four feet in height had graphically demonstrated that at the combined overall height, the statue would not be fully visible from outside the main entrance's archway to the Exposition grounds. Based on the height study, both Dawson, the on-site representative of the Olmsted Brothers, and the supervising architects required the pedestal be reduced in size to just ten feet tall.

On June 14, 1909 (Flag Day), Taft's monumental statue of George Washington in bronze was unveiled to the public.[14] The statue itself was impressive, measuring fourteen feet

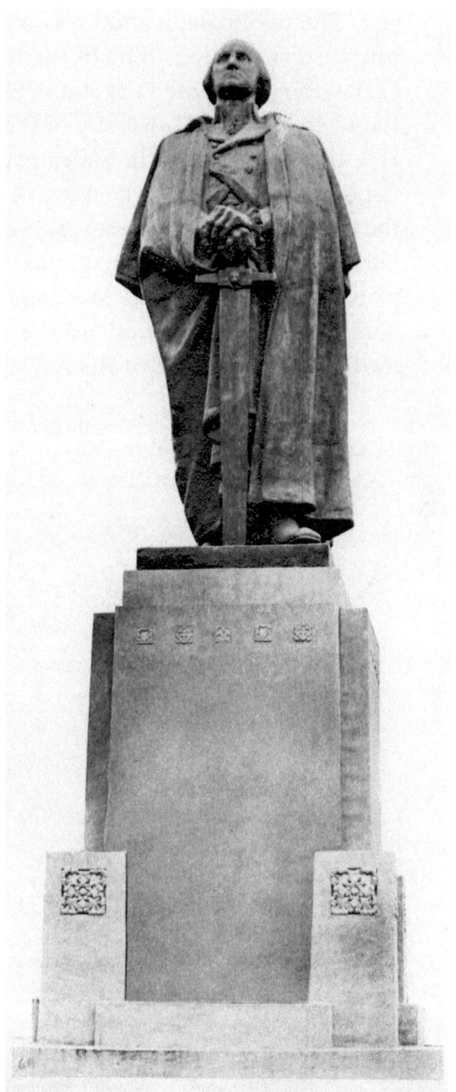

George Washington by Lorado Taft. **1909. Undated photograph. Seattle Public Library.**

in height and five feet across at the base. It was dramatically covered with a large American flag for the unveiling (a common practice used for the dedication of many Seattle statues that later followed). As a final complimentary detail, a small drinking fountain was installed in front of the statue at the west end of the Puget Plaza square.

The public dedication was met with much fanfare. Edmond Meany provided an oration, "Life of Washington," to the assembled crowd. Eliza Ferry Leary presented the statue for the D.A.R., while Dr. Kane accepted it on behalf of the University of Washington. Acting Governor Marion E. Hay also accepted for the State of Washington. J.W. Slayden from the State Legislature and George Dickson of the Washington State Commission for the Exposition also joined in taking credit for the statue. The D.A.R. members hosted a reception that followed to celebrate, inside the newly completed Washington State Women's Building on the Exposition grounds. Taft, however, did not attend the dedication, nor did he visit the statue during the public run of the A-Y-P Exposition.

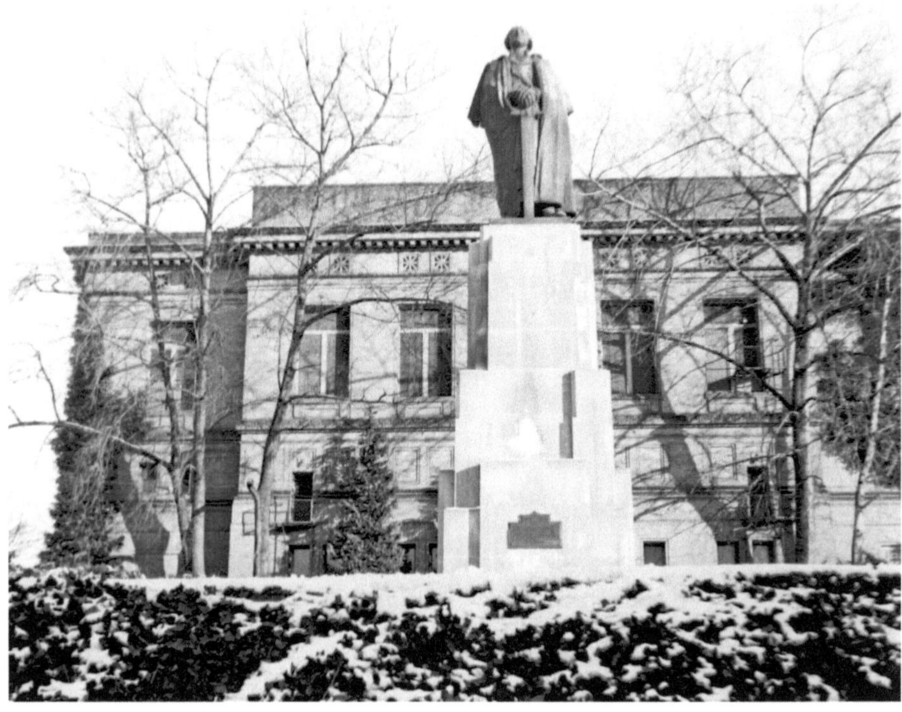

George Washington by Lorado Taft, in foreground of Meany Hall, University of Washington. Undated photograph. Seattle Public Library.

The sculptor's final version of the George Washington figure had differed very little from his earlier clay and plaster models. One minor change was that the folds in the drapery of Washington's cloak were more pronounced in the final bronze cast produced at the American Art Bronze Foundry Company in Chicago and then shipped by rapid freight to Seattle, where it arrived just days in advance of the Exposition's opening date on June 1, 1909.

In September 1909, Meany's office coordinated the final payment of $7,500 still owed to Taft for the statue's successful completion. A "state warrant" was issued to the sculptor similar to those that had been paid out to fund other Exposition expenses, but the sculptor had trouble cashing it in back in Chicago. Distressed by the financial run-around Taft had experienced with the warrant, Meany soon saw to it that it was cashed by a local Seattle bank and the funds delivered to the sculptor in Illinois.

During the next four and a half months that the A-Y-P Exposition was open, the George Washington statue greeted a total of 3,740,551 visitors.[15] While the Exposition's conclusion on October 16, 1909, marked the end of the grand event, the statue continued to endure as a lasting legacy on the UW campus.

Unfortunately, the decision to hold off on acquiring the permanent pedestal that Taft had recommended as far back as 1905 remained an ongoing point of contention between the sculptor and the University. The wooden pedestal made for its display during the Exposition (envisioned as a temporary measure) remained in place after the Exposition concluded. A plea sent to University of Washington president Henry Suzzallo from the D.A.R.'s original Rainier Chapter for a new pedestal went unheeded. Meany wrote several times to Taft in 1920, extolling the ongoing efforts by the Architecture Department and Administration to find (and fund) a suitable solution by way of a new pedestal design. Substitutions of other, less costly materials for granite were considered and rejected. New attempts made by the D.A.R. to raise funds from the public to pay for a new base likewise were fruitless.

By September 1920, the wooden pedestal had deteriorated to a point where it was no longer a sound support. The statue was removed from its unsound mooring and kept in the same spot it had occupied during the Exposition, sans its elevated status. Taft was not pleased.

Years later, sculptor James Wehn recalled Taft's poor reaction to seeing his Washington statue "in the mud."[16] Nor was there a solution offered by the University anytime soon, to remedy the situation of the statue's public presentation. When Taft visited the University of Washington on March 16, 1920, as a guest of Phi Beta Kappa, he gave two public talks on the beautification of American cities with new sculpture. His remarks given at Meany Hall stressed that Americans were "fed up with cathedrals" and wanted to create their own artistic style for new public artworks across the country, with much of this sentiment driven by American service-men—doughboys—recently returned from the European battlefields of World War I.[17]

The subject of Taft's talks was a bit ironic, given that the George Washington statue was now displayed in a manner not originally intended by the sculptor. The effect was magnified by the statue also having retained such prominent visibility near the main campus entrance. In an attempt to spur some action towards a new pedestal, Taft forwarded a new ink drawing made by Pond & Pond of Chicago to Meany's office that showed an elevated central platform for the statue decorated with an elaborate series of interlocking vertical panels and corner medallions.

When the sculptor returned to Seattle two years later in 1922, the statue's position and low-level display was unchanged. For the next twelve years, Taft "always felt like staying away from Seattle" owing to the lack of respect shown for his work and the great leader it represented.[18]

As with many of the University's dealings with the public on topics of history, it was Professor Meany who led efforts to remedy the need for a new pedestal for the Washington statue. But progress was still slow nonetheless. The first attempt at a solution did not occur until 1930, when the University had the statue re-installed onto a new concrete base meas-uring ten feet square. Not only did the base still lack sufficient height to elevate the statue, it also was deemed too small. The figure's feet comprised the widest part of the statue, which measured five feet across by three-and-a-half feet deep.

Meany publicly decried the new base, citing the feet as appearing disproportionate in size to the new display and the concrete stand as "not adequate."[19] In the year that followed, the professor continued his efforts to secure a new pedestal with the support of University of Washington president M. Lyle Spencer. On December 23, 1931, the pair approved a revised version of Taft's original design for a new, limestone faced base that now measured twenty-eight feet in overall height. The plan for the new display of the statue also called for its being repositioned on the cam-pus, between Meany Hall and the University library.

As had been the case with the original plan for the statue from 1905 to 1909, funding continued to be the major obstacle to seeing the pedestal design to completion. But a secondary issue of where the statue should be permanently located on campus also continued to complicate and further delay University planning for an improved display.

By 1934, the question of placement for the statue appeared to be resolved, at least to Taft's satisfaction. He returned to Seattle and checked into the Olympic Hotel on November 14, 1934, to give a public lecture later that same evening at Meany Hall. With the help of Charles Saunders, the UW Board of Regents had recently approved a plan to relocate the George Washington statue from its present site to the campus north entrance at 17th Avenue Northeast.

The funding challenge was finally resolved a year later, when the UW secured support from the Works Progress Administration (W.P.A.) in the amount of $21,182 to have the new pedestal constructed and installed. The University contributed another $3,123 to pay for new landscaping around the statue. In October, Taft answered in reply to the news he received from R.W. Lahr at the W.P.A. that the funding was finally in place:

> It is indeed good news that you send me. I had begun to think that the promises made last fall were a benevolent "confidence-game" intended to make me feel happy while visiting in Seattle. Now I know better. I thank you! I am very grateful to you for your efforts in behalf of my "much discussed" statue of Washington. I hope it will look better on the pedestal designed for it...[20]

Taft returned by invitation from the Seattle Art Museum in the winter of 1935 to again offer a lecture on "Sculpture of the Italian Renaissance" at Meany Hall.

While the funds were awarded by the W.P.A. in 1935, it took another three years to see the new pedestal constructed and Taft's statue of Washington finally raised twenty-four feet above the ground. In the ongoing saga of where best to place the statue, it was determined that the final location of the statue needed to be changed yet again. On August 9, 1938, the statue was soft-wrapped in blankets and moved by a car-mounted hoist just one block north to a new spot near the west campus entrance where it was raised onto its newly constructed sandstone pedestal.[21] In the following year, the State of Washington celebrated its Golden Jubilee of fifty years as a state with W.P.A. projects that included the George Washington statue commemorated in a promotional poster.

While the statue had regained its elevated status as a signature monument for the University of Washington campus and indeed, the city of Seattle, the final outcome proved to be a sad irony for the sculptor. Taft did not live to see the final re-installation of his lone public sculpture made for the city. He died on October 30, 1936, in Chicago, almost three years before the statue was rededicated on February 22, 1939, by the state's W.P.A. administrator, Don G. Abel.

Since February 22, 1910, the D.A.R. had an annual practice of placing bouquets of flowers at the base of the statue to commemorate the birth of George Washington. This observance was held for many years afterwards, with the D.A.R. further donating a plaque for the pedestal's base in 1984. While the plaque noted the original Rainier Chapter of the D.A.R. as the sponsor of the statue and its placement as part of the A-Y-P Exposition of 1909, Meany was given special recognition for securing Taft as the sculptor. It also remains as a reminder of Meany's role in the advocacy, design or installation of nearly every other public sculpture that originated with the A-Y-P Exposition.

With the exception of a short period from 1969 to 1970, when the University was undergoing a construction period and the pedestal was again replaced, *The Universal Washington* has remained on prominent

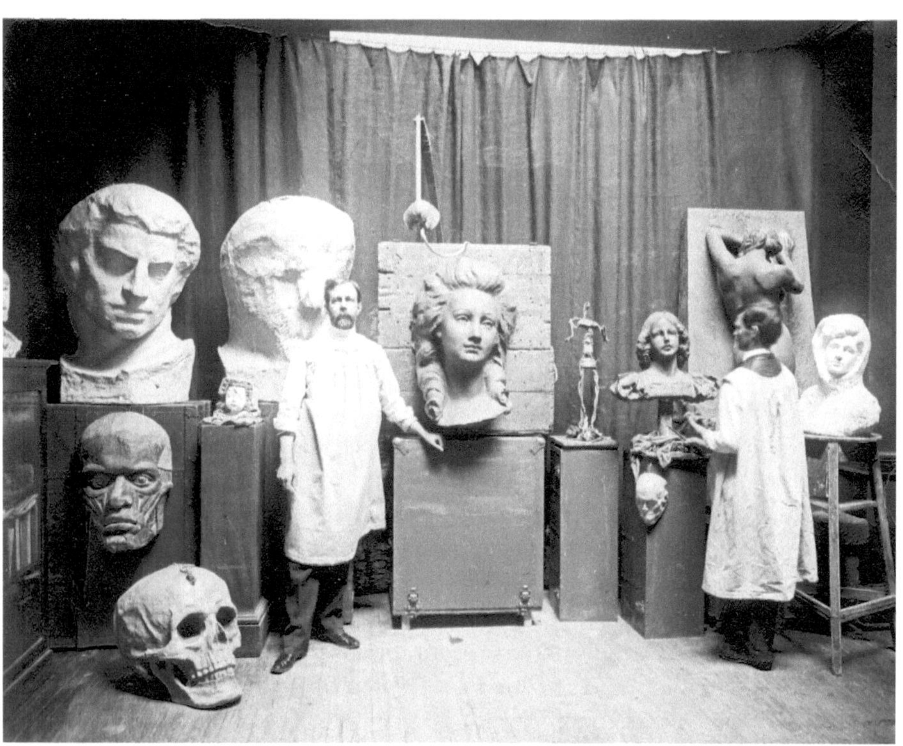

Taft in studio, Chicago. **Photograph ca. 1910. Courtesy University of Illinois Archives.**

display as the first public sculpture created for the University of Washington.

Taft's legacy as the first sculptor to contribute a public statue to Seattle is just one of many such artworks he created over his long career for cities across the United States. These other works have included a second statue of Washington as the central figure of a sculpture group for Chicago's Heald Square begun the final year of his life. The monument was later completed by Leonard Crunelle, Nellie Walker and Fred Torrey.

Yet the importance of the monumental George Washington statue, as both a historical monument from the A-Y-P Exposition and as a representational portrait, bears a unique meaning for the citizens of Seattle and the state. That Taft was able to accomplish his original design in a period of four years speaks to his abilities as a sculptor and his willingness to take on new challenges with public monuments. Equally important, his efforts helped to establish a new presence of public sculpture in Seattle as a reality, which in turn aided other sculptors that followed.

While not a local sculptor, Taft brought a passion for art to the city in ways beyond his statue for the University of Washington. His repeat visits to the campus to offer lectures on sculpture and art in America provided a much needed voice to inform and inspire others, including a new generation of women sculptors who sought to make their own mark in the male-dominated field of sculpture as an arts profession.

Taft was the first. Others would soon follow him out west or else rise from amongst the city's own to create new sculptures for all to see.

2

Richard E. Brooks
(1865–1919)

When the University of Washington's Board of Regents hired John Charles Olmsted and Frederick Law Olmsted, Jr., in 1906 to develop a plan for the UW campus to host the Alaska-Yukon-Pacific (A-Y-P) Exposition, they were not the first group to have expressed an interest in the brothers' vision for enhancing Seattle public spaces. The Olmsted firm had already generated a family legacy of public parks and campus landscapes across the nation, including Central Park for New York City in 1857 and the grounds of the United States Capitol in 1873.

Both the Seattle Chamber of Commerce and the Board of Park Commissioners worked with the City Council to commission John Olmsted to prepare a report that examined several park areas within the city for future landscape development. During the summer of 1903, Olmsted spent several weeks touring the city's park spaces. The Olmsted report that resulted was approved by the Parks Board and adopted by the City Council on October 19, 1903.

The Olmsted plans were a key factor in determining the future of another prominent piece of statuary made early in Seattle's history of public art. This sculpture was the monumental statue cast in bronze of William Henry Seward by the sculptor Richard E. Brooks.

Like Taft, Brooks was not a native to Seattle. He was originally from Massachusetts, had spent his youth living near a granite quarry, and worked first at a terracotta company before going on to start his own business in Boston designing architectural ornamentation and cemetery monuments. He had a natural aptitude for sculpture and excelled at portraiture early on in his career. At age twenty, he first studied sculpture with the aid of Truman Howe Bartlett, which ultimately led him to pursuit of further studies in the arts overseas.

Again, like Taft, the Boston sculptor looked to Paris, France as a source of new inspiration and further instruction. He left the United States in 1893 to join the sculptors Jean-Paul Aubé and Jean-Antoine Injalbert at the Académie Colarossi. His first public commission for a sculpture bust occurred a year later: a self-portrait commissioned by Massachusetts Governor William Russell that was installed in the State House.

While Taft had remained in Paris for only a couple of years, Brooks stayed on in Paris to produce many more public sculptures. He established a studio in the city, and continued to model life-sized portraits in bronze, including a statue of Colonel Thomas Cass produced in 1899 that received a gold medal at the Paris Exposition of 1900.

While it was not unique for American sculptors to travel to Europe for studies and even to produce work, Brooks developed a unique reputation as an accomplished sculptor, living afar yet still much in demand by his countrymen back in the States. He produced a series of portrait medallions showing the mayors of Boston, commissioned by another mayor of that city, Josiah Quincy. Bronze statues of Charles Carroll and John Hanson were both completed in 1902, at the request of the State of Maryland, and installed a year later in the prominent National Statuary Hall in Washington, D.C., as the two sculptures allocated from that state for display.

However, the winter months of 1906 found Brooks away from his Paris studio, residing in New York at 9 East 17th Street.[1] It was fortuitous timing indeed for a group of civic leaders from Seattle, of a collective mind to see a new monument added to the city. While concurrent efforts were underway by the local chapter of the Daughters of the American Revolution (D.A.R.) to commission a statue of George Washington, members of the Seattle Chamber of Commerce had come together to plan a monument to another figure of Northwest history.

On October 31, 1906, Chamber member Gerhard Beninghauser submitted a motion at the Chamber meeting that underscored his interest in a new statue of William Seward, and furthermore "that the subject was prosecuted in a manner which would insure the erection of such a monument, in the near future."[2] During the meeting, the assembled members voted unanimously to adopt a resolution put forth by W.T. Dowell that called for the creation of a Seward Monument Committee to see such a monument was made for the city of Seattle. Initially, the committee was comprised of seven members, including Beninghauser (who was a local watchmaker and jeweler) and Judge Thomas Burke, who was named Committee Chairman.

A week later at the next Chamber meeting, the monument committee was expanded to sixteen total members, with the number now including additional prominent local figures such as Edmond S. Meany; Charles D. Stimson, of the Stimson Mill Company in Seattle; and John H. McGraw, the second Governor of Washington in 1892. In an address to the group, Burke was eloquent in the merit of such a monument dedicated to Seward and the legacy provided to the Pacific Northwest as a region: "He foretold at a time when the World regarded them as uninhabitable wilderness, the part of Alaska and the Pacific coast were to take in the World's commerce."[3]

Burke spoke of Seward's foresight in securing the Alaska purchase as the treaty signatory for the United States on March 30, 1867. During Seward's long career of public service, he was both Governor of New York and a United States Senator, and appointed by Abraham Lincoln as Secretary of State from 1861 to 1869. In his own day, some referred to the purchase of 586,412 square miles of territory in the north as "Seward's Folly" for the price paid to the Russian Empire to acquire the land which became the Alaska Territory.

The passage of time had borne out the wisdom of Seward's counsel on the acquisition and its importance to the people of the Pacific Northwest. In Seattle, work on the A-Y-P Exposition had been underway ever since it was first proposed by a group called the Alaska-Yukon Pioneers in 1905. The Olmsted Brothers firm from Brookline, Massachusetts, had been hired in 1906 to develop the University of Washington campus in anticipation of hosting the Exposition. Funding was anticipated through the State Legislature and local citizens, and the University of Washington's Board of Regents was also in support of the Exposition. The Regents signed a lease with the Alaska-Yukon-Pacific Exposition Company on September 27, 1906, which secured the campus grounds as the site for the Exposition to open in 1909. The Chamber's actions that same fall towards a new monument of Seward no doubt had the Exposition clearly in mind, given Seward's historical role as the primary figure responsible for the addition of Alaska as a national resource.

Not just the University grounds were undergoing rapid change. To implement John Olmsted's report of 1903 that called for the development of parks throughout the city, a bond issue of $500,000 was submitted to a vote of the people in 1906 and authorized. Whereas the city had only six improved parks in 1904, by 1911 this number had been increased to sixteen, with another twelve playgrounds also added.[4] Volunteer Park received the most extensive treatment, with $30,922.95 allocated for new walks, drives, ponds and a music pavilion, along with other amenities.

This park would play a key role in the future of the Seward monument, once the A-Y-P Exposition officially ended on October 16, 1909.

The Seward Monument Committee met officially for the first time on November 14, 1906, at the regular meeting at the Seattle Chamber of Commerce. Among the business discussed, was a communication received from the Valdez and Copper River Mining Districts, which pledged donations of ore to help make a copper pedestal for the monument. The committee also discussed how a statue of Seward would be coordinated as part of current efforts involving the A-Y-P Exposition.

As these discussions progressed over the following month, there were several important developments that took place involving both the Exposition and the statue. The Alaska-Yukon Pioneers were enlisted to help with the commission for the statue, as part of the Monument Committee's efforts towards an active campaign for securing funding for the project by public subscription.

By late fall, Meany had also decided to take a leave of absence from the University beginning in January of the New Year, as an emissary of Seattle to secure support for the Exposition back east to cities such as New York and Boston. Among those he was scheduled to visit, was General William Seward, the statesman's son, who resided at the family's mansion in Auburn, New York. To aid him in this visit, another member of the Monument Committee, the president of the National Bank of Commerce, M.F. Backus, wrote Meany a letter of introduction to the General. The letter outlined the importance of Meany's planned visit to Auburn "for the purpose of seeing the monument now standing in Seward Park."[5]

Meany's visit to Auburn was helpful both in how it served to inform the Seward family about Seattle's monument project and as a fact-finding trip for Meany, to see another public statue to Seward done in 1888 by the sculptor Walter G. Robinson. Furthermore, it also helped to secure New York State's interest in the A-Y-P Exposition, which led to the installation of a New York Building as one of the East Coast states represented at the Exposition. It was no coincidence that the design for this building was modeled as a replica of the Seward mansion in Auburn.

Meany's trip served another purposed as well with respect to the Seward monument. While in New York, Meany received a letter from Monument Chairman Burke, which served as the connection between the proposed statue and the selection of Brooks as the choice for the commission:

> While you are in New York, I wish you would call on Richard E. Brooks, the sculptor ... you will recall that Mr. Brooks is the sculptor I spoke of before the committee at the last meeting. He has won high distinction as a sculptor at home and abroad.

> I am personally acquainted with him and all other things being equal I should prefer to see him selected as the sculptor of the Seward statue.... I believe he would give us a statue of Seward of which we would all be proud.[6]

Burke also asked fellow committee members Charles D. Stimson and James D. Hoge to also call upon Brooks and review work in the sculptor's New York studio.

A consensus was reached several months later, at the March 8, 1907, meeting of the Seattle Chamber of Commerce. The assembled committee members selected Brooks as the official sculptor for the commission to create a new bronze statue of William Seward for the A-Y-P Exposition. The reputation of Brooks as a national figure in sculpture was paramount to the decision, with his service as the chairman of the board of judges on sculpture at the St. Louis Exposition of 1904 cited as just one example of his excellence in the field. His recent accomplishments of statues commemorating Robert Treat Paine (in Taunton, Massachusetts) and Oliver Wendell Holmes (Boston Public Library) were regarded with equal measure.

The committee had arrived at a cost estimate for the new statue and pedestal at $20,000, with work by the sculptor to take two years to complete in time for the opening of the A-Y-P Exposition in Seattle. Some debate had also centered on where the new statue should be placed in the city both during and after the Exposition, with the downtown location of Pioneer Place advocated by Thomas Burke. Given the importance of the A-Y-P Exposition, it was decided the statue should be temporarily installed on the grounds of the University, at least for the duration of the event.

On June 17, 1907, the committee ratified the contract with Brooks for the new statue and its pedestal. The revised cost was now $18,000, with $15,000 of the total amount going to Brooks for the work and the balance of $3,000 towards a foundation under his direction. The sculptor also called for the statue's bronze composition to include both gold and silver, similar to the type of alloy found in "the finer work of the ancient Japanese."[7]

True to the approach he had used previously for the portrait statues of other famous Americans, Brooks modeled his figure of Seward with lifelike detail and in monumental scale. The completed figure stood twelve feet tall, and presented a stern-faced Seward holding an unfurled scroll symbolic of the 1867 treaty agreement for Alaska. Behind the figure on the left side, a globe was included as further visual testimony to Seward's world view of the United States as a global leader. The hem of Seward's coat billows out, as if the man has been caught in the act of motion, conveyed forward and evocative of progress as an action. This effect of forward motion was further reinforced by the sculptor, in his placement of Seward, left foot forward and overhanging the edge of the statue's base, as if the figure were frozen in the act of stepping off the platform.

Some distinction is owed to Brooks in his choice of foundry as well for the Seward statue. The bronze casting was accomplished not in the United States, but in Paris, where the sculptor had a studio there. When it finally arrived to Seattle, the decision to have it on view in front of the newly constructed New York Building was not accomplished as originally planned by the Seward Monument Committee. As had also occurred with Lorado Taft's statue of *George Washington* placed at the A-Y-P Exposition's main entrance, the elaborate pedestal that had been planned for the Seward statue was not ready. A simple, elevated pedestal round in form was made from concrete, with the bronze statue then lowered into place on top. On the base were placed the inscription "Let Us Make the Treaty Tonight" in reference to Seward's famous passage extolling the purchase of Alaska, with "Seward" placed below in the center of the base.

On September 10, 1909, the statue was unveiled to an audience of over 3,000 people, with General William Seward giving a speech in honor of his father's historic accomplishment in securing the "golden north" for the country. The unveiling was attended by the majority of the Seattle Chamber of Commerce members, many of which had also served on the Seward Monument Committee. Former Washington Governor John McGraw was counted among the latter and in attendance with his granddaughter, Harriet May Baxter, who unveiled the statue that day. The Exposition's official photographer, Frank Nowell, captured the moment shortly after the unveiling, with the elderly Seward seated, legs crossed and bowler hat on one knee, while the young Harriet stands next to him, still holding the cord used to pull the cover from the statue and a serious look on her face.

During the evening of the statue's unveiling day, a dinner for the visiting dignitaries was hosted by Benjamin Wilcox, the Chief Executive Officer of the New York State Building. Judge Burke served as the toastmaster, while John E. Chilberg, president of the A-Y-P Exposition, and Seattle mayor John F. Miller, provided addresses of welcome and accepted the statue on behalf of the A-Y-P Exposition and the City of Seattle, respectively.

For Brooks, the Seward statue was an unqualified success. He received a gold medal for the statue from the A-Y-P Exposition in recognition of his achievement. No small part of this goes towards the talent of Brooks as a sculptor, and in particular, his monumental public sculptures of his-

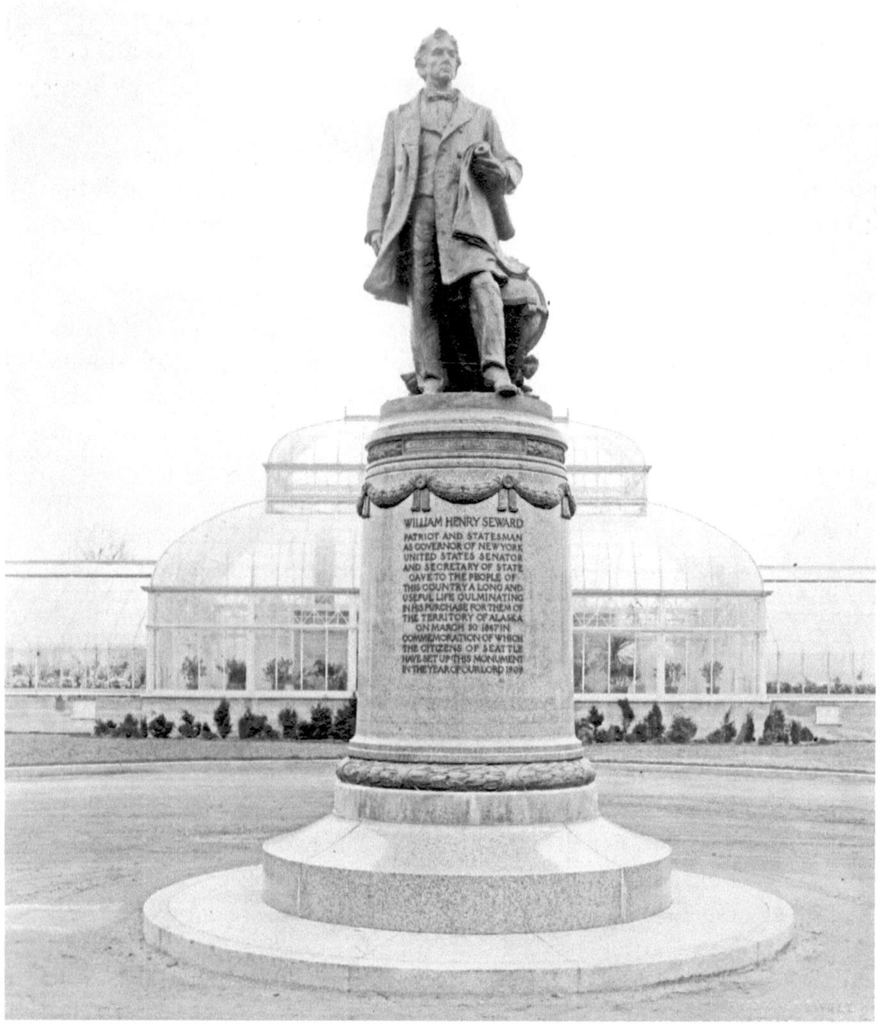

Seward statue, Volunteer Park, by Richard E. Brooks, 1912. Seattle Municipal Archives.

torical figures. Taft was succinct in his praise of Brooks, as "a sculptor of much skill."[8]

Another aspect that contributed to both the support of the statue as a public sculpture project and its widespread acceptance by the Seattle citizenry was the subject of William Seward and his ties to the Pacific region and the timing of a statue in his name while the A-Y-P Exposition was a citywide event.

The success of the statue was also the result of the Seward Monument Committee and the Seattle Chamber of Commerce ability to raise most of the $15,000 required to pay Brooks. Unfortunately, it was not until the statue was moved to its new location in Volunteer Park in 1910 that the balance of the funds was secured to pay for a new, round pedestal made from granite. This pedestal included bronze trim along its top edge which, like the temporary pedestal at the Exposition, included Seward's famous phrase. An additional band of ornamental festoons circled the pedestal near the top, while a bronze plaque on the front of the pedestal boasted raised letters in copper: "William Henry Seward / Patriot and Statesman / As Governor of New York United States Senator and Secretary of State gave to the people of this country a long and useful life culminating in his purchase for them of the Territory of Alaska on March 30, 1867." Etched into the granite below the plaque was a generalized acknowledgment of those who produced the statue: "Erected by the Citizens of Seattle / 1909."

The location of the statue post–Exposition was again discussed at a meeting held on October 7, 1909, of the City Council's Street Committee. Burke reiterated his position that the statue belonged in an "open park" space and suggested placing it downtown at Pioneer Place, in front of the old City Hall.[9] However, the area in question was part of an estate bequest from Henry Yesler which called for a library to be placed there. Both library trustees at the meeting as well as Maurice McMicken, Secretary of the Yesler estate, were opposed to placement of the Seward statue, and told Burke as much. Recent updates made as part of the 1903 Olmsted report for parks citywide also argued for the statue's re-installation instead at Volunteer Park, as a more suitable site.

In its annual report released by the Board of Park Commissioners in 1910, the section which described Volunteer Park also mentioned its latest acquisition: "The Seward Monument has been placed at the head of the main concourse."[10] While the Seward statue was now afforded a new pedestal and prominent display, the city had gained its second, permanent public sculpture.

This latest addition to the city's public art collection was instructive, where the Parks Board was regarded as an important part of city government on such matters. The dramatic growth in the number, size and scope of the city parks in the past several years also mandated that the city's charter reflect new measures and guidelines for the Board of Park Commissioners to function effectively in its role of municipal oversight.

The city charter as amended and published in 1911 included a comprehensive "Article XIII" for the Department of Parks, which established a park fund consisting of "such gifts, bequests and devises as may be given, bequeathed or devised to the City of Seattle for the purpose of parks, parkways, public squares, play or recreation grounds, or any ornamentation thereof."[11]

The article continued on to establish the role of the Board of Park Commissioners as the governing municipal body authorized to manage both the city's park system and public squares, including funding sources and any direct appropriations from the City Council made in support of the parks.

On the topic of public artwork, the article language was also clear. While Taft's statue was designated part of the University of Washington and exempt from the Park Board's oversight, the new statue by Brooks did come under their guidance, given its dedication as a city sculpture and placement in a city park. Section three of the Department of Parks article spelled this out with respect to how all future sculptures would be reviewed and acquired by the city for display. The language stated in no uncertain terms that the Board of Park Commissioners had authority on city lands "to erect and maintain buildings, monuments and structures therein, and shall have the power of censorship over any statuary, monuments or works of art that may be presented to the city, and shall in the name of the city accept all devises and bequests...."[12] This proviso would be the primary regulation that governed municipal review of public sculpture going forward, until Resolution No. 152 was passed years later on November 14, 1929, which established Roanoke Park and public squares at street intersections as the only locations sanctioned for new public sculpture.

In the meantime, Brooks capitalized on his reputation as a sculptor with a prestigious monument in Seattle. His opportunity came with the demise of a noted member of the Seward Monument Committee, John H. McGraw, in 1910.

McGraw was a bit of a local legend in Seattle. One account described how in 1886 McGraw, who was Sheriff at the time, deputized 400 local citizens in order to prevent a mass round-up of Chinese laborers by vigilantes bent on racial purity in the Pacific Northwest. McGraw's public stand against such blatant repression held firm, even in the face of gunfire.

McGraw was also known for taking a controversial stand in favor of a city-supported shipping locks and canal project to interconnect Elliott Bay, Lake Union and Lake Washington. With McGraw's vocal support as Mayor of Seattle, the project was realized and the Ballard Locks eventually opened in 1917.

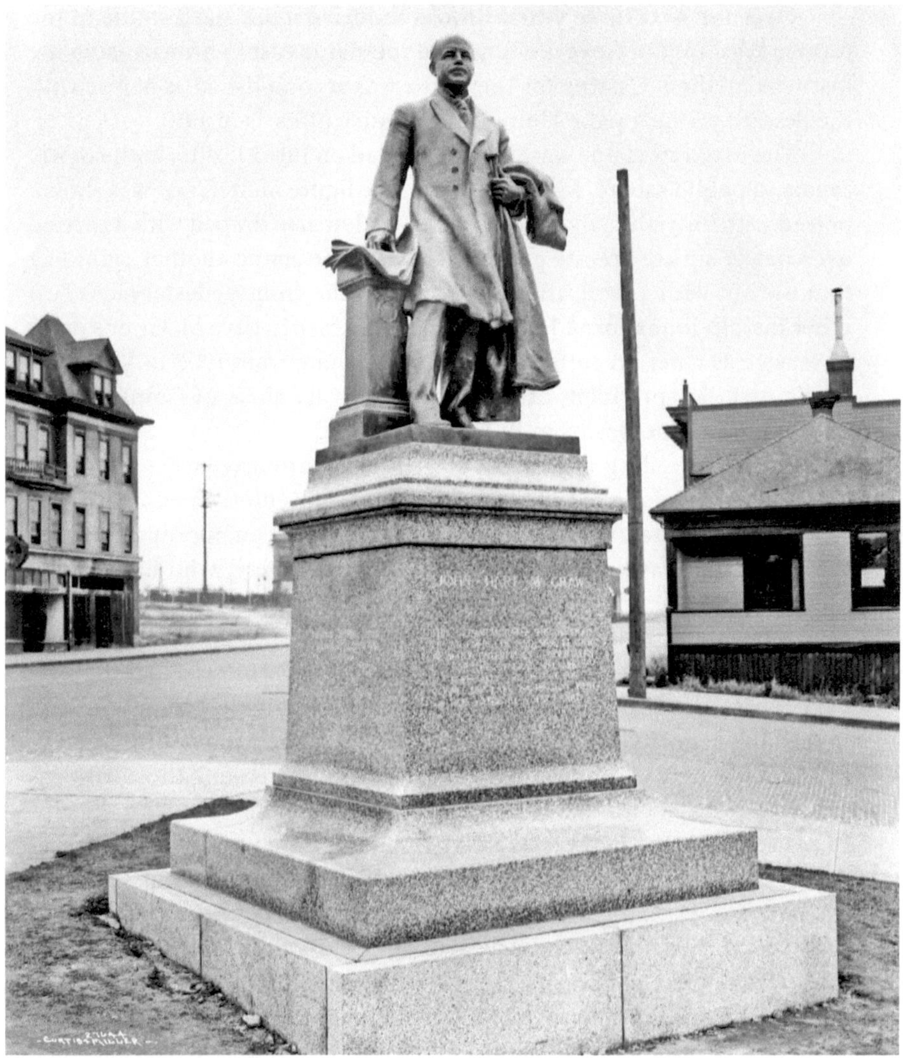

John McGraw **by Richard E. Brooks. Undated photograph. Courtesy Lawton Gowey and Paul Dorpat.**

A site was selected by a group of private citizens that included McGraw's family to place a new monument. Through funds provided by this group, land was purchased at the intersection of Westlake Avenue North and Stewart Street. The land eventually became one of the smallest parks in the city park system. For Brooks, the commission to model a statue of McGraw was also entirely funded by these same private sources.

Over the next three years, Brooks modeled a life-sized statue of the former Washington Governor and had the statue cast in bronze using the lost-wax method. Casting for the statue was accomplished as before with the Seward statue, by the Hohwiller Foundry of Paris in 1912.

The McGraw statue was finally unveiled on July 22, 1913, in the newly renamed public square, McGraw Plaza. The figure of McGraw was shown poised with his right hand upon a table, the left arm draped with a carried overcoat. A square granite pedestal elevated the statue another eight feet into the air, with a dedication inscribed on the front pedestal face. Two other inscriptions adorned the pedestal sides, which gave McGraw's dates of service as chief executive of Washington State from 1905 to 1907, and as the first vice-president of the Associated Chambers of Commerce of the Pacific Coast cities from 1908 to 1909.

At the unveiling ceremony, Professor Meany gave a testimony to McGraw's influence as a public figure in local law enforcement, and most recently, of McGraw's timely assistance in securing an appropriation for the new Lake Washington Ship Canal. John Chilberg, who had known McGraw and counted him a political ally during the A-Y-P Exposition, gave a tribute as well extolling McGraw for his statesman-like qualities. Dr. Stephen Penrose, president of Whitman College, offered that the statuary represented "an abiding inspiration to the coming generation, and that of the majority of colleges and universities each is but a monument to some big man."[13] Judge C.H. Hanford, who was among those citizens who had privately funded the memorial, presented the statue to the city. In his remarks, the judge made sure to mention that both this work and the statue of William Seward were the result of the "eminent sculptor" Richard Brooks, and that Seattle was "fortunate" in have two such statues to its credit.[14] The statue was accepted on behalf of the city by J.M. Frink, President of the Park Board.

For Richard Brooks, the McGraw statue would be his final achievement in major public statuary for a city. Yet both statues have continued to endure and signify Seattle's first efforts at historical sculpture and public art for the city. Minor adjustments to each work have added to their character and history over the past century. In 1922, the Parks Board contracted with architect D.R. Huntington to move the McGraw statue a modicum distance from its original spot in the plaza, for repaving of the streets (achieved without incident). The Seward statue was plagued over time with the loss of its raised copper letters on the dedication plaque, first in 1930 and twice more, with repairs made a third time in 1952 by the sculptor James Wehn. Not long after the formation of the first Municipal Art Com-

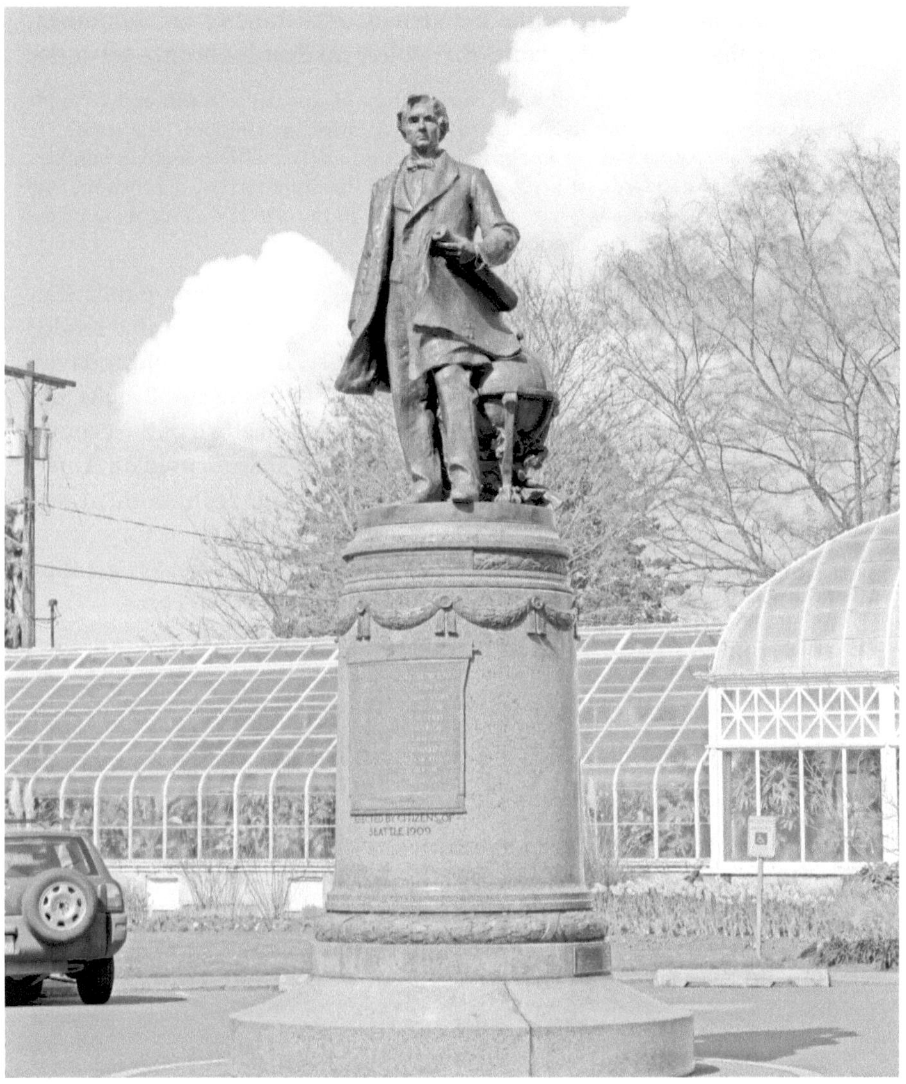

William Henry Seward by Richard E. Brooks. 1909. Fred F. Poyner IV, Photographer (2014).

mission in 1955, a proposal to relocate the Seward memorial to Seward Park was studied by the group and subsequently rejected.

In 1971, the Superintendent of Parks and Recreation for the City of Seattle, Hans A. Thompson, Sr., replied to a letter posted to *The Seattle Times* which criticized the appearance of the McGraw statue. Thompson explained the rationale for the maintenance schedule of the monument and how that was best determined as policy for Seattle's bronze artworks:

> The responsibility lies within the jurisdiction of this department, and a simple cleansing without abrasives is all that is permitted to "maintain" the statue. To remove the patina and restore the finish to its original condition would be contrary to aesthetic standards set up by sculptors and the Seattle Arts Commission, who claim that the patina is what gives "character" to the statuary ... we abide by the standards set by the professionals.[15]

Today, Seattle is the only West Coast city that can claim public statuary done by Brooks' hand. They were of a design and quality that rivaled the two statues produced for the State of Maryland that stand today in the National Statuary Hall in Washington, D.C. In this regard Brooks represented the ideal of American sculptors active at the turn of the century that were engaged in a creating unique sculptural style focused on American historical figures and subjects while borrowing from both Beaux-Arts and neoclassical hallmarks found in European art.

With Brooks—and now the city's Parks Board—Seattle's progression as a city of art continued, with the promise of more yet to come.

3

Finn Haakon Frolich (1868–1947)

Of the three great sculptors who created public sculptures for Seattle in 1909, Finn Frolich contributed both the most in number and the most diverse in terms of individualized portraits and neoclassical figures of an allegorical description.

Born in Oslo, Norway, on August 13, 1868, to a family of means, Frolich left his home in Kristiania at the tender age of nine to work his way at sea. He eventually jumped ship in Brooklyn, New York, on July 15, 1886, after most of the ship's crew had succumbed to plague. Frolich soon found his calling in the fine arts, after he answered a local ad placed by the studio of sculptor Daniel Chester French.

As French's apprentice, Frolich worked out of the senior sculptor's New York studio for the next six years on important commissions, including sculptures for the World's Fairs in Paris, St. Louis, and Chicago. Frolich also traveled to Paris, where he studied at the École nationale supérieure des Beaux-Arts in 1895. No less than the eminent American sculptor Augustus Saint-Gaudens offered instruction to the young Frolich during this time in The City of Light.

Several traits emerged which clearly directed Frolich's path as a sculptor. He was an adventurer with a world view, an international perspective, and a sense of the global community, as evidenced by his desire for exploration, his gravitation towards the World's Fairs as venues, and his blending of American and European training in the arts. His work was global in nature: a great portrait head of South African president Paul Kruger completed just after the end of the Boer War; and another horse and chariot sculpture group done with Alexander Phimister Proctor for the American Building at the Paris Exposition. No challenge too great seemed to give Frolich pause.

He was successful as a sculptor and quickly established an international reputation towards this end. In his comprehensive examination of sculpture in the United States, Lorado Taft characterized Frolich as an accomplished figurative sculptor, one who "knows how to make a convincing soldier."[1]

While abroad, he earned an honorable mention for exhibition of work at the Salon and received a silver medal at the Paris Fair from the Société Nationale des Beaux-Arts. Frolich naturally gravitated towards venues that were cosmopolitan in scope and huge draws for audiences to see his work, such as the Columbian Exposition held in Chicago, 1893, and the Louisiana Purchase Exposition in St. Louis, 1904. He was equally accomplished at producing more permanent monuments for public spaces, such as a statue of General Corcoran placed in Central Park, New York, and other military monuments at Weber and Attleboro, Massachusetts.

Frolich, like the sculptor Alonzo Victor Lewis, desired to create monumental figures in bronze with heroic proportions and emphasis on presenting the individual larger than life. He adopted this approach to the modeling of his own sculptures from the start, after having learned it firsthand from the French for sculptures such as *Republic*, a seventy-foot–high statue for the Chicago World's Fair. These experiences ultimately helped to prepare the sculptor for his most challenging period of work to date, as the Director of Sculpture for Seattle's Alaska-Yukon-Pacific (A-Y-P) Exposition of 1909.

While the planning and construction work for the exposition had been officially underway since 1906, Frolich's arrival to Seattle occurred two years later, in June 1908. However, this was not his first visit to Seattle: the sculptor had come to the city in 1898 to found a new school of design, but his stay was a brief one and the school unrealized. Unlike many of his other travels, his return to the west was spurred on not by the promise of a new commission, but rather the lack of one:

> I had separated from my first wife, and there didn't seem to be another sculpting commission for me on the horizon in New York. I came off a drunk one morning in 1908, on 42nd Street in front of the Grand Central Station. I went into the ticket office and asked the agent what kind of places they had and he asked, "What kind of place do you want?" "The farthest away from here you got." So he gave me a ticket to Seattle.[2]

Frolich wasted no time in making his mark on the local arts scene. He soon established a studio called the Beaux-Arts Workshop in the old (Territorial) University Building, and helped to start the Northwest Society of Beaux-Arts as an arts colony on the eastern shore of Lake Washington.

Modeling in clay became a means to create not only new busts and statues, but also a way to engage with local artists and performers, first through his workshops and later, sessions on stage with "live modeling in clay" performed for audiences at the Alhambra Theatre.[3]

Yet it was the A-Y-P Exposition where Frolich really capitalized on his reputation as a worldly sculptor. In the summer of 1908, the architects of the Exposition, John Galen Howard and John Debo Galloway, presented Frolich with a design made by another member of their firm, Édouard Frère Champney, which called for a monumental fountain sculpture for placement at the head of the Cascade Court in the center of the Exposition grounds.

The Champney drawing had been completed on April 11, 1908, and presented the *Spirit of the Pacific* fountain as a neoclassical design drawn to one-eighth-inch scale. This detailed sketch had the main winged figure nine feet tall, with the other figures slightly smaller in size. The main figure was also an allegorical one named after the sculpture's title, and presented the woman semi-nude, with a torch held aloft in the left hand and left foot raised, as if to take off in flight from the globe. Below the *Spirit* figure and the globe, a grouping of four female statues were drawn around the fountain's central column, holding hands and very similar in appearance to models of statuary from ancient Greece. These female figures were symbolic of races viewed as primary to the Pacific region and vital to Seattle, and were represented as Japanese, Chinese, Alaskan Eskimo, and the South Seas. The cement basin of the fountain was in turn supported by a group of four other figures, male and nude, placed at the four corners of the compass points.

When compared to another Howard and Galloway architectural drawing that showed the elevated plan for the cascades water feature on the grounds, the fountain's scale was significantly larger: thirty-eight feet high overall, with the main figure twelve feet tall and other statuary eight feet tall. This second architectural drawing, numbered "A98" confirmed the placement of the fountain group sculpture as part of Howard and Galloway's Exposition plan.

By August, Frolich had completed his plaster scale model for the cascades fountain. The model still showed two groups of four figures, each group supporting and surmounting the fountain's main basin. The first group of four female figures mirrored the respective identities of their male counterparts below and placed in a similar orientation around the shaft rising from the basin in the center. However, in Frolich's model, the women now had appearances that more realistically depicted their regions of origin in terms of native clothing worn, with racial characteristics in the faces. At the apex of the fountain's font was a globe topped by a heroic female statue called the *Spirit of the Pacific.* Frank Nowell, the official photographer of the A-Y-P Exposition, visited Frolich's studio and captured a view of this model. The photograph was later reproduced in many prints and postcards sold during the exposition as souvenirs.

The October 1908 edition of the *Alaska-Yukon Magazine* also ran Nowell's photograph of the fountain maquette by Frolich, and stated the completed sculpture would be thirty feet high and also announced its placement on the grounds at the head of the cascades rapids.

Early drawings of the Exposition grounds done by Howard and Galloway in 1908 confirm that this fountain sculpture was initially included as a feature inside the basin at the head of the Cascades water feature. One of these drawings showed an aerial view of the Court of Honor and surrounding buildings with the fountain in the center. The drawing also showed a second, larger column monument identified as the Alaska Monument, placed within the same courtyard and in front of the U.S. Government Building.

The skill of Frolich as a sculptor was immediately apparent to Howard and Galloway, with a two-fold result: he was named as the official Director of Sculpture for the Exposition and was given approval to continue his efforts towards a centralized fountain sculpture group. In short, the model "was approved with enthusiasm by the architects of the Exposition, and Mr. Frolich was urged to begin work with little delay on the larger cement piece ... 80 feet in height."[4]

The location for the modeling of the enlarged fountain sculpture group was Frolich's studio abode inside the old University Building. But the space presented challenges, not least of which was a need to remove the upper floor on one side in order to accommodate the size of the monument's design for casting into cement.

Another challenge was the University of Washington Regents plans for continuing to lease the old site for additional revenue. By October 1908, the old University Building required either $10,000 for relocation from its site downtown, or faced being torn down to make way for "modern business blocks."[5] While the uncertainty of the old University's tenure remained in question, it continued to serve the sculptor's needs as a studio until it was finally torn down in 1910.

Meanwhile, in the first few months of 1909, Frolich's direction towards completion of *Spirit of the Pacific* took a divergent turn with respect to the grounds plan for the Exposition. The cascades water feature, a series of falling risers with rapids that lead to a large geyser basin called the Arctic Circle, was completed by December 1908. Surrounding the cascades in a semi-circle, were seven temporary buildings designed in a Beaux-Arts style: architecture with great colonnades, pediments and arched roofs with flourishment and other elaborate details. Each of the seven buildings represented a different regional identity or industry and was listed on the official A-Y-P Exposition map as Government, Alaska, Hawaii, European, Oriental, Agriculture and Manufacture.

The fountain sculpture group originally envisioned for this area and first modeled by Frolich was never enlarged or cast into cement. Priority for the head of the cascades was directed towards the Alaska Monument surmounted by a large American eagle sculpture. This monument became Frolich's focus as a means to incorporate other elements from the earlier *Pacific* sculpture group, such as the retention of the four female sculptures representing the Pacific regions. Now, these were placed as individual sculptures around the base of the column, and arranged at the compass points as before.

That Frolich was comfortable with changing various elements in his monumental sculptures for the A-Y-P Exposition was also seen in the evolution of the Alaska Monument. An article about the sculptor's work on this centralized feature of the Court of Honor described an alternate view of the monument in February 1909:

> The Alaska monument will rise eighty-five feet from its base. It will be a fluted and ornamented Greek column, crowned by an American eagle with outflung [*sic*] pinions, perched upon a globe engraved with the signs of the Zodiac. At its base will be placed the three figures of which Mr. Frolich is now working out the details. They will symbolize mining, hunting and the fisheries. Completed at the hands of Mr. Frolich, the shaft and the three figures will be clothed in Alaskan gold.[6]

The article continued on to mention that Frolich's sculpture of a winged female figure, now called *Spirit of the North*, was to serve as the third figure around the column base and once completed, placed on temporary view in the lobby of the Hotel Washington in Seattle. The article's description of this particular figure was akin to the one designed for the earlier fountain sculpture.

By the time of the A-Y-P Exposition's opening on June 1, 1909, the central fountain of the cascades had not been completed or installed, while the Alaska Monument stood in the main Court of Honor in front of the Government Building. It reflected a column design, fluted and topped with a globe and an American eagle sculpture with wings raised, similar to the one that also adorned the front pediment entrance on the Mines

Building on the Exposition grounds. Both the capital and the base of the column were adorned with festoons, while the base had an added reverse swastika design which symbolized Korean spiritualism. Frolich retained the earlier element from the other fountain sculpture which had identified four female statues representing four races of the Pacific, and placed these around the base of the column at the four compass points. Only a simple water spout had been installed as a fountain element in the lower Arctic Circle's Geyser Basin, at the foot of the cascades rapids. The Geyser Basin fountain had been completed a year earlier, in August 1908, and like the monument placed in the Court of Honor, had been originally envisioned by John Olmsted and included in his plan for the Exposition.

Despite the omission of the monumental fountain sculpture from the Exposition's construction phase, Frolich was credited for seeing the Alaska Monument to its successful completion. It was an impressive feature visible for miles in every direction, and in a nod to the original Olmsted Brothers preliminary plan for the Exposition (the 1906 version had called for an electric tower at the monument's site) both the top of the monument and its base were illuminated with lamps at night. Like many of the temporary buildings constructed on the exposition grounds, it was torn down at the conclusion of the Exposition on October 16, 1909.

In addition to the Alaska Monument, Frolich completed several other sculptures for the A-Y-P grounds during his tenure as the Sculpture Director. A series of five animal sculptures were planned for placement around the Arctic Circle, at the foot of the cascades rapids. These animals were monumental in size, cast into cement and placed on raised pedestals at a viewer's head height and faced out from the basin's pool. The association to Alaska was to be represented by sculptures which showed a grizzly bear, polar bear, a "glacier bear," and a wolf, while one of these sculptures in particular, a puma, was evocative of the South American continent.[7] However, just as the *Spirit of the Pacific* fountain sculpture had only elements of its design added to the Alaska Monument column, so too the plans for these animal sculptures underwent an evolution in their final execution by Frolich. While placement of the completed sculptures remained the same around the Arctic Circle, only four heroic animal sculptures were cast into plaster and the composition of these adjusted as well. Of the original five, only the wolf and the polar bear were retained; the puma from South America was now a mountain lion, and the grizzly bear replaced by an ox.

Contrary to early descriptions published in the local press, none of the sculptures Frolich modeled for the exposition were covered in gold.

While an impressive exhibition of gold valued at $1 million was on public display in the Alaska Building, the majority of the statuary and other sculptures on the grounds were cast in either plaster or cement. The records of the Roman Bronze Works foundry in New York show that Frolich did place a casting order on July 19, 1909, at an incurred cost of $731.[8] This was one of two orders the sculptor placed with the foundry to have models cast into bronze for the Exposition.

In addition to the four reclining women sculptures around the Alaska Monument, Frolich also modeled two monumental sculpture busts that were unique in their departure from the allegorical figures, as portraits of real individuals. These works also proved to be Frolich's lasting legacy to the University of Washington grounds and the public sculpture of Seattle.

Through the advocacy of several prominent local citizens, including J.M. Hawthorne, Alden J. Blethen, and Judge Thomas Burke, a committee was formed with the support of the Minnesota Club (from that Midwestern state) for a new monument in honor of railroad magnate James Hill for the Exposition. As the Director of Sculpture, Frolich was enlisted to model a monumental size bust of Hill in clay, which he accomplished both by live modeling of Hill during a ten day period at Hill's home in St. Paul and through the use of photographs of the magnate. By March 1909, the bust was completed in Frolich's Seattle studio with plans already in motion for its placement on the Exposition's grounds:

> To a few of the more fortunate, a private view of the Hill figure has been given … of these, Mr. Hill's closest friends have declared that it is so faithful a likeness, down to the minutest detail of resemblance and personality, as to be startling. The monument will be placed inside of a reservation 100 feet in diameter, which forms the central part of what is known as the Klondike Circle … this is only a temporary location and upon removal of the temporary structures after the close of the exposition the monument will be changed to a permanent site which will be determined upon by the president and regents of the University.[9]

Both Judge Thomas Burke and C.W. Corliss were among those who previewed the bust, with the latter quoted as saying the portrait quality was of such a fine quality that "it was Mr. Hill himself."[10] Endorsements from such prominent citizens of Seattle served to bolster Frolich's status in the community and further validate his selection as lead sculptor for the A-Y-P Exposition.

The sculptor's portrait of James Hill showed the subject as an elderly man, a statesman in appearance while true to his likeness, with a beard, mustache and balding head forming a strong realistic presentation. The collars of a suit coat completed a picture of a man dignified and professional; modern, and yet still keeping with a style prevalent in the American sculpture of this time period.

The choice of Hill as subject for a public sculpture bust for placement on the Exposition grounds emphasized the importance of this figure to the development of Seattle's transportation infrastructure and economic development of the Pacific Northwest as a region. Hill was known as "the Empire Builder" and his railroad companies, beginning with the Great Northern in 1893, connected the city with the rest of the country and made expanded trade with the Pacific Rim countries all the more possible. Such advocacy went to the heart of why the A-Y-P Exposition was held in the first place: not only as a centennial celebration of the Klondike gold discovery of 1897, but also as a way to highlight Seattle's connectivity to the Pacific Rim regions.

As a sculptor, Frolich lived in an era when it was not unheard of to propose a public sculpture to a man of such prominence as Hill (even if the subject were still living). The rationale for a new monument was reinforced further by additional benefits reaped by the city both directly and indirectly from Hill's efforts, following the formation of the A-Y-P Exposition Company on May 7, 1906. In this same year, the magnate had opened the King Street Station, "which became the main portal for those visiting the A-Y-P three years later."[11] The A-Y-P Exposition Company also sold stock shares in support of funding the fair, amassing $650,000 in revenue on October 2, 1906. Hill's company, the Northern Pacific Railway, was one of these that purchased 2,500 shares of the stock in a single day. And in acknowledgment of his standing in the community as a business leader and proponent of the exposition, Hill was the keynote speaker at the opening of the Exposition on June 1, 1909. To the assembled crowds in attendance that day, Hill proclaimed Seattle as no longer an isolated community, an achievement made possible through both connectivity and a wealth of natural resources. He characterized the Exposition as symbolic of this achievement, and called it "'The Fair that Faces Forward.'"[12]

Local support for a bust of Hill was a united front. Letters of support poured in to the monument committee from Seattle Mayor, John Miller, N.H. Latimer of the Dexter Horton & Company Bankers, E.W. Andrews of Seattle National Bank, and Frolich advocate Donald Mitchell, of the Western Academy of Beaux-Arts. Another letter to J.M. Hawthorne from railroad contractor H.C. Henry seemed to summarize the feelings of many towards Hill and the promise of a new monument in his name:

Believing as I do that the entrance of Mr. Hill's railway into this city determined its supremacy for all time as the leading city of the Northwest, I am sure its citizens will be glad to assist in showing their appreciation of his services by honoring him in the manner proposed by the committee of which you are chairman ... it is fitting that a statue in his honor should be erected by his beneficiaries now.[13]

Frolich's clay bust was enlarged and cast into bronze by the Roman Bronze Works in New York, which undertook the casting for other public monuments across the country. The completed bust was six feet high and placed on a granite pedestal twelve feet high from its base. During the time of the Exposition, the monument was placed near the Klondike Circle, in a prominent location near the main entrance and between the Palace of the Fine Arts Building and the Mines Building. By coincidence or design, the bust by the Norwegian-American sculptor was located in front of the Swedish Building, aligning the Nordic identities of both artist and architecture.

In addition to the portrait bust, four additional bas-relief plaques in bronze were mounted to the four sides of the pedestal base. Three of these—the front and back plaques and the one on the left side—were designed by Frolich and cast by the same foundry that had done the bust cast in bronze. The front plaque showed a steam locomotive pulling a train of cars, while the reverse side plaque showed the steamship *Minnesota*—both designs a testimony to Hill's origins back east and his legacy as a railroad man. The side plaque illustrated a view of the state seal of Minnesota, in its original version depicting an Indian on horseback and a farmer tilling his field, a musket and powder horn within reach.

The fourth bronze plaque on the right side of the pedestal, showed the seal for the State of Washington, with George Washington's portrait in the center. This particular plaque was done for the Exposition by Seattle sculptor James A. Wehn, who was noted for modeling many portrait medallions of both U.S. Presidents and other historical figures from the Pacific Northwest.

At 3:00 p.m. on August 3, 1909, the bust of James Hill was unveiled on its pedestal at Klondike Circle. As a symbol of Hill's international connections in commerce, the bust with his likeness was jointly covered with the American flag, Japanese flag and Union Jack of the United Kingdom. Governor John A. Johnson of Minnesota, who had traveled to Seattle to give the Minnesota Day address at the A-Y-P Exposition, did the honors of the unveiling. Hill was not in attendance at the unveiling. He pleaded that pressing business in St. Paul required him elsewhere, and sent his appreciation in a letter that praised the "energy and fairness of Seattle."[14]

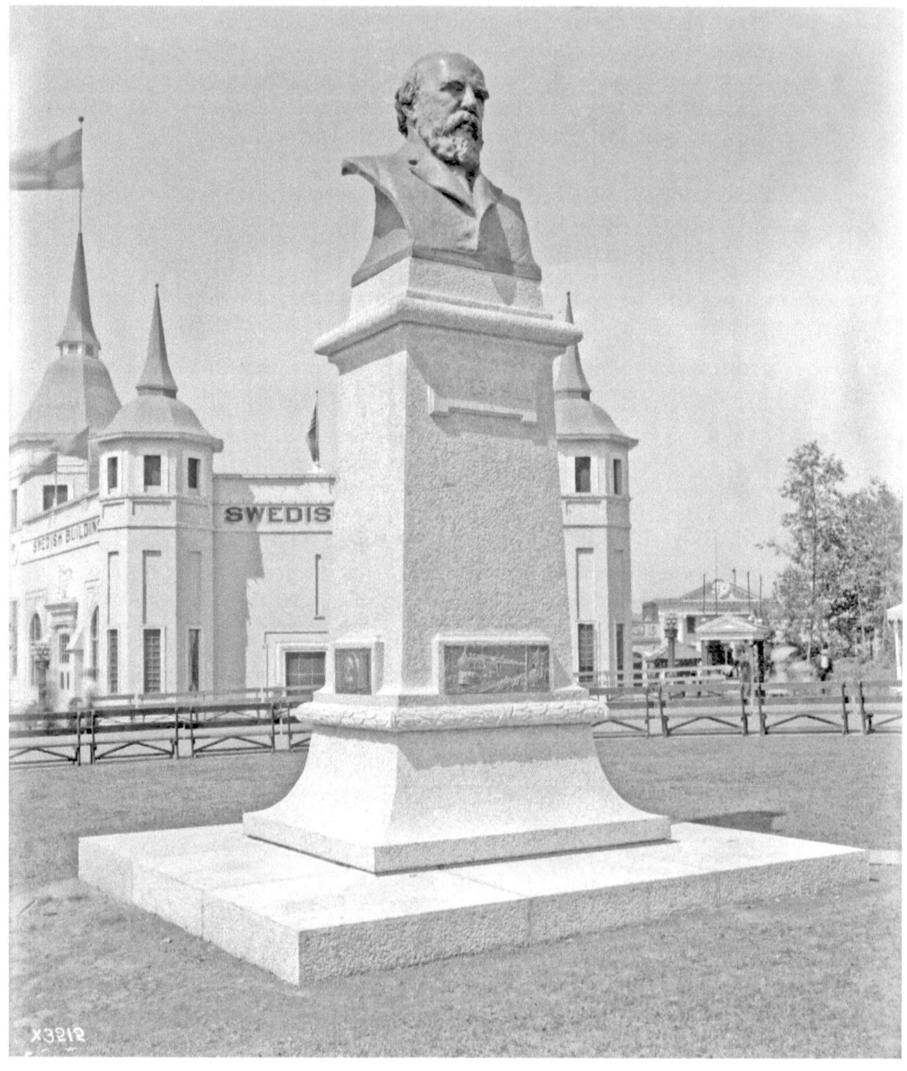

Bust of James J. Hill by Finn H. Frolich at Alaska-Yukon-Pacific Exposition. 1909. **Special Collections, University of Washington Libraries.**

While the Hill monument committee had solicited project funds from the public in the months leading up to the opening of the exposition, it was the Minnesota Testimonial Committee which underwrote the final cost of the commission. As a result of their efforts, the University of Washington officially accepted the sculpture as a gift from the people of Minnesota.

Nor was this the only copy produced of the bust. In 1925, the sculptor James Wehn was commissioned to model in plaster a twenty-two-foot-high copy for the Great Northern Employee's Club in Superior, Michigan. When finally completed, it was cast into bronze by the local foundry of Leon Morel, Sr., in Seattle, and shipped back east to Michigan.

The Hill bust has the distinction of being one of a handful of new public statuary and sculptures which mark the "Golden Age" of public sculpture for the city of Seattle. It has continued in this regard as a lasting, permanent sculpture at the University of Washington. It was relocated once, in 1953, to its present position on the north side of More Hall.

Frolich created one other large scale sculpture bust during his time spent on the A-Y-P Exposition that was a lasting contribution to the University's grounds. While engaged on the design for the *Spirit of the Pacific* fountain in the fall of 1908, Frolich secured a commission for a large statue of the Norwegian composer Edvard Grieg for Prospect Park, in Brooklyn, New York.

With a commission of a fellow Norwegian already underway, Frolich used his connections with the local Norwegian-American community in Seattle to garner support for a new sculpture bust of his Grieg portrait for display during the A-Y-P Exposition. A Grieg Monument Committee was formed with C.M. Thuland as Chairman, and three other members: Seattle City Councilman H.P. Rude, W.B. Olson and G. Nygard. Similar in scale to the bust done of James Hill, the Grieg bust was modeled first in clay, then cast into plaster and unveiled as part of the Norway Day festivities held on August 30, 1909, in the Exposition's Amphitheater.

In addition to the dedication of the Grieg bust, a Viking boat replica had also been built for the Exposition by a group of local Norwegian-Americans from Bothell and Ballard that included carver H.L. Erickson, Gunnar Lund of the *Washington Posten*, millwright Jacob Mohn, fisherman Albert Ness, merchant Gerhard Ericksen, and boat builder Sievert Sagstad. The vessel—appropriately named *Viking*—was based upon "the lines of one of the oldest of the Norse ships ... boats of similar design still used in some of the Norwegian fisheries."[15] On the appointed day of the Exposition, the boat was sailed down Lake Washington with a crew which included re-enactors from Tacoma dressed as Vikings in chainmail and helmets, as well as Norway's feudal king Sverre Sigurdsson and his queen, Margareta Eriksdotter. Over 7,000 people greeted the ship's arrival to the Exposition on the western shore of Lake Washington.

After Norway Day had concluded, Frolich was asked for his bill specific to the costs incurred for the Grieg sculpture. Ever the bohemian and

Norwegian at heart, the sculptor had decided on a different form of payment:

> I am a loyal son of Norse. My work was for the fatherland. You might give me that Viking ship out in the lake. I don't know what I would do with it, but the sight of it arouses a tingling in my blood. I'll put power in the craft, and she'll be able to weather most any storm.[16]

Frolich took official ownership of the boat on September 14, 1909. The sculptor envisioned sailing the *Viking* back to his birthplace in Kristiania (Oslo), Norway, with a crew of fellow Norwegians, which included several actors and actresses and a local Norwegian Captain, Ole Brude, in time for celebrating the centennial of Norway's independence on May 17, 1914.

Frolich's dream of a global cruise back to his native homeland was never realized. Funds were never raised for the voyage and in 1915 the Bothell contingent brokered the sale of the boat to the Alaska Packers Company in San Francisco. Once relocated to the Bay area, it took part in the Panama-Pacific Exposition's Norway Day held on June 3, 1915, and changed owners several times over the next two decades. It was finally destroyed by a fire while on display in Balboa Park in 1936.

Interest in the Grieg sculpture bust, however, continued amongst the Norwegian community in Seattle well after the Exposition concluded. Funds from the local community were raised totaling $4,000 to see a six-foot-high copy of Frolich's design cast into bronze. Once again, Frolich relied on the services of the Roman Bronze Works in New York to complete the casting of the Grieg bust into bronze.

At the unveiling held on September 30, 1917, the sculpture was presented by H.P. Rude, chairman of the Grieg Monument Association and accepted by Professor Edmond Meany on behalf of the University. The sculpture was called a gift from the "Norwegian citizens of the Northwest" to the University of Washington.[17] Festivities also included songs sung that day at the monument's location in front of old Meany Hall, with two compositions by Grieg: "Velkomssang av Grieg" and "On the Sea," performed by the Pacific Coast Norwegian Singers. The bust remained on the University of Washington campus, but was relocated twice: first to Governor's Grove, then later to its present site on a raised pedestal of Washington State granite in the Grieg Garden.

In the final report of the Alaska-Yukon-Pacific Exposition commission, Frolich was not mentioned anywhere in his capacity as Director of Sculpture. Nor were there any official payments recorded to him in the report's summary of receipts and disbursements: no salary was collected by the sculptor, and no expenses were reimbursed to him directly. In contrast, the report clearly identified the costs for Lorado Taft's bronze statue of George Washington. The statue alone had cost $8,010.40, with a total cost of $14,500 for its placement on Exposition grounds.[18] Other sources (including Frolich's niece) reported the sculptor made $35,000 as a result of his sculpture work for the A-Y-P Exposition in 1909.[19] Another estimate placed the cost of the Hill bust at $8,000, with part of these funds allocated to the sculptor. Regardless of the financial compensation, the event helped to expand Frolich's reputation as a sculptor on the West Coast.

After the conclusion of the Exposition, Frolich continued to live in Seattle at a "Viking camp" (no. 14) that had been setup in Madison Park. Despite having been a founding member of the Northwest Beaux-Arts Society that had purchased fifty acres of forested property on Lake Washington to create an artists' colony, Frolich never lived on the site. He did create one more public sculpture for the city of Seattle as part of the new central library sponsored by Andrew Carnegie in 1906. Among the features of the new downtown library was a fountain designed by the Beaux-Arts architect, M. Somervell. Frolich was commissioned to sculpt and cast a lion's head in concrete. The sculptor completed the new sculpture, with the fountain installed November 16, 1910, in front of the new Seattle Public Library on Fourth Avenue.

When the library was later demolished in 1957, the lion's head was salvaged from the site by longtime Seattle arts patron Ann Gould Hauberg and moved to her home on Bainbridge Island.

For Frolich, his professional life as a sculptor often was inseparable from his personal life, as witnessed by his love of the bohemian lifestyle, wanderlust for new places, and character towards his wives. Soon after the divorce to his first wife, Ragnhild Eleabora, was granted on May 21, 1910, he married his second wife, Helen, in Victoria, BC, on July 5, 1910. This second attempt at marriage fared no better than the first. At this time, Frolich was forty-eight and his newlywed wife age twenty-five. The couple quarreled constantly while living at a boarding house in Seattle, with the sculptor accused of verbal and physical abuse. The public charges of cruelty and non-support against Frolich were substantiated by both the boarding house operator, Mrs. Thompson, and one of Helen's stenography office co-workers at the Alaska Building.[20] Rumors of infidelity circulated about the young mother by the sculptor added more fuel to the fire.

In her filing for divorce from the sculptor only a year later, Helen claimed her husband had failed to support the family, which by now included the couple's six-month-old infant daughter, Virginia. She filed for a divorce on March 3, 1911, yet it was Frolich who made matters infinitely worse by then kidnapping his own daughter only two days before the final divorce hearing in court on Saturday, July 15, 1911. Prior to the act, Frolich had confided to a friend that he had learned of his wife's plans to leave him for South Dakota, and to take Virginia with her.

Helen prevailed in gaining an uncontested divorce and sole custody of the daughter, and Frolich soon came to his senses and returned the child unharmed. No criminal charges were brought against him, but the damage to his reputation was done. He remained in Seattle another four years, but never created another major public commission for the city.

The sculptor left the Pacific Northwest in 1915 and headed to California where he established a studio in San Francisco, ostensibly to offer his services for statuary at the Panama-Pacific Exposition held that same year. After the move south, Frolich became good friends with the writer Jack London, and London's wife, Charmian, at the author's Glen Ellen ranch in Sonoma County, in Northern California. Frolich was one of many artists, writers, activists, and other intellectuals that visited London and stayed at the ranch: in one group photograph, Frolich stands on the far left, beside Johan Böjer, Douglas Doty and Upton Sinclair, wearing his signature beret and wire-rimmed glasses. For his part, London encouraged these associations, and in Frolich's case, also became a regular patron of the sculptor's work.

Frolich was welcomed at Glen Ellen for his boisterous, outspoken nature, and shared a love of the sea with London as well, as both of the men were sailors. London biographer Irving Stone has

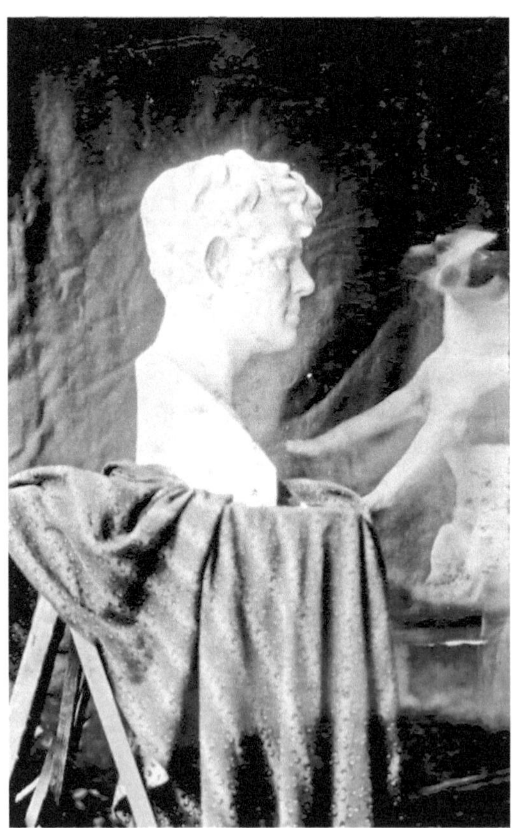

Bust of Jack London by Finn H. Frolich. Ca. 1920. The Huntington Library, San Marino, California.

described Frolich as London's "court jester and sculptor" at Glen Ellen.[21] In this capacity, he produced many sculptures for the couple, which included a portrait bust of Jack London that today marks the entrance to Glen Ellen as a state park. A copy of this bust was later cast into bronze by the Oakland Port Authority when it built Jack London Square.

During his time in the Bay area and visits to Glen Ellen, Frolich remarried to his third wife, Kala. Despite the custody ruling in Seattle, Virginia Frolich came to live with her father at Glen Ellen, along with Frolich and Kala's young son, Guilford.

When London committed suicide in 1916, Frolich was asked to engrave the author's name on the gravestone at Glen Ellen. The friendship at an end, the sculptor moved his family to Los Angeles in 1920 in a Ford Model T, where he built a new studio in the Hollywood neighborhood that was ever-after known as "London House" in honor of his friend. The sculptor's time in L.A. over the next two decades was a mixture of commercial and fine art projects. At long last, he seemed to have found a permanent home. He produced over 100 statues for the motion picture industry, while continuing to sculpt historical portrait busts and reliefs, notably a monumental bust of the Antarctic polar explorer and fellow Norwegian, Roald Amundsen.[22]

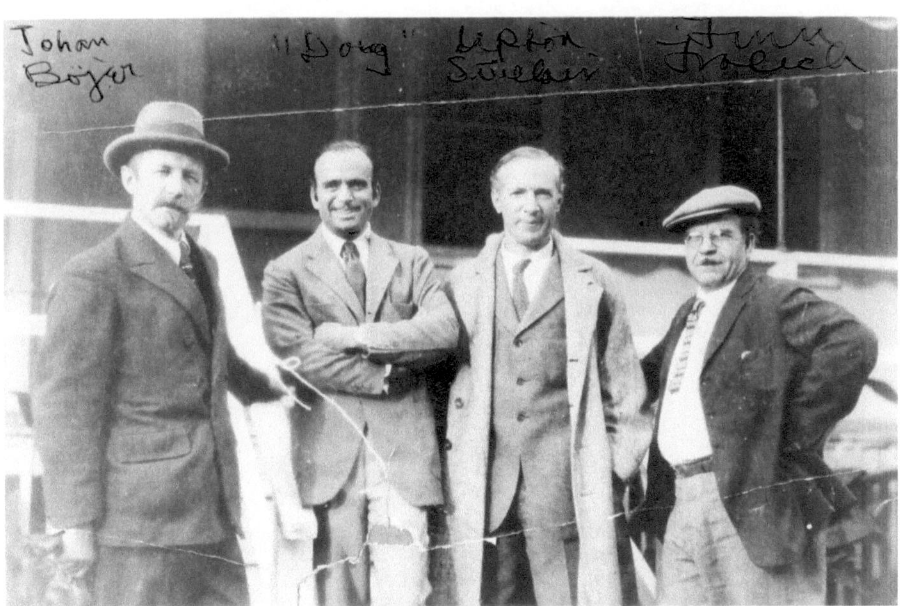

Johan Böjer, Douglas Z. Doty, Upton Sinclair, and Finn H. Frolich. **Ca. 1925. The Huntington Library, San Marino, California.**

The sculptor died at the age of 79 in 1947, at Salinas, California. His legacy as one of the creative minds that helped to insure the success of the A-Y-P Exposition of 1909 and more specifically, his two monumental sculpture busts to Hill and Grieg at the University of Washington, have remained a lasting tribute to early efforts to produce public sculpture for Seattle.

4

Max P. Nielsen
(1864–1917)

Of all the sculptors who have contributed public monuments to Seattle, Max P. Neilsen may be the most enigmatic. He was active between 1907 and 1917, and in that ten-year timespan completed five portrait medallions and one small statue in bronze for the city. His subjects for these works were well known to the local citizenry and included such luminaries as city father Henry Yesler and park activist Sherwood Gillespy.

Nielsen was a newcomer to both the Pacific Northwest region and indeed, the country, hailing originally from Denmark. He first arrived to the United States by ship from Copenhagen to New York, on May 17, 1905. He came out west that same year, as a sculptor contributing to the ornamentation of buildings at the Lewis and Clark Exposition held in Portland, Oregon.

During Seattle's first "Golden Age" of public monuments, memorials and statuary between 1905 and 1915, Nielsen played a notable (albeit brief) role as a contributing sculptor. Just as the majority of the public sculptures created during this timeframe were connected in one way or another to the Alaska-Yukon-Pacific (A-Y-P) Exposition of 1909, so too did Nielsen owe his beginnings as a Seattle sculptor to this event. His arrival to the city coincided with the groundbreaking held in 1907 at the University of Washington, site of the future Exposition buildings, exhibitions and landscaping.

Nielsen was hired as a plasterman, one of many who came to Seattle between 1907 and 1909 to model, sculpt and cast the many architectural ornaments that decorated over twenty-five buildings designed in a Beaux-Arts style for the Exposition. Many of these craftsmen also came from European countries, such as Italy, France and Norway. The Portland Exposition had also proven his abilities as a sculptor in such regard, so the relocation north to Seattle from Oregon was a timely one.

47

These craftsmen created elaborate medallions and crests, fluted colonnades and capitals with acanthus motifs, urns and archways that adorned the facades and pediments of buildings, and beautified the surrounding grounds. Among these buildings so adorned was the Agricultural Building on the west side of the Arctic Circle's Geyser Basin. Done in a French Renaissance style, it covered 60,000 square feet of ground and included 100,000 square feet of interior floor space. The building was undertaken for the Exposition by the architectural firm of Graham and Meyers of Seattle, with oversight by the firm of Howard and Galloway who in turn had been secured by the University of Washington's Board of Regents on May 21, 1907, as the architects in charge of executing the Exposition's building plans.

Nielsen was among those plaster craftsmen who worked on the decorations for the Agricultural Building. While the building did not survive past the Exposition's end date as a permanent structure on the University of Washington campus, Nielsen did develop a close association with the newly formed Beaux-Arts group first established under Frolich in 1908. Nielsen kept a studio in the old University Building downtown, which also housed studios for others in the group, including Frolich. Through this network of sculptors and other artists, Nielsen was later able to model a small statuette called *Umbrella Man* which was cast into plaster by the Milani Brothers, who had also come from Italy for the A-Y-P Exposition. Beginning in 1910, these copies were sold to the public at a low cost of one dollar apiece.[1]

However, Nielsen's initial foray into the local arts scene was not limited to the A-Y-P Exposition or the Beaux-Arts group alone. In the fall of 1907, the Dane learned of a new public call for a sculpture design planned for a fountain at the intersection of Fifth Avenue, Cedar Street and Denny Way. The project was the first public art commission offered by the City of Seattle.

Nielsen submitted a competing design with the subject of his statue the namesake of the city, Chief Seattle, of the Suquamish and Duwamish Tribes. However, the sculptor took his inspiration from another design which had already been published in local newspapers after it was released by the same city committee that was supervising progress on the project. This was the design for the statue of Chief Seattle by sculptor James Wehn, originally provided to committee member Clarence Bagley in July 1907.

Despite the committee's desire to accept the Wehn statue without qualification, the city had a requirement for competitive bids on the project, which prompted the advertisement for other designs "for an erection of a piece of statuary and pedestal in connection with an ornamental fountain."[2] While the announcement did not call specifically for Chief Seattle as the subject for the statue, the local press regardless published sketches of the Wehn design that had been released by one of the committee members.

Nor was Nielsen the only sculptor who took the idea of Chief Seattle as the figure for the project statue and made it his own. Two others—James John Frederickson and C.E. Dorisy—also presented models of the Chief in similar poses for review by the committee in October 1907. Of these sculptors, Wehn had a low opinion as to both their general skill and in particular, how they had appropriated his design: "The men who had submitted the copies of my study had arrived for work at the Exposition and were known as plastermen; such workmen do ornamental work and plaster casting, often they attempt to pass as sculptors."[3] Wehn's design for the Chief Seattle statue ultimately prevailed, leaving Neilsen to continue his efforts on the plaster ornamentation for the buildings of the A-Y-P Exposition.

Towards the end of his career, Wehn had characterized the others who had submitted alternative versions of his Chief Seattle statue as "scavengers."[4] But in 1908, he proved to be of a more forgiving nature towards his fellow sculptors, at least where Nielsen was concerned.

Recognizing the Danish sculptor's experience in working with plaster casting, Wehn did include Nielsen on his project for the first city-commissioned statue. More than a year after the competing designs fiasco, Wehn hired Nielsen to undertake the large scale plaster work for the mold of his life-sized clay model. The $100 he paid to Nielsen also covered the cost for one ton of plaster of Paris used to cast the figure of Chief Seattle into three sections, with each piece later recast in bronze by a local Seattle foundry. The work was completed successfully in December 1908. It would not be the last time the two sculptors' paths would cross on public sculpture projects of mutual interest.

After the conclusion of the A-Y-P Exposition in October 1909, Nielsen remained in the city and continued to work out of his studio in the old University Building. By this time, the sculptor had successfully completed a number of new portrait commissions both as sculpture busts and medallion reliefs. Of the former type, Nielsen modeled portraits of Mark Twain, Colonel Harvey Scott, editor of *The Portland Oregonian* newspaper, and both a bust and death mask of the late U.S. Congressman Francis Cushman from Tacoma, Washington, in plaster. His medallion subjects included Cushman, and a dual portrait medallion with the profiles of Mr. and Mrs. Louis Schoenfeld, founders of the Standard Furniture Company. Unfortunately in the case of the last commission, which had been intended as a surprise present to Louis Schoenfeld on his seventieth birthday, the father died twelve days prior to the medallion's arrival from the foundry back east. Nielsen produced another portrait plaque in bronze of Charles Henry Cobb, with this work installed in the lobby of the Cobb Building in downtown Seattle.

The years immediately following the A-Y-P Exposition in Seattle were lean ones for Nielsen. In 1910, public notice of judgements for sale by a debt collection agency posted in the local newspaper included one for Nielsen, in the amount of $67.13. In that same year, the sculptor also lost the site for his studio, when the old University Building was finally torn down. Despite these setbacks, Nielsen remained in the Pacific Northwest to continue his work as a sculptor.

During his time in Seattle, Nielsen was successful in his specialization of modeling portrait medallions for subjects accomplished in the areas of government and business. He produced relief medallions in bronze of both C.F. White and E.A. Stuart, which like the Cobb medallion, were installed in the lobbies of their namesakes' buildings. The sculptor modeled a bust of John L. Wilson, who served as a United States Senator for Washington State between 1895 and 1899, as a newly commissioned memorial in 1912.

Not all of his efforts towards commissions bore immediate support. In the case of the Cushman bust, his clay model design took three years to finally see it cast into bronze. The bust was unveiled at the Washington State Historical Society on January 16, 1912, with Seattle businessman John Arthur offering the key note address commemorating the sculpture to the Society's permanent collection in Cushman's memory. Funding for the bust casting was a conglomeration of sources that made contributions to the cause and included the local Grand Army of the Republic (G.A.R.) Posts, the Relief Corps, the Independent Carpenters' Association, George W. Tibbets (on behalf of the veterans in the Orting Home), the Pacific Coast Lumberman's Association, and many others.[5]

The portrait commissions Nielsen was able to secure were supplemented with public exhibitions of his work with other groups, such as an exhibition sponsored in 1913 by the newly formed Washington State Art Association at their gallery on Fifth Avenue. Among the thirty-eight paintings and five sculptures accepted by the jury for display, was Nielsen's series of portrait medallions in bronze of Dorothy Elizabeth Baker, Chester F. White, John L. Wilson and Carrie Bell Turner Cobb.

Nielsen continued to exhibit his medallions and small sculptures with the Art Association over the next two years, and received an honorable mention for his juried entry in the 1915 exhibition that included fifty-three Northwest artists. The year also marked the creation of the most elaborate monument of his career: the fountain, statue and medallions dedicated to Sherwood Gillespy at Jefferson Park. The completion of this memorial sculpture heralded the end of Seattle's first major era of public sculpture added to the city.

Just as the A-Y-P Exposition had served as a catalyst for the creation of Lorado Taft's monumental bronze statue of George Washington and Richard Brooks' statue of William Henry Seward, the statue and medallions modeled by Nielsen for Jefferson Park were part of a larger effort to transform public lands throughout the city. As the Exposition was also the first of its kind for Seattle, so too was the development of Jefferson Park, intended as the first public golf course for the city.

The origins of the park dated back to 1898, when the city purchased 235 acres from the State of Washington that at the time was designated State school land. This area became known as the Beacon Hill Park, with the land purchased to serve as a twin reservoir water supply from the Cedar River and also as a cemetery site. Beacon Hill (and Beacon Avenue, which runs through the park land) was named after Beacon Hill in Boston by M.H. Young of the Union Truck Line Company that operated an electric car line in the same area.

It was not until 1907 that Park Board Commissioner Edward Cheasty proposed the idea for a nine-hole golf course as a feature of a new municipal park on Beacon Hill. Over the next two years, the Parks Board moved incrementally towards endorsement of Cheasty's idea. The park was renamed in 1908 in honor of President Thomas Jefferson. Sherwood Gillespy was also enlisted by Cheasty as another proponent of the golf course. Gillespy had come to Seattle in 1896 to work in the dry goods business. He eventually became the manager of the Mutual Life Insurance Company, and as their agent negotiated the purchase of the Mutual Life Building.[6]

The fact that Gillespy was originally from New York and a Scotsman, as well as well-traveled and therefore familiar with the success of golf as a pastime in other cities, helped in his advocacy of a new public golf park for Seattle. In 1909 the City Council directed the Parks Board to have the Olmsted Brothers "determine the feasibility of a nine-hole golf links on the city-owned property on Beacon Hill."[7] That same year, the city designated twenty-one acres in the park for future use as a nine-hole golf course.

Seattle historian Don Sherwood has suggested that the plan developed by the Olmsted brothers was actually for an eighteen-hole golf course and first submitted to the city in 1911. An alternate version held that the Olmsted brothers instead submitted a plan for only a nine-hole course in early 1912 to the Seattle Parks Board.[8] In either case, by the fall of 1912 the city had abandoned the idea of the nine-hole course in favor of an expanded eighteen-hole links and hired Robert Johnstone from the Seattle Golf Club to design the course. Johnstone's plan for this course covered ninety-six acres, of the park's total 137 acres of land.

Gillespy, who was largely responsible for garnering city-wide support for the project both at the Park Board level and through a petition signed by "several thousand citizens," did not live to see the city's first golf course park come to pass.[9] His death on May 10, 1912, preceded Johnstone being hired to do the golf course by several months.

Fortunately for the city, it had a ready-made labor force available in the form of convicted criminals housed in the City Police Stockade on the property. The stockade's construction (along with an isolation hospital or "Pest House" which housed those suffering from contagious diseases) pre-dated the designation of the land for park purposes. Construction on the golf course began in 1913, with the prisoners undertaking much of the manual labor to transform the wooded landscape to fairway greens. By the fall of the next year, most of the major work on the golf course had been completed. The year 1914 also saw the end of Edward Cheasty, who in addition to Gillsepy had been a major supporter of efforts to have a golf course offered in Seattle.

The loss of both Cheasty and Gillespy was felt especially by the golf community in Seattle, and efforts were begun in 1914 through a memorial committee to create a new memorial to Gillsepy in particular, who was regarded by many as "the father of the public golf movement in Seattle."[10] The committee began a fundraising effort led by Dr. Frank Shaw and committee treasurer N.B. Solner, with donations of one dollar requested as the standard contribution. The group was successful, and raised $1,000 towards the design and casting in bronze of two portrait medallions and a small-sized statue as part of a granite drinking fountain memorial.

Over the course of several months, Nielsen modeled the two medallions and the main statue's figure of a young male golfer posed with golf club over left shoulder in mid-swing. On February 18, 1915, he placed his first casting order with the Roman Bronze Works foundry in New York, with a cash deposit of $168 paid in full for the completed order on March 1, 1915.[11]

The memorial fountain was installed in front of the golf course clubhouse, on the Beacon Avenue side. A polished granite base had two bronze

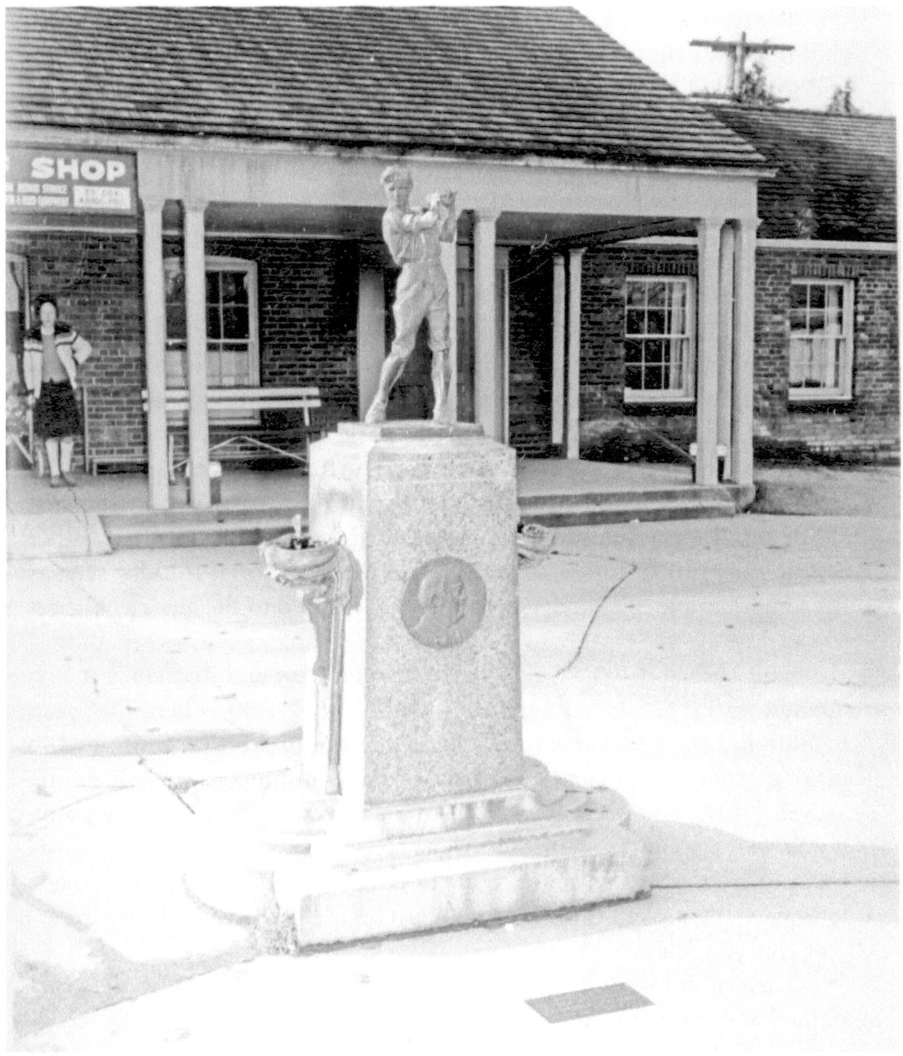

Sherman Gillespy Fountain. Photograph 1950. Seattle Municipal Archives.

cast sconces for drinking fountains placed on either side, while the opposite sides were adorned with a bronze portrait medallion of Gillespy's profile and another medallion bearing the inscription: "a kindly, lovable man;
an ardent golfer, the father of the idea of a municipal golf course for the
City of Seattle."[12] Further details on the portrait medallion included the
sculptor's initials, "MPN," and Roman Numerals around the top edge
which signified the birth (1853) and death (1912) years of Gillespy.

For the fountain's central element, Nielsen modeled a figure in period clothing of the time: shirtsleeves rolled to the elbows, "Plus fours" breeches and shins clad in stockings. The statue was twenty-six inches high when cast in bronze and showed the golfer frozen in the act of motion: the figure's right foot with heel raised, after having completed a full swing with his driver golf club and head canted over the right shoulder looking downrange after the ball. When installed atop the four-foot-high granite base, the memorial had a total height of just over six feet.

The Jefferson Park Golf Course officially opened to the public on May 12, 1915, with the Nielsen memorial in place to greet the arrival of several hundred people. Its completion also marked the memorial committee's intent to make a gift of the fountain to the city of Seattle. A year after the sculpture's dedication at the park opening, Nielsen was still receiving high praise for the work in news articles promoting the Washington State Art Association's latest exhibition of paintings in the city. While not done at the same monumental scale as statues made by other Seattle sculptors of this time period, Nielsen's memorial is today seen as the lone example of statuary which he contributed to the city's public art scene.

The Jefferson Park Golf Course has likewise endured since it first opened to the public. Attendance in 1962 was 97,000 golfers that year, notable in that it was one of the few city enterprises that continued to make a profit year after year. The memorial continued as a stable fixture as well for the site, with a few adjustments over the years. At one point, it was relocated to the south side of the clubhouse, where it greets visitors today in front of the entrance to the building. In 2012, repairs were made to replace the broken off golf club and to fix the fountain with new reservoir components added.

Nielsen enjoyed his greatest success as a city sculptor in the years immediately following the end of the A-Y-P Exposition. The public recognition afforded to him for the Gillespy memorial helped him to create one other public sculpture for Seattle. True to his strength as a portraitist, this was a bronze plaque made in honor of one of the first pioneers to the area and city father, Henry Yesler.

Seattle served as the seat for King County government and in 1911, voters approved the construction of a new building downtown to house both the city and county offices as well as serve as a courthouse. The Beaux-Arts style which had been a popular architectural design for many of the buildings in the A-Y-P Exposition again found favor in the new County-City Building through Seattle architect A. Warren Gould. The site for the construction of the new five-story building was also significant as a historical landmark, since it was once occupied by Henry Yesler's pioneer home.

The inspiration for adding a plaque with Yesler's likeness to the building's façade originated from local historian and University of Washington history professor Edmond S. Meany. In the spring of 1915 Meany wrote to the King County Commissioners, extolling the legacy of Yesler and urging them to include "a bronze tablet to the pioneer's memory."[13] Meany's advocacy went further to suggest that local sculptor James Wehn was an accomplished portraitist for medallions of this kind and should be the person chosen to complete a new plaque for the building.

In April 1915, Professor Edmond Meany at the University of Washington wrote to his close friend, James Wehn, to confide details to help secure the commission:

> Henry S. Yesler—Builder of the first steam sawmill in Puget Sound at Seattle in 1852, Mayor of the City and prominent citizen of the State, after forty years of useful life in this community, died in his beautiful home on this site in 1892.—In memory of the honored pioneer this tablet is erected in 1915 by the Board of Commissioners of King County.
>
> The arrangement above is only for my convenience and need not influence your plan of sculpture. It is possible the names of the Commissioners may need to be added. I will notify the Board you are working on this. Yours faithfully, Edmond S. Meany[14]

As prominent a sculptor as Wehn was at this time in the city, and in spite of his apparent inside track with Meany's office, the Board of Commissioners instead selected Nielsen as the sculptor for the job. The timing for Nielsen's involvement was perfect as far as the new commission, with the sculptor just finishing work on the Gillespy memorial for the high profile Jefferson Park.

Nielsen's close association with the sculptor Finn Frolich and the Northwest Beaux-Arts group may have enhanced the selection process by the King County Commissioners in his favor. In a similar fashion, his past experience with Beaux-Arts style of architecture from the Portland and Seattle Expositions would have appealed to the architect Gould's stylistic choice for the building design.

By November 17, 1915, Nielsen had completed the Yesler plaque and sent the plaster mold to the Roman Bronze Works foundry in New York, with an incurred cost of just twenty-three dollars for the bronze casting order. His payment on February 22, 1916, settled up well in advance of the new building's completion and dedication several months later on May 4,

1916. Nielsen's final design for the plaque showed the pioneer in three-quarter profile and in the twilight years of life. It measured thirty-four inches high by twenty-five inches wide and was installed near the building's entrance on Third Avenue.

Another detail that Nielsen had included as part of the dedication text on the plaque was the historical connection between Yesler's home and the present site of the building, with the concluding line citing 1892 as the year the pioneer perished while at home. When an expansion of the building added six floors in 1930, the plaque remained on the façade where it may still be viewed today.

For James Wehn, the loss of the county's commission was only a momentary setback. In the following year, the "First Sculptor of Seattle" was able to regain the attention of local government officials with his own Yesler portrait design by securing a new commission for a bronze medallion installed at the Yesler Public Library (Douglass-Truth Library) in Seattle.

The Yesler plaque on the County-City building proved to be Nielsen's last public monument for the city and the final sculpture of his career. Little else is known about Nielsen's personal life and time spent in Seattle. His mother, Karen Madson, was an American citizen and lived for a time in Denmark with Nielsen's father, a Danish national. She followed her son back to the United States two years after his arrival in 1905. Nielsen had two brothers and one sister, all of them living on the West Coast. His death at Swedish Hospital on March 7, 1917, at the age of fifty-three was a tragic loss to the Pacific Northwest arts community. Equally tragic is the prospect of his obscurity today as a sculptor of note.

Such a fate has not yet come to pass, so long as public monuments such as the Gillespy memorial endure. Other sculptures by Nielsen in public collections allow posterity to witness and marvel at the skill and historical value they embody. This sentiment was well summarized in the remarks from Bishop Frederic W. Keator at the 1912 unveiling of the Francis Cushman bust:

> Possibly for those of us who knew him as he worked and as he went in and out among us, it was not necessary that there should be any such monument as this, and yet we know full well how easy it is for the memory of man to be forgotten, and so for those who are to come after, for the rising generation, it is most important that we should place these outward and visible memorials, so that those who come after can look upon him and know his features and his face as we know them. So it seems to me that it is most appropriate that there should be this Hall of Fame and in it there should be found a place for this lasting memorial of Francis W. Cushman.[15]

This vision of public sculptures as having intrinsic historical, cultural and artistic value was shared by Nielsen and other sculptors who lived in Seattle or came to the city. Through their combined efforts, many statues, busts, reliefs and portrait plaques were contributed to the city's landscape.

5

James A. Wehn (1882–1973)

While the Alaska-Yukon-Pacific Exposition of 1909 was a transformative event for Seattle in many ways, it notably served as both a source of support and a venue for the display of several new public sculptures and monuments for the city. In the span of just a handful of years leading up to the Exposition and immediately after its conclusion, these works by such accomplished sculptors such as Lorado Taft, Richard Brooks and Finn Frolich enhanced the University of Washington and other public spaces with new historical, cultural and artistic representation and vitality.

The sheer multitude and combination of exhibitions, buildings, attractions, landscaping, infrastructure elements, cultural activities and historical re-enactments had achieved and far exceeded the Exposition's main stated purpose at its inception: "to exploit the resources of Alaska and the Yukon Territory, make known the vast importance of trade of the Pacific Ocean, and demonstrate the marvelous progress of Western America…"[1]

It was also in part through the Alaska-Yukon-Pacific (A-Y-P) Exposition that another sculptor was able to create another public sculpture for Seattle. But unlike those statues and busts that had found more immediate life during the days of the Exposition, the memorial sculpture created by Seattle sculptor James A. Wehn was not a reality until 1926. This was the monument to the Confederate war dead installed in Lake View Cemetery sponsored by the United Daughters of the Confederacy (U.D.C.).

The origins of the Confederate soldiers' monument date back to the founding of the U.D.C.'s Robert E. Lee Chapter no. 885 of Seattle in 1905. The group had an interest from the start in acquiring land in a cemetery within the city, for the purpose of interring deceased veterans who had fought for the Confederate cause in the American Civil War.

The process of collecting funds for the land purchase was slow, especially given that Seattle had no pre-existing cemeteries of Civil War dead on the Confederate side. Lake View Cemetery in Seattle does have a small section with 219 Union soldier graves on the north edge of the grounds. The spot was marked by a simple stone pylon marker in the center of the gravesites, put into place by the local Grand Army of the Republic (G.A.R.) members comprised of former Union Army veterans.

While the Seattle G.A.R. membership was an established group in the Pacific Northwest, in the years leading up to the A-Y-P Exposition of 1909 they had little interest in joint memorial commemorations or remembrances with their Southern counterparts. One exception to this was the G.A.R. observance of Memorial Day in Seattle, where the Robert E. Lee Chapter sent flowers as a token of respect.[2]

The A-Y-P Exposition presented the U.D.C with an opportunity to raise additional funds for a new memorial site, by hosting a "Dixie Day" celebration to bring together supporters of Confederate veterans while enlisting support from visitors who traveled from the Southern states to see the Exposition.

It took another two years, but eventually the Sons and Daughters of the Confederacy were able to finally purchase a plot inside Lake View Cemetery in 1911. It was the only such plot dedicated to Confederate soldiers in the Pacific Northwest. By 1922, seven veterans who had died in the interim period were buried there. Also by this year, the local U.D.C. chapter had committed to raising the monument's cost of $1,800 by asking other chapters nationwide for financial contributions, with $494.55 collected to date.[3] As had been the case with the plot purchase, funds were again slowly acquired: in 1925, the Washington Division reported at the thirty-second annual U.D.C. convention that another $190 had been collected for the Seattle monument fund.

When the sculptor James Wehn first entered into the odyssey of the monument at Lake View Cemetery is difficult to say. Around the same time as the purchase of the cemetery plot, he successfully modeled a profile portrait relief of the Confederate General and U.D.C. Chapter namesake, Robert E. Lee, and gave this to Professor Edmond Meany at the University of Washington. This portrait medallion figured prominently into the monument design Wehn completed fifteen years later.

By early 1926, the Robert E. Lee Chapter had enlisted the services of both Wehn and Edmund C. Messett of the Sunset Monument Company in Seattle to jointly design the monument. The sponsors had also purposely selected a stone from a site across the country that offered both lasting quality as a material and symbolic of Confederate veteran identity. Messett was instructed to carve the base, posts and lintel pediment of the monument from a single piece of granite from Stone Mountain, Georgia. By no coincidence, this was the same site where in 1916, Gutzon Borglum had first begun his own large-scale relief carving for the United Daughters of the Confederacy that was to show Generals Lee and Jefferson Davis leading a procession of horse-mounted generals and cavalry.

Messett had worked with Wehn before on other public sculpture projects, notably the memorial bench at Sluiskin Falls commemorating the first ascension of Mount Rainier by Hazard Stevens and P. B. Van Trump on August 17, 1870. The monument also memorialized Sluiskin, the Native American guide after which the Falls were named, who waited for the two climbers at the spot where the bench was placed. Messett's company, the Sunset Monument Company, was also just one of five companies in the Puget Sound region that was capable of doing the type of granite stone cutting needed for the new Confederate monument planned for Lake View.[4]

On February 26, 1926, the steamship *Monticello* unloaded the ten-ton stone in Seattle. While Messett oversaw the carving process, Wehn modeled several sculptural details that would adorn the assembled stonework at the gravesite. In all, the sculptor produced a "Southern Cross of Honor" for the top pediment at its center; the insignia of the U.D.C. for the stone cross-brace between the lintel posts; and a pair of crossed muskets with a copy of the 1911 portrait medallion of General Lee at the center of the base. All of these sculpture elements were cast in bronze from plaster models prepared at the sculptor's studio in the Leschi neighborhood of Seattle. Once it was finally assembled, the monument stood fourteen feet high.

On May 23, 1926, the monument was unveiled at Lake View Cemetery and dedicated to the Confederate Soldiers of America. At the ceremony, Mrs. May Avery Wilkins, president of the Washington Division of the U.D.C., declared how the new monument marked "consummation of a dream of Southern women in the Northwest of more than two decades ago."[5] Veterans from both North and South attended the ceremony, along with others who had served in the Spanish-American War and World War I. The solidarity of those veterans in attendance served as a visible reminder of the sacrifice made by all men in war, and was an observation not unnoticed by newspaper accounts of the event.

The keynote address at the monument dedication was provided not by any Seattle city official, but rather the Mayor-elect of Tacoma, Melvin

G. Tennant. The day also underscored a reality of this particular monument: that as a privately funded affair, it was a memorial with sculpture but not one planned or intended for widespread review in a public space.

Such was not a concern for James Wehn. As a sculptor, he had established a business practice of producing portrait medallions, plaques, busts, masks and other figurative sculpture as commissioned by private parties. Sometimes these were intended as cemetery markers, while others were for families to view in the privacy of their own home. The monument he co-designed and provided the bronze ornamentation for was the largest sculpture work of his career. It was also the first memorial to Confederate veterans placed within the city.

From the time he was a young boy, Wehn was a Seattle native. His upbringing in the city bore witness to trials such as the Great Seattle Fire of 1889 and triumphs such as the discovery of gold in the Klondike in 1898. He walked the streets with Princess Angeline, the daughter of Chief Seattle of the Suquamish and Allied Tribes, and as a young sculptor, was befriended by the likes of Clarence Bagley and Edmond Meany, who shared his passion for Northwest history and promotion of the arts. It was in this era, not long after Wehn's return to Seattle from an apprenticeship to the Chicago sculptor August Hubert, that these men were captivated by the young sculptor's idea for the city's first officially commissioned piece of public sculpture. This was the fountain statue of Chief Seattle (Sealth; Si'ahl), a Native American of renowned character and leadership in the Pacific Northwest.

A special committee had been formed by the City Council in early 1907 to commission a sculptor to create a new statue for the intersection of Fifth Avenue, Cedar Street and Denny Way. The committee's members included Bagley, Dr. James E. Crichton, Arnold Zbinden and Reginald H. Thomson, and was charged by the city to pay for the sculpture with approximately $3,000 in funds left over from the recently completed Denny Hill regrade project.

Through an intermediary Wehn met Bagley and offered his vision for this new statue as one that served as a historical monument to the Chief of the Suquamish and Duwamish tribes. The sculptor described the figure of Seattle at the moment when he first greeted the Denny party of settlers in 1851 on a beach at Alki Point, dressed in a Hudson's Bay blanket and his arm raised in friendly greeting. The concept was an immediate success with Bagley and the others. Despite a city government provision that required additional designs from other sculptors after the fact, Wehn's design for the Chief Seattle statue was finally accepted and the commission awarded to him in January 1908. It was the first public sculpture commission made by the city for a public space.

In his memoir about making the Chief Seattle statue, Wehn spoke with pride about his achievement and acknowledged that much of the work to model and cast the sculpture still lay ahead of him:

> The elation one feels after working hard to accomplish something worth while [*sic*] was mine. But not for long. A sculptor bidding on a piece of work in the medium of either marble or bronze knows through experience which firm is most capable or reproducing his work in permanent form.[6]

The unexpected competition over securing the statue commission was only the first of several challenges Wehn faced. He soon found himself at odds with the city appointed committee over the selection of which foundry would be used to undertake the bronze casting of the plaster mold, once that was ready. It was the city's position that the job should go to a recently started foundry in Seattle, as a show of support for local businesses. Wehn was unconvinced that the foundry (operated by Leon

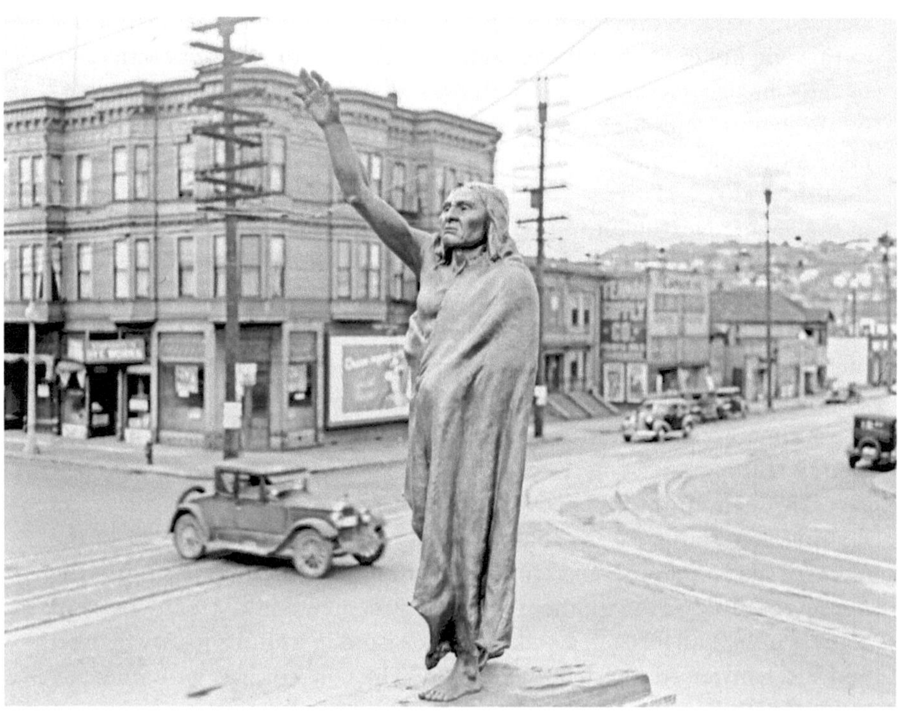

Chief Seattle by James A. Wehn at Fifth and Denny Way. Photograph 1936. Seattle Municipal Archives.

Morel, Sr., a Frenchman recently arrived to Seattle) had enough experience in fine art bronze casting to complete a quality cast using the lost-wax method preferred by the sculptor.

The sculptor's choice of the Gorham Manufacturing Company with its foundry in Providence, Rhode Island, was subsequently overruled by

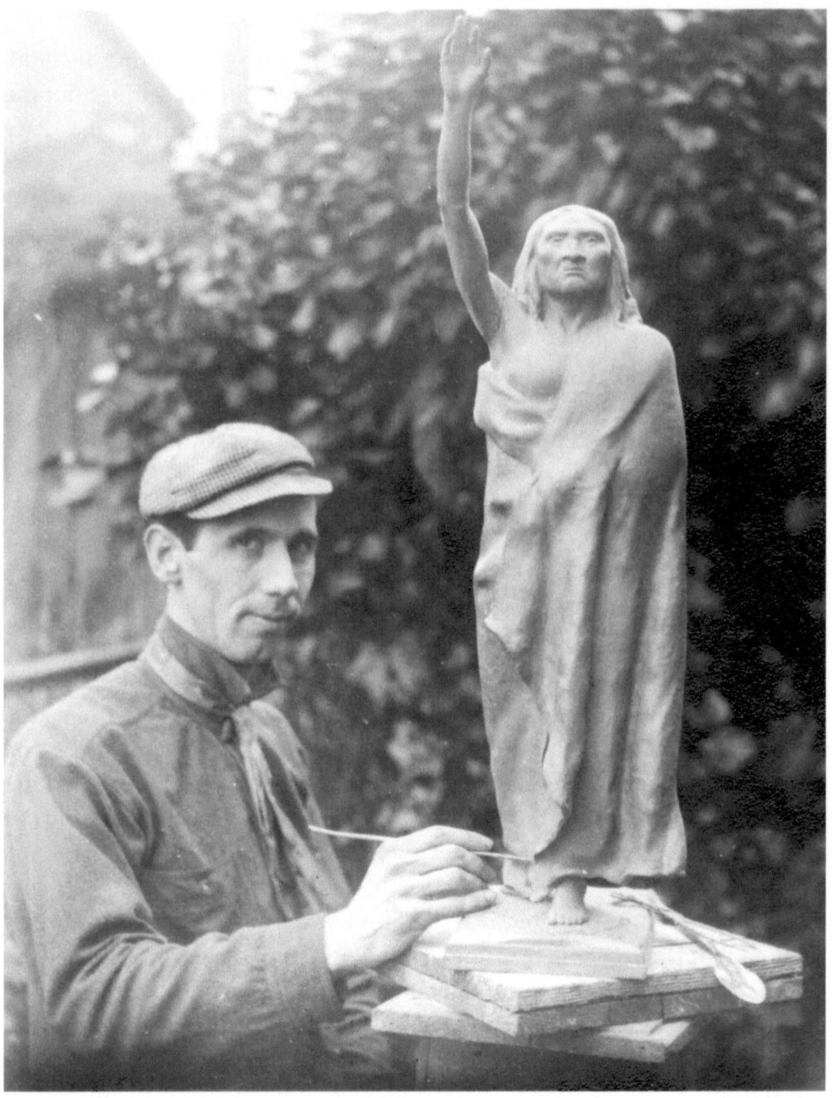

James A. Wehn with study for Chief Seattle statue. **1907. Photographer unknown. Special Collections, Washington State Historical Society.**

the committee. His concerns about the quality of the bronze casting went beyond the immediate result:

> What kind of sculptor was he in the first place, they would have every right to say, to do such work ... as long as the statue stands as a public monument, the question will be raised "Who was the sculptor, not who were on the committee, not who were the foundrymen [sic]. Wehn will be criticized long after all of those who were associated with the erection of the statue are gone."[7]

Research about his subject was also a challenge. Starting in 1908, James paid regular visits to many of the local reservations throughout the Pacific Northwest to study Native American physique, culture and daily life. These visits included tribal communities across the Pacific Northwest: the Suquamish Tribe's Port Madison Reservation; the Duwamish River valley and other ancestral Indian lands in the southern Puget Sound area, such as those near present-day Tukwila; the Tulalip Reservation, just outside Everett; Indian lands to the east, including the Muckleshoot Reservation; and those further north, such as those settlements found in the Upper Skagit Valley region. These visits gave the young sculptor a chance to escape the confines of his studio and helped him keep in shape for the physical labor required to work a ton of modeling clay for the Chief Seattle statue.

Wehn also gained insights into his statue model through Bagley, who had personally known the Suquamish Chief and provided the sculptor with the only studio photograph known to show the figure, taken in 1865 by the E.M. Sammis photography studio of Seattle.

It took the sculptor most of 1908, but by December of that year, he had completed a seven-foot-high model of Chief Seattle in modeling clay. A plaster cast was made for Morel's foundry, which called for the statue design to be cast in four sections of bronze and then welded together. The plan was contrary to Wehn's original plan to have the bronze work done in a single piece, using the lost-wax method of fine bronze casting. In spite of his reservations, the plaster model was delivered to Morel in January 1909.

A full ten months later, the sculptor's worst fears were proved true. The head of the figure lacked the original detail and clear features of the Chief's portrait Wehn had so laboriously modeled. The torso, right arm and legs sections had imperfect edges and gaps, which would require patchwork to the bronze where the seams joined together to complete the full statue. Recasting was not an option, given that by this time Morel and his business partner, Richards, had spent more than half the project's funds and also demanded additional payment to continue the foundry's work.

The sculptor eventually persuaded the Committee members to forgo further involvement of the local foundry, and struck a deal with them to remodel the entire figure once more at no additional cost for his labor. The city would pay compensation for the plaster used to make a second model to be sent back east, and the statue's granite pedestal that was already on order. As part of this new arrangement, the second casting of the statue in bronze would be done by the Gorham foundry in Providence, Rhode Island, and paid for by the city.

Before commencing work on the new figure, Wehn paid one last visit to the Morel foundry:

> The foundry was built on a raised ground, about five feet above tidewater, with a pleasant view of the sound and part of the city waterfront. While I appreciated the view, the five feet above tidewater interested me more from the point of utility ... with the help of a borrowed wheelbarrow I proceeded to dump my plaster cast of the Chief Seattle statue into the tidewater...[8]

By the time he started the modeling process using another ton of clay in his studio, a full three years had passed since the award of the commission. It took another year to again model the statue, have it cast into a plaster waste mold, and then shipped to the Gorham Company foundry. Per the foundry's instructions, only the arm was provided as a separate plaster piece for casting into bronze. The rest of the figure would be cast in one section, with the arm and pedestal base added as separately bronze cast pieces. The shipment of three crates departed from Seattle on March 30, 1912, via the Great Northern Railway.

Wehn's statue of Chief Seattle was successfully cast by Gorham and returned back to Seattle on October 24, 1912. It had a golden patina, and stood at seven-feet, two inches tall on its pedestal. Much to the pleasure of the statue committee members, it would be ready for unveiling on Founder's Day, November 13, 1912.

On the day of the statue's dedication, the sculptor offered some words of encouragement to the assembled onlookers, which included many Native Americans who shared their identity and heritage with the figure raised in bronze. For Wehn, it was a moment of professional triumph, but also one of homage to the statue's subject and pride he felt as a citizen of Seattle:

> Brother Tilikums, I wish to thank you for the honor that you have extended me today, in accepting my humble labor—the modeling of this statue of Chief Seattle, the City's first great Tilikum: and I further wish to extend my thanks to the Honorable Mayor Cotterill for his acceptance in behalf of the City, and of Mr. Cheasty in behalf of the Park Board. I wish to express my gratitude for having been chosen as the first sculptor to erect the first monument in our city.[9]

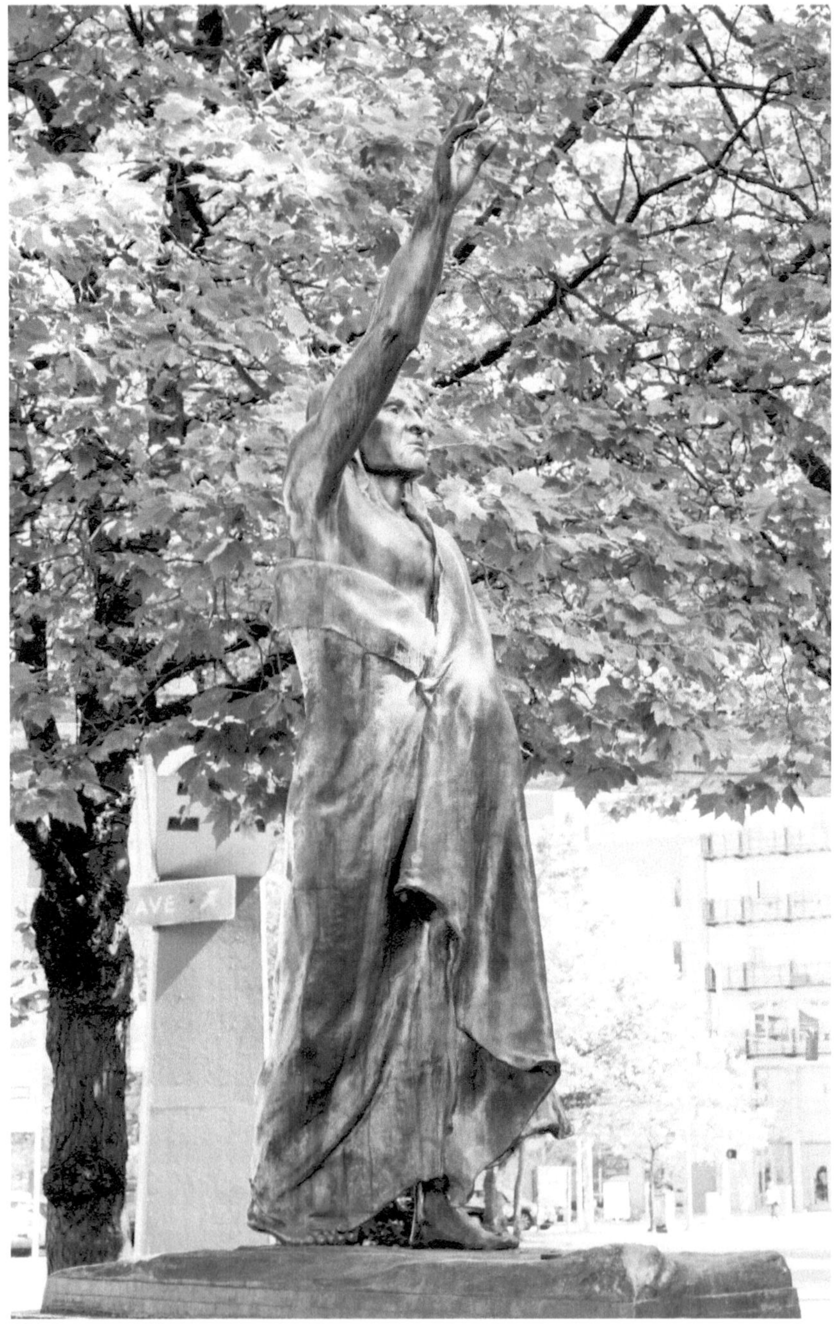

Chief Seattle by James A. Wehn. 1912. Fred F. Poyner IV, Photographer (2011).

In the final tally of his financial compensation for the fountain statue, Wehn collected between $600 and $800, after expenses. The greater benefit, however, came to him in the years that followed this initial success, in the connections made and reputation that assisted in his securing many new commissions, both public and privately funded.

It should be stated that while Wehn achieved his lifelong ambition of becoming a sculptor, in his personal life he endured more than a few losses close to home. During his childhood, he lost two brothers: the first to a diphtheria epidemic in Indianapolis, before the Wehn family moved to Seattle in 1889; the other brother, age fourteen, to a drowning accident on Lake Washington in 1895. His mother suffered a stroke on the day she learned of her eldest son, Harvey, had died by drowning, and in later years required home care by James.

In 1917, Wehn's first wife, Florence, was brutally murdered not three blocks from where the couple briefly lived on the west side of Queen Anne Hill in Seattle. The sculptor was questioned by police, but quickly dismissed as a suspect. The murderer was never caught.

The 1930s saw Wehn's studio endure economic hardships that were shared throughout the country during the Great Depression. The bachelor sculptor continued to work tirelessly to create new sculpture pieces, many which were installed throughout the city. In 1928, he designed and modeled the twin dolphin seal emblem that today decorates dozens of lamppost bases on city streets downtown. Three additional portrait busts in bronze of Chief Seattle were ordered by the Parks Board, to decorate fountains in Pioneer Place, Westlake Boulevard and Fourth Avenue, and Occidental & King Streets. All told, the sculptor created at least fourteen different portraits of Chief Seattle for various medals, medallions, plaques, busts and statues, including one that was adopted in 1936 as the official seal of the city.

Over a career that spanned seventy-five years, Wehn created over 225 medallions, portrait busts, plaques, statues, reliefs and public sculptures in his Seattle studio. Over fifty of these number found their way into public venues around Seattle, including schools, building lobbies and facades, city parks, cemeteries and the University of Washington.

In 1949, Wehn married his second wife, Lillian, who had been a sculpture student of his in the Sculpture Department at the University of Washington. Wehn had started the department in 1919, and remained as an Associate Instructor in Modeling and Sculpture until 1924, when he left to pursue a growing demand for work from his own studio. Years later, Lillian's professional connections to Seattle Public Schools aided her hus-

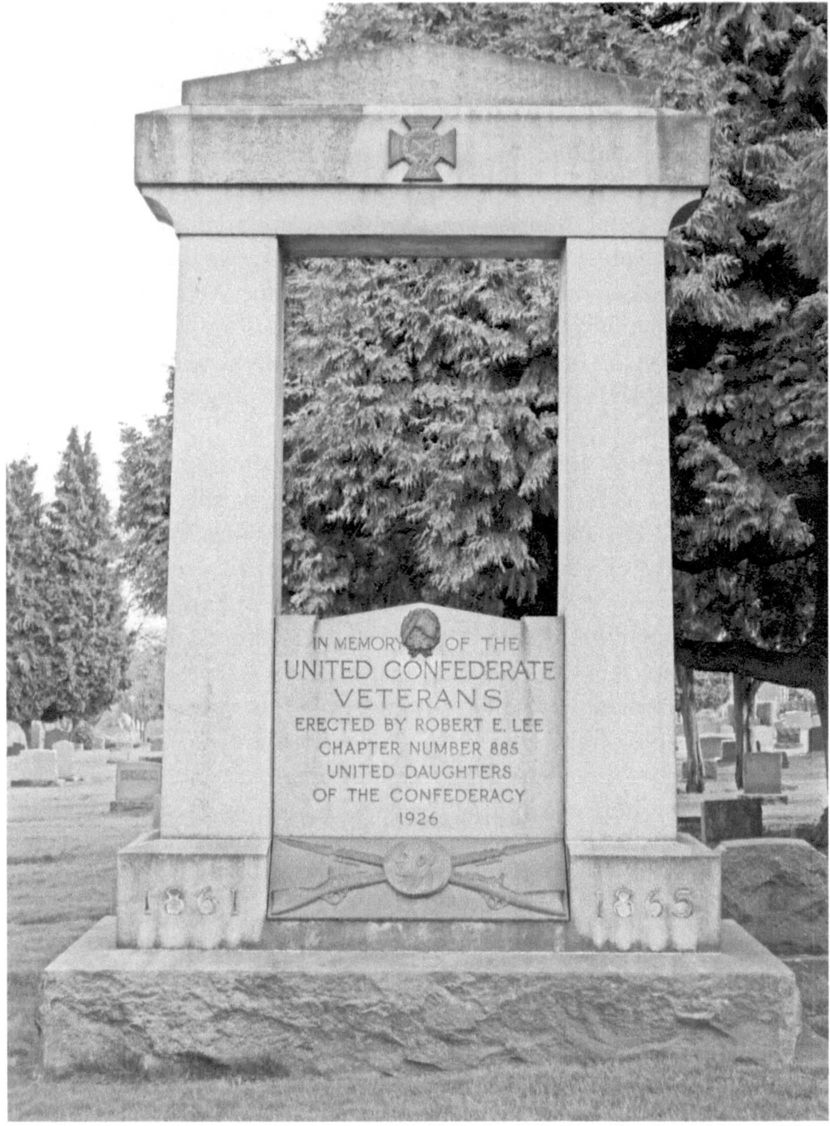

United Confederate Veterans (U.C.V.) Memorial **by James A. Wehn. 1926. Fred F. Poyner IV, Photographer (2014).**

band in securing over a dozen portrait plaque commissions through the schools. One of these works—a portrait plaque of Nathan Hale for the Nathan Hale High School—was completed shortly before his death in 1973 at the age of 91.

James Wehn's bronze statue of *Chief Seattle* that has stood at the intersection of Fifth Avenue and Denny Way since 1912 was an impressive effort on several fronts. In his own lifetime, James Wehn claimed the title of "First Sculptor of Seattle" in large part based upon this work as the first public sculpture commissioned by a committee of the City Council in 1907. He was also the first, true "local" sculptor from Seattle to gain such a publicly commissioned work. Arguably as well, his choice of a Native American as a figure of historical importance and regional identity for the statue was also a first for the city, where public sculpture was concerned. In this singular respect and in the totality of his sculpture work, Seattle is fortunate to have received a lasting legacy.

6

Allen George Newman
(1875–1940)

The period of the 1920s was an active one for Seattle, in terms of the number of new statues and other sculpture monuments that were either in development as projects, or were fully completed and installed in parks and other public spaces around the city. Similar to Seattle's earlier "Golden Age" of new historical statuary added during and shortly after the Alaska-Yukon-Pacific (A-Y-P) Exposition of 1909, this second wave of monuments was achieved by a combination of sculptors both already living and working in Seattle, and others who heralded from cities across the United States.

Collectively, all of these men and women have defined the statues, historical monuments and portraiture sculptures found throughout Seattle, and thus are known to us today as Seattle sculptors. Some, like James Wehn and Alonzo Victor Lewis, were long established in the Pacific Northwest, with homes and studios located in the city's environs. They were well-known to the citizenry not just for their artistic creations (and temperaments) but also their personal connections to the local community. Both of these men are counted among the sculptors who provided new monuments to Seattle between 1909 and 1929.

Other sculptors like Alice Carr moved to Seattle later in life, and made a contribution to the public sculpture of the city, only to then move on with their lives and careers. Still others came and stayed for a short duration to design and install a single new sculpture for a city park, such as the New York sculptors Hermon A. McNeil and Richard Brooks, or the imminent Lorado Taft from Chicago.

There was yet another type of sculptor responsible for producing new public sculpture for the city. These were sculptors whose work was produced in locations far removed from Seattle, with the subjects of these works impersonal but with enough commonalities to make them desirable as new acquisitions for the city. In this category, Seattle has included the work of the sculptor Allen George Newman.

It was Newman who provided the very first war memorial sculpture for the city, titled *The Hiker*. While this statue was installed in 1926 at Woodland Park, the history surrounding the figure depicted in the memorial dates back to the turn of the twentieth century, when the city was drawn into conflicts that demanded lives and land on a most intimate level. For his model, Newman selected a soldier characteristic of the volunteer infantry who served in the Spanish-American War (1898), the Philippine-American War (1899–1902; also called the Philippine Insurrection) and the Boxer Rebellion in China (1899–1901; also called the Yihequan Movement).

Even though its military subject had direct ties to the history of Seattle, the statue was not commissioned specifically for the city alone. During his lifetime, the sculptor had at least twenty-one copies of the soldier design cast in bronze. Most of these statues were cast either six feet tall or the more heroic proportion of nine feet tall, and were installed in town squares, veteran's cemeteries and public parks. A third cast size was made as a collectible statuette, done in an American Beaux-Arts style and smaller in size at a height of twenty-eight inches. Copies of this smaller version have since been collected by institutions including the New York Historical Society and the Munson-Williams-Proctor Arts Institute.

Newman's statue is unique among the other public historical statuary of Seattle in another respect. From amongst the larger castings that were installed across the United States, the six-foot-high version of *The Hiker* found in Woodland Park was the only copy installed on the West Coast. The majority of the twenty other versions of the statue were placed in cities and towns along the eastern seaboard, with six copies in New York and another four in Rhode Island.

The proliferation of *The Hiker* design throughout the east ties directly back to the sculptor's family origins in New York City and his early training as an artist.

Born on August 28, 1875, Allen George Newman III came from a well-off family that lived in New York during the winters and spent summers at the family's estate at Garrison-on-the-Hudson. Newman's father owned and operated the Capron Brass, Iron, Silver and Bronze Foundry in New York. From his father, Newman learned through observation the hands-on techniques for working metals, while the influence of Newman's mother was more indirect:

From early childhood he displayed an interest in the Foundry, which was taken for granted by a family largely wrapped up and united in their interests. Besides, his mother, Ada, had prayed for months before his birth that she would have a son, and that he would be a sculptor.[1]

At the age of fifteen, Newman required an operation for appendicitis and to recuperate, spent six weeks in Florida on his aunt and uncle's citrus plantation. During his convalescence, he spent time carving a set of alligators out of orange wood—the first sculpture of his career. Upon his return to New York, he completed high school and entered City College, where his studies focused on the Romantic languages.

In some interesting comparisons, both Newman and the sculptor James Wehn had very similar experiences as young adults that helped to shape their future lives as sculptors. Both men suffered from maladies in their youth, which restricted them to bed and in doing so, focused their attention on art to pass the time (in Wehn's case, his poor constitution had him remain indoors, where he worked with watercolors to paint still-life compositions). Both men also had fathers who were active in the foundry business. Both of them were encouraged by other arts professionals to continue working in the fine arts, based on their initial artworks done while in recovery. Both sculptors returned to live and work from their parents' homes, in order to care for their elderly and infirmed mothers. And tragically, both men suffered personal loss of family close to them early in life. Wehn lost two brothers and later his first wife to a murder that went unsolved; Newman lost his second child to strep throat in 1905.

For Newman, a mentor was found by way of a family connection, through the intervention of John Q.A. Ward, dean of American Sculptors and whose stepson had married Allen's sister, Marion. Ward had opportunity during a family visit to see the alligator carvings from Florida, and based on this offered encouragement to Newman and also took him in as a new studio apprentice in 1897. For the next four years Newman worked under the direction of Ward, notably as an assistant on the modeling of an equestrian sculpture featuring General Mark Sheridan for the New York State capitol in Albany. During this time, he also completed his studies in sculpture at the Columbia University's Academy of Design.

It was also during this time that Newman first developed his concept for *The Hiker*, as a contemporary subject. In 1898, the Spanish-American War was underway in Cuba. The sculptor's modeling process would take the next six years to complete and longer still before any copies of the statue were cast into bronze.

Newman's design for the statue showed a lone infantry soldier, dressed in the uniform of a volunteer Army recruit destined for tropical climates. The shirt had a wide collar, worn open at the neck, and the sleeves rolled up to the elbows. A wide-brimmed hat sat cocked to the left side on the soldier's head, while the belt worn at the waist was worn slung on the hips to the opposite, right side. Sturdy boots extend almost to the knees, with the pants tucked inside at the boot brims. In the soldier's right arm, a Krag rifle was cradled in the bend of the elbow, with the right hand holding the stock near the gun trigger.

While the soldier can be clearly identifiable as a "hiker," which served as the moniker of infantrymen of the Spanish-American War, the sculptor had deliberately omitted any specific details that identify the figure beyond his generalized role, so that even uniform rank insignia were left off the shirt. Newman's intent was to show this could be any American fighting man who had endured long marches or "hikes" through tropical jungles.

That Newman used soldiers returning from Cuba—and later starting in 1899, from the Philippines—as models for his statue, was a practice the sculptor continued for commissioned work throughout his career. When he created his statue of *Justice* placed on top of the Florida Capitol Building in Tallahassee, Newman used his live-in, African-American maid at the time as the figure. Once completed, he told her, "Cora, now you are truly emancipated."[2] In another instance, Newman encountered a former Civil War-era Colonel on the streets of New York and asked the man to pose for the modeling of a statue dedicated to General Sterling Price, completed in 1914 and installed in Keytesville, Missouri. For a third public monument, Newman used his mother, brother and sister as models for a sculpture group titled *Women of the South*, destined for Jacksonville, Florida.

Newman's models for *The Hiker* were taken from assorted interviews the sculptor made with returning soldiers from the conflicts abroad, some of them on sick leave recovering from malaria and other diseases rampant in the exotic climates. The sculptor spent "several months collecting data on the Cuban and Philippine campaigns preparatory to commencing his work."[3] These efforts at using live models mark the sculptor's first efforts in such regard towards the completion of a design for a public sculpture.

Unique as his statue design was, Newman's figure of the soldier had some marked similarities to the artwork produced during this same time by another American artist, Fredric Remington. As a war correspondent in Cuba while the Spanish-American War was underway, Remington made many drawings and paintings of American infantrymen and cavalry soldiers fighting on the front lines, marching in formation, and in different states of posing in uniform. Some of these drawings were published in editions of *Harper's Weekly* magazine during June and August 1899. Clearly evident in many of these are the same rifles carried, wide brim hats worn, and the open collared shirts found in the Newman statue.

No written evidence indicated that Newman and Remington ever corresponded, or met to discuss the work of either artist. However, one drawing done by Remington in particular strikes an uncanny resemblance to Newman's soldier. Identified as number 02412 in the Remington catalog raisonné developed by the Buffalo Bill Center of the West, the drawing appeared in *Collier's* March 25, 1899, edition, shows an American infantry soldier posed with right hand on hip, with the left hand leaning on the business end of a Krag rifle. The figure's shirt, pants, belt, hat and boots are all realistic details found in the Newman statue, while only a bedroll slung diagonally from the left shoulder to the right hip was an additional detail seen only in the Remington figure. Even the soldier's stern expression and slightly bent knees are comparable to *The Hiker*.

Several major life events for Newman coincided with his progress on the statue's final design. He was awarded the Prix de Rome, a scholarship for three years of study at the Academy in Rome, but declined so that he could marry a childhood sweetheart, Florence Allan, on March 28, 1900. A year after his marriage saw the arrival of his first child, daughter Ramona. By this time, Newman's professional association with Ward had ended, and the young father applied his artistry as the head of the jewelry design department at Tiffany's in New York.

Personal events again conspired to keep Newman on the East Coast. In 1902, the sculptor was offered a teaching position as an Art Instructor at the University of St. Louis. However, not long after accepting the appointment, the sculptor's father and namesake died, leaving Newman's elderly mother alone at the family's 71st Street & West End Avenue residence in New York. In part owing to a sense of duty to care for his mother, Newman declined the role in St. Louis and relocated his wife and daughter into their ancestral home. The year also saw Newman open his first studio in the city.

On July 2, 1902, the Philippine-American War officially came to an end. The conflict had lasted for three years, one month and two days, and claimed 4,234 American dead with another 2,818 wounded.[4] Many more Americans would later perish from tropical diseases brought home, following their return to the United States. Yet it would be another two years until Newman had his design for *The Hiker* copyrighted and ready for casting in 1904.

The first copies of the statue were produced by the John Williams foundry in New York and made at a reduced scale with a height nearly two and a half feet tall. These early copies went by several titles, but were collectively all identified as the same figure. *The Hiker* was a name given to the typical infantrymen, while other, alternate titles such as *Rough Rider* and *Soldier with his Rifle* referenced the same fighting man, his hat cocked to one side with the right foot forward and hand on hip. The original maquette of the design cast into bronze in 1904 was owned by Judge Louis Martin of Clinton, New York, acquired by him in 1921 for the veterans of New York State. Many years later, this first edition of *The Hiker* was donated to the collection of the Munson-Williams-Proctor Arts Institute in Utica, New York.

Three years after the initial castings were completed the first public exhibition of Newman's signature sculpture was planned for the rotunda display in the New York State Capitol Building. However, while the New York State Historian confirmed that the design was intended for display during the Jamestown Exposition hosted at the State Capitol, a list of the artwork and other materials post–Exposition omits *The Hiker* entirely.[5]

Despite the inconsistencies over the Exposition record, Newman succeeded in seeing his first life-sized casting of the statue in bronze installed at a veteran's cemetery in Providence, Rhode Island. In 1911, the City Council had put aside land at North Burial Ground for those servicemen that had served in the Spanish-American War. In the following year the statue was installed and dedicated as a new memorial at the site. It was the first of many copies produced for the sculptor by the John Williams, Inc. foundry, with two more installed in the same year as the Providence statue: one in Washington Park, on Staten Island and the third copy at Bayonne Park, New Jersey.

The Adjutant General of Rhode Island, Charles Wheaton Abbot, Jr., himself a veteran of the Philippine-American War, presided over the official dedication of the first *Hiker* in Providence. He offered an eloquent description of the finished work, and its effectiveness as a model which combined both realistic, physical details of the serviceman with idealized elements symbolic of the identity and the sacrifices made by the infantrymen as a whole:

> The head is strongly poised on a sinewy column. The shoulders are broad, the chest full and deep. The flanks are thin, the hips narrow. The muscular legs show great marching capacity, which is helped by a tendency to plant the foot Indian fashion to the front. There is a suggestion at the bow of the knee that he could ride a horse. His trusty Krag is not the first gun he has handled. You will not find that position in the manual, though the muzzle is elevated. It is equally handy to be

aimed, clubbed or lunged. His head turns naturally a little to the right to balance the hat brim falling to the left. But the face, smooth shaven as was the mode—every part is strong, every feature clean cut, and all perfectly balanced. The lined cheeks show that in his 28 years he has lived. He is no saint. He is no molly-coddle. He is an American soldier. He is a disciplined man at arms, the wonder of the world today wherever such foregather.[6]

The official unveiling of the statue in Providence and the other locations was attended by many veterans of the Spanish-American War, and had the net effect of securing their endorsement of Newman as the sculptor responsible for the official monument to the group's history and legacy. The design also received high praise from Lorado Taft, considered by many at this time to be the foremost authority on American sculpture. In the years that followed, these endorsements had a direct effect in Newman's ability to secure commissions for new castings of the statue in bronze for other cities, including Seattle.

The Hiker was a common thread that linked Seattle to places like Monongahela, Pennsylvania, and Riverside Park in Wichita, Kansas. In one way or another, Newman's soldier statue served to commemorate the Spanish-American War as a shared memorial sculpture and in the majority of cases had a similar role in commemorating the Philippine-American War and the Boxer Rebellion as well.

Veteran's groups from each locality were the primary advocates who called for *The Hiker* to be installed, especially after 1907 when the first smaller scale bronze castings were in public circulation. This was also true for Seattle, with efforts to secure a copy for the city underway by members from the United Spanish War Veterans of Washington and Alaska in January 1926.

Members of both the local Fortson-Thygesen Camp no. 2 and the Louis C. Roop Camp purchased the statue from Newman at a cost of just $3,000, which was the standard price the sculptor had charged other sites for copies of the six-foot tall statue. A public campaign was begun by the group in early 1926, but the veterans were still raising funds with entertainments at their location at 1616 Third Avenue as late as October 1926, several months after the statue was unveiled in Woodland Park.

The Woodland Park site was already a prime location for Newman's statue in several respects. The park had a direct historical connection to the Philippine-American War as a troop staging area. In a competition between Pacific Northwest cities to see which would serve as the launching point for over 1,100 men and their horses, Seattle won out over Tacoma when the U.S. Army's Quartermaster Department announced its decision on July 25, 1899. For the next several months, the Third Cavalry Regiment under the command of Captain Robinson had its camp "pitched on the high ground in the northwestern part of the park" while an added fence protected the southern portion of the park yet still allowed the camp's horses free access to water at Green Lake.[7]

The next month, soldiers bound for the Philippines crowded aboard the *St. Paul*, one of several steamer troopships that had been retrofitted at Moran's dock to carry troops along with 8,000 horses for the voyage to Manilla. Crowds of civilians gathered on the docks to bid the soldiers farewell. A Seattle photographer, Norwegian-American Anders Beer Wilse, was hired by the Captain Robinson to document the activities of Third Cavalry Regiment, with the *St. Paul*'s loading just one of these many views.

The assault on Manilla on August 13 had resulted in heavy fighting, and many American casualties. The same month also saw the return of the First Washington Volunteers Regiment from the Pacific, with many of these soldiers sick or wounded, and slated for recovery in the camp hospital. News reports from the front were both complimentary of the American effort and described the harsh conditions endured by the troops:

> The soldiers knew on Friday night that an attack was to be made. Reveille was sounded at four o'clock. The troops arose singing and cheering. For weeks they had been encamped in swamps or lying in ditches filled with water, exposed to tropical rains. They had waited patiently for the order to attack and when it came the demonstrations were unanimous along the lines. Through four lines of intrenchments [*sic*], extending for two miles, the enemy was driven in a panic to the walled portion of Manilla. This the Spaniards surrendered. The casualties on the American side were confined to the land side. Not a man of the fleet was injured.[8]

When the war finally ended nearly three years later, public celebrations were held throughout the city of Seattle. Veterans of the First Washington Volunteers Regiment marched in Pioneer Square, while the surrounding buildings were festooned with banners and American flags.

For Seattle, the end of the war marked a beginning of the process of transformation for one public space. In the minds of many citizens, Woodland Park was already identified as a site associated with a military presence. As the years passed and veterans of these conflicts gathered in the city to meet and remember, one corner of the park became symbolic of that shared memory.

Memorials are derived from memory, but require the tangible, the familiar, the historical, in order to provide both continuity and satisfaction for the viewer. This process continued in incremental leaps over the course

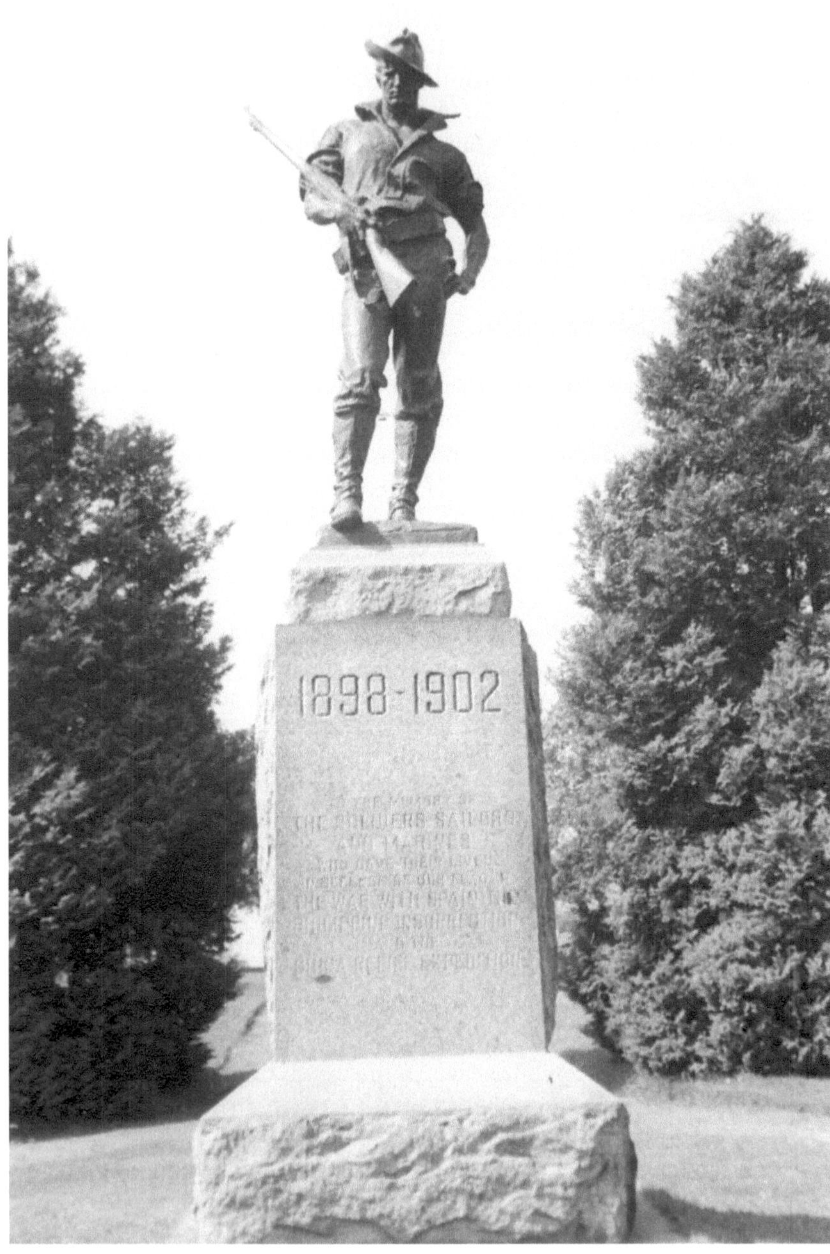

Spanish-American War Memorial by Allen G. Newman at Woodland Park. Undated photograph. Werner Lenggenhager, Photographer. Seattle Public Library.

of the next twenty-four years in Woodland Park. In 1911, two naval cannons from the USS *Concord* were loaned by the U.S. Navy to the United Spanish War Veterans for display in the park. These guns in particular were desirable given their history of use at the Battle of Manilla Bay on May 1, 1898, during the Philippine-American War. Even when pressed to have the guns turned over for the scrap metal drive during World War II, the veteran's voiced their opposition to the Board of Park Commissioners, citing the organization's sentimental interest and the question of legal ownership by the Navy.[9] The pair of six-inch cannons remained in place.

However, mementos of the conflict would alone not suffice where a monument to the veterans of the Spanish-American War era was concerned. In 1914, the Parks Board set aside a plot of land in the southwest corner of the park for "commemoration and exhibit" specifically as an area for the United Spanish War Veterans of Seattle.[10] Two years later, an eight-foot-tall, granite pedestal was added to the veteran's plot which bore a carved memorial inscription to those who had served: "1898–1902 / To the memory of the soldiers, sailors and marines who gave their lives in defense of our flag in the war with Spain, the Philippine Insurrection and the China Relief Expedition."

A total of 445,000 Americans served in the combined military forces of the United States, in all three campaigns. Men in regiments on the western half of the country were sent to the Philippines, which included the First Washington Volunteers. It was members from this group, and specifically the Fortson-Thygesen Camp, which finally secured a copy of *The Hiker* for Woodland Park to place atop the granite pedestal already on site. As it had done previously for other cities, the Williams foundry completed this latest bronze casting in 1926.

On Memorial Day, May 31, 1926, Seattle became the fourteenth city in the United States to install a copy of the statue by Newman. The combined height of the monument was now at fourteen feet and included a bronze relief plaque on the back side of the pedestal, dedicated as a memorial to those lost on the USS *Maine*. Charles Keck was the sculptor for the USS *Maine* plaque, which was replicated by the Williams foundry for several other *Hiker* monuments around the country.

On the day of the statue's unveiling, veterans John Witherspoon and Jackson Silbaugh presented the sculpture to the city. It was officially accepted by Mayor Edwin J. Brown, as the first official war memorial of the city.[11] Two wreaths were placed at the base of the statue by members of the Grand Army of the Republic (G.A.R.) and United Confederate Veterans (U.C.V.), respectively.

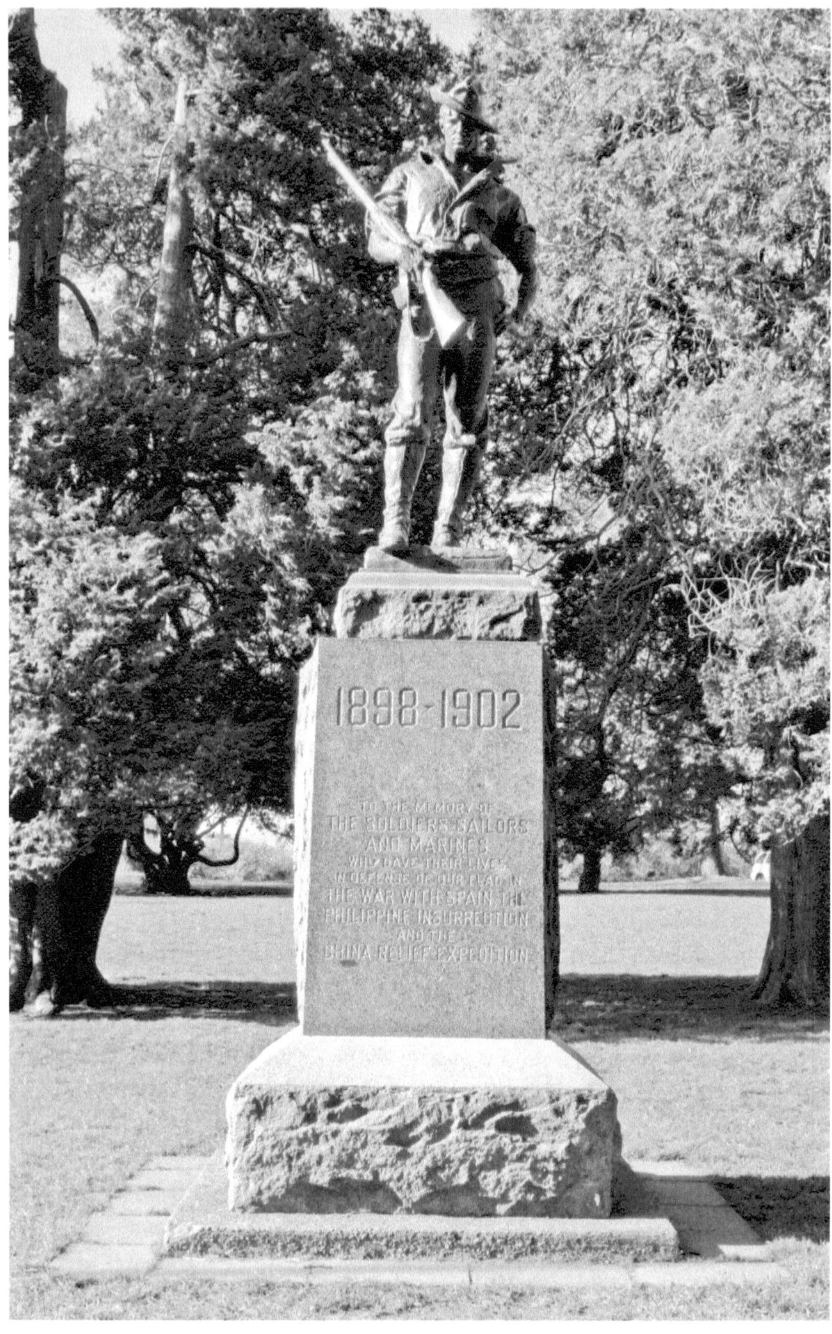

The Hiker by Allen G. Newman. 1926. Fred F. Poyner IV, Photographer (2016).

For years after its dedication, *The Hiker* served as a gathering place for veterans to come each Memorial Day in Seattle. The practice continued following the end of World War II, with the Fortson-Thygesen Camp members contacting the Seattle Park Board each year for assistance by providing park benches and tables for visitors on that day. By 1957, the membership of the two United Spanish War Veterans posts had dwindled to just 340 members.[12] With this decline, *The Hiker* became less and less prominent in the public's eyes as a gathering place in memorandum of the war dead. Even the name designation for the day honoring America's military war dead had changed. When first held in 1868, the day once known as "Decoration Day" was gradually replaced with "Memorial Day," until the latter name was officially declared a federal holiday in 1967.

Newman went on to create many other great public sculptures during his lifetime, but most of these were east of the Rocky Mountains. He did produce a statue dedicated to the pioneers of Oregon, placed at the State Capitol in Salem, as well as four earlier statues done for the Panama-Pacific Exposition at San Francisco's Golden Gate Park in 1915. As one more interesting life parallel to the sculptor James Wehn, it was likely that Wehn witnessed firsthand Newman's statues that decorated the four massive arches at the Exposition's entrance. The young sculptor was recently married to his first wife, Florence, and the newlyweds were visiting the Exposition while in San Francisco on their honeymoon.

Notable as well was Newman's career trend as a sculptor to focus on military figures and subjects for several monuments, including a World War I era "Doughboy" soldier statue which overlooked the Hudson River in Rhinebeck, New York; busts or statues for several generals (e.g., *General Sheridan*, Scranton, Pennsylvania; *General Russell*, West Point, New York); and sculptures which portrayed the history of the Confederacy (e.g., *Women of the Confederacy*, Jacksonville, Florida). The sculptor was also an accomplished medalist and exhibited several of these at the World's Fair in New York during 1938–1939. His statue of *The Hiker* was the only public sculpture he produced for Seattle.

Newman died in 1940, but in a final tribute to both his creativity and the men of Company G, a final heroic bronze copy of *The Hiker* was installed posthumously in the city of Ypsilanti, Michigan. Another city that, like Seattle and many others in his day, looked to honor its military war dead through observance cast into bronze.

7

Hermon Atkins MacNeil
(1866–1947)

Of all the public monuments in Seattle—those which include statuary or other sculpture as inherent to their design and purpose, historical and otherwise—the Thomas Burke Memorial represents the last such tribute installed in the city, both in monumental scale and individualized focus on a prominent citizen. In one of the great ironies of early public art in Seattle, this memorial sculpture was not done by a sculptor from Seattle, but rather one of international training and achievement who briefly came west to share his talent in the medium: Hermon Atkins MacNeil.

One could also say that the public memorial MacNeil created wasn't one commissioned by the city, but was the end result of the collective efforts made by friends of Burke from the community who were well organized, financially well-off, and like Burke, were respected civic and business leaders in their own right. As a group, they were united in their lifelong connections to Thomas Burke while he was alive, and remained so following his death. The end result was a shared vision to see a memorial to his great character set in stone and bronze. To understand MacNeil's success as a sculptor in creating the memorial, it is necessary to understand the man who so inspired others to see it come to pass.

These two men, Burke and MacNeil, were not dissimilar in many respects. They were both originally from the East Coast. Burke was born in Clinton County, New York, on December 22, 1849; MacNeil was born in Prattville, Massachusetts, on February 27, 1866. The value of academic study was not lost on either man. Burke earned his law degree from the University of Michigan in 1870 and remained a stanch alumni supporter of the University in the years that followed. As a sculptor, MacNeil had studied at art institutions both in the United States and overseas in Europe.

During their lives, both men regarded the United States as their home, yet traveled across the country and abroad in the course of furthering their professional and personal interests. While Burke was meeting with Great Northern railroad magnate James Hill in St. Paul to review prospective plans for a new railroad tunnel in Seattle, MacNeil was working on a new commission for a medallion design for the upcoming Pan-American Exposition in Buffalo, New York. Burke made several visits across the Pacific Ocean to help establish trade and cultural ties to East Asia; MacNeil's portfolio of public monuments included more than a dozen cities, including Chicago, Albany, Portland, Columbus, Charleston, Hartford and the nation's capital in Washington, D.C.

Both men enjoyed being close to the water. Later in his career, the sculptor had a studio at College Point, on Long Island, New York, where he lived and worked with his wife Carol, and the couple's two boys. While Judge Burke had a law practice in Seattle, he and his wife, Caroline, would often escape to a rustic, two-story lodge they named "Illahee" on the shores of Lake Washington. The couple collected and displayed numerous examples of hand-woven baskets, carved paddles and other items of Native American culture which decorated the lakeside retreat. Meanwhile, MacNeil displayed a similar passion for Native American life by modeling many of his own sculptures after figures with tribal identities from across North America.

Neither MacNeil nor Burke was a stranger to the international scene. The sculptor had been trained in the Beaux-Arts style of sculpture in Paris, and in 1919, took a post as a resident professor at the American Academy in Rome. For Burke, a sojourn to Europe in 1899 was interrupted when railroad plans put forth by James Hill required the Judge's immediate return to Seattle. The exchange between the two men paints Burke in a favorable light with respect to his putting the public good ahead of his own interests:

> Jim Hill showed him the plans for the present tunnel under the city and the present Union Station, and said the project could not well be put through without Judge Burke's presence. "That is a perfect plan," said Burke. "Consider me on my way home." "It's too bad to interrupt your trip," said Hill. "By no means," replied Burke. "Going home with good news like this will be a pleasure."[1]

And both men were equally successful in their respective chosen professions and public causes. Burke served as Chief Justice of the Washington State Supreme Court, and an accomplished civic activist for education and railroad infrastructure for both Seattle and the state of Washington. As a proponent for the railroads, he served as a partner in the Seattle, Lake Shore & Eastern Railroad and later served as attorney for James J. Hill's Great Northern Railway to Seattle.[2] Burke was a successful advocate as well for both the University of Washington and Whitman College, and was conferred an honorary LL.D. degree from the latter institution. His reputation as a civic leader for Seattle's interests as a port city likewise extended to connections he forged with trade groups and representatives in both Japan and China (a trait which would later find expression in his memorial). On one such occasion, at a banquet sponsored by the Seattle Commercial Club on December 28, 1905, Burke gave a speech to the assembled members at the Stander Hotel on the Orient and its importance to the trade with Seattle and the Pacific coast.

Burke's friend and biographer, Charles T. Conover, described the judge's accomplishments on the international scene and the value of these especially for relations between Japan and the United States:

> He had been decorated by the government of France with the Cross of the Legion of Honor, by Belgium with the Order of the Knights of Leopold, by Japan with the Third Order of the Sacred Treasure and the Fourth Order of the Rising Sun, for his efforts for world peace and international amity and understanding. To the people of Japan he was doubtless the best known and best beloved American, and he was on terms of intimacy and mutual regard with her public men and business leaders.[3]

MacNeil first obtained his arts instruction at the Massachusetts Normal Art School in 1886, then continued his studies and earned honors from both the Julian School and at the École des Beaux-Arts in Paris. While in the great city, he exhibited a bust in the Salon in 1890. His return to the states in 1893 heralded several new commissions, all completed in the decade that followed. Several of these public monuments focused on highly detailed figurative sculptures of Native Americans, such as a statue of Chief Manuelito for Gallup, New Mexico (1895) and another depicting Chief Multnomah commissioned by the family of former mayor David Thompson, for the city of Portland, Oregon (*Coming of the White Man*, 1904). The sculptor was equally skilled in modeling reliefs for medallions, as he was modeling monumental figures for statuary. In the year before he completed the Manuelito statue in bronze, the sculptor finished four bronze reliefs depicting incidents from the life and death of explorer Père Marquette for the Marquette Building in Chicago.

In 1893, MacNeil lived in Chicago and prepared sketch models for the Columbian Exposition under Philip Martiny. In the two years that followed the World's Fair, he taught art at the Art Institute of Chicago. A contemporary of MacNeil noted that even early on in his career, the sculptor was unsatisfied with "modern sculptural themes" such as those afforded by his time spent in Paris, and that he "wanted to do things more original and more truly expressive."[4]

A new opportunity to further explore sculpture as a medium came for MacNeil in the fall of 1895, when he was one of two American sculptors awarded the first-ever Rinehart scholarship for study abroad. Before leaving for a four-year period to study under sculptor masters in Rome, he married Carol Brooks, one of his former pupils.[5]

The statuary and reliefs MacNeil produced during his stay at the Villa dell' Aurora marked him as a sculptor both talented and distinctly American, in his choice of figures from tribes of the American Southwest such as *The Moqui Runner, A Primitive Chant* and *The Sun Vow*. Of the first statue, Lorado Taft called it "savagery personified."[6] Details of anatomy, pose, clothing and adornments in these works were modeled to perfection, dramatized and beautiful, yet deliberately stopped short of transformation from an authentic character to a classical idealization seen in many European neoclassical sculptures of that time.

MacNeil and his wife departed Italy in 1899 to Paris, where the sculptor gained further accolades for his work decorating the United States Building at the Paris Exposition of 1900 (he was awarded a silver medal for his sculptural reliefs). The couple returned to the states in the following year, where MacNeil became an industrial arts instructor at Cornell University in Ithaca, New York. He continued working from his studio at Long Island for the remainder of his life, returning to Chicago later only on a temporary basis to contribute new sculpture monuments to its urban landscape.

Great as they were at their vocations, both Burke and MacNeil were also diverse in their talents. Burke was a recognized authority on the law; an orator; a leader in the community, and a man who literally helped to change the urban landscape of Seattle in the arena of railroad infrastructure. A vocal proponent for the city, he addressed an assembled mob during the anti–Chinese riots of February 1886, and called for calm and reason to prevail for the sake of both minority rights and the reputation of Seattle. While the occasion was still marked by violence, it also marked Burke in the eyes of many as a man of moral conviction and bravery.

Burke's list of professional associations was reflective of a strong work ethic as well as an ability to forge ties within the community, and oftentimes, as the initiator of such efforts. He was the last surviving founder of the Seattle Chamber of Commerce, an organization he contributed to going on fifty years since its inception and finally led as its president in his later years. Both the Associated Chambers of Commerce of the Pacific Coast and the United States Chamber of Commerce likewise benefited from his leadership. Nor was Burke one who actively sought out fame through publicity. In a letter to Edmond Meany in 1915, he clearly articulated his objections to the professor over a request to have his portrait published in a local newspaper:

> I understand and fully appreciate the value of the historic work you are doing in that line, especially for those whose retirement long since from active participation in affairs makes a record such as you are writing of value and interest for future reference; but as I am still active in business and civic affairs, such a publication as you contemplate would be an actual embarrassment to me in my work. That distinction should be reserved for *old men*.[7]

MacNeil's range of activity as an artist was no less daunting by comparison: he contributed designs to the Society of Medalists and the United States Mint; modeled the portraits of great national figures in stone such as the monument to President William McKinley in Columbus, Ohio; and sculpted allegorical figures as architectural elements, like the figure of *Justice, the Guardian of Liberty*, on the east pediment of the United States Supreme Court Building. MacNeil incorporated the same level of detail in his modeling of smaller scale portrait busts, with two of these done during his time spent in Rome paramount examples. His female bust *Agnese*, whose subject was of a patrician beauty from that city, was noted by Lorado Taft as being "among the finest works yet produced by an American."[8] Other contemporaries of MacNeil agreed with this assessment of his work, and the bust received a gold medal for the sculptor at the Pan-American Exposition in 1901.

As much as either predetermined by fate or as mutual interests would have it, MacNeil and Burke became acquainted with each other on at least one occasion. At a banquet held in 1905, Burke remarked on his appreciation for MacNeil's work designing public monuments. He told the young sculptor while sitting next to him, "I want you to make a monument for us someday."[9] Burke's declaration was prophetic and sadly ironic, as it would be MacNeil who was selected to design a Seattle memorial to the judge twenty-two years later.

The news of Burke's demise in New York on December 4, 1925, came as a shock to his home city. As a prominent citizen, he had come to embody the sense of the "Seattle spirit"—a term first coined from the days of the Alaska-Yukon-Pacific Exposition—especially where this involved support of the arts and civic improvements. Telegrams and notes of consolation to the judge's wife, Caroline Burke, poured in from longtime associates and friends alike. Seattle investment banker J.D. Lowman sent one such telegram while staying at the Roosevelt Hotel in New York. Similar messages of condolence came from many of his other associates among the academic institutions, businesses and municipal government branches of Seattle. Several also came from notable Japanese citizens who had either known Burke personally, or were familiar with his record of service promoting good trade relations between Japan and the United States. Seattle historian Clarence Bagley recalled one such telegram from the Japanese ambassador to Washington, D.C., which expressed profound sentiment at the loss: "have always followed with high appreciation the self-sacrificing activities made by Judge Burke in the interest of international peace and particularly in that of friendly relations between our two countries."[10]

As Thomas Burke finished the last speech of his life to the Carnegie Endowment for International Peace in New York, MacNeil witnessed the dedication of his war memorial sculpture *The World War* in Flushing, New York. Not lacking for commissions, the sculptor was also soon engaged in a new monument destined for Chicago, where he revisited the subject of Père Marquette. He spent the first eight months of 1926 completing a monumental statue for the windy city, with it installed on Marshall Boulevard in August of that same year.

Almost immediately following Burke's funeral, a memorial committee was formed in Seattle from amongst his professional associates and friends to begin the process of raising funds for some kind of a public memorial and to also determine what form that memorial should take. Investment banker J.D. Lowman was appointed as chairman, while members Theodore Haller, A.S. Kerry, C. Wills and Joshua Green were appointed to a finance committee to manage memorial funds. M.F. Backus, president of the National Bank of Commerce, was named as the fund treasurer.

The prospect of a statue or other sculpture was soon discussed by members of the committee. By no surprise, it was an idea publicly endorsed by a sculptor already active in Seattle, Alonzo Victor Lewis. More specific direction by others called for the statue in whatever form it took, bronze or otherwise, to face east towards the Orient and include the last words of Judge Burke, "'I urge international justice and courtesy'" upon it.[11] These last two suggestions were made in no small part as acknowledgment of the great strides Burke had made in his life towards promoting goodwill with Japan.

But the statue concept was only one idea of many being proposed. Other prominent figures came forward to advocate for alternatives to a personalized memorial. F.C. Babcock of the Parks Board recommended a new park be constructed on the site of the old Providence Hospital downtown. Kerry was initially a proponent of taking the funds collected in order to apply them in a takeover of the Cornish Arts School, and renaming it "The Burke Memorial School."[12] Professors and administrators from the University of Washington put forth suggestions for the founding of new institutions on campus devoted to either the social sciences or a museum in Burke's name that focused on Pacific Rim countries. Stephen Penrose, president of Whitman College, announced that the trustees of the college would seek to establish a much-needed new library after Burke.

In May 1926, the memorial committee announced that plans for a statue with an estimated cost of $100,000 would serve as the public monument to the late judge. The decision was made by unanimous committee vote, and more to the question of what kind of memorial to undertake, had already been somewhat predetermined by Caroline Burke. Within six months of his death, Burke's wife had made the decision to bequeath the bulk of the Burke family fortune to the University of Washington for a new memorial building. In addition to the promise of a future campus building, Caroline contacted the Memorial Art Company in Seattle for services to have a new Burke family mausoleum constructed with stone columns, base, architrave and ornamentation. Over a year later, the company was still writing to the widow, petitioning for her business. The mausoleum was finally completed at Evergreen Washelli Cemetery on a hill overlooking the entrance to the cemetery on August 11, 1928. The mausoleum's design included an oblong portico measuring fifteen by forty feet, with a cost of $50,000 (coincidently, the same amount as the final cost for the Burke memorial sculpture).

Following the committee vote, no sculptor had yet been selected, nor had a location for the statue been determined. Suggestions for the latter question offered both Volunteer Park and a small park at Highland Drive and Seventh Avenue West as possible sites.[13] As to the funding for the memorial, these were to be raised by public subscription. Perhaps owing to both the prospect of unsecured income and other efforts underway at the time to promote his monumental *Doughboy* soldier statue, the sculptor Lewis was not engaged by the memorial committee to undertake the Burke monument as a new commission.

Nor as it turned out, would other established sculptors in Seattle be offered the commission. In the same month that the committee announced its plans for a new statue, sculptor James Wehn completed his first large-scale monument to veterans of the Confederacy installed at Lake View Cemetery in Seattle. While impressive as a memorial, Wehn's piece consisted of a granite archway produced locally with the help of the Sunset Monument Company, and embellished with a bronze "Southern Cross" and a bronze portrait medallion of Confederate General Robert E. Lee. What the United Confederate Veterans (U.C.V.) memorial offered in terms of size at twenty feet high by ten feet wide, it omitted in design as far as any statuary elements which were clearly desired by the Burke memorial committee's leadership. Notwithstanding the fact that Wehn had worked as a sculptor in Seattle since the turn of the century, most of his commissions up until 1926 had involved small-scale portrait medallions, wall reliefs and sculpture busts, with the notable exceptions of his *Chief Seattle* bronze statue completed in 1912 and the more recently completed U.C.V. memorial. While competent as a sculptor and a local familiar with the legacy of Judge Burke, Wehn was not solicited as a sculptor for the Burke monument commission.

The Burke committee's desire to see statuary as a major element to the memorial had the net effect of widening their search of prospective sculptors to a national level. No record of any public call for submissions was undertaken by the group, but there was clearly an expressed desire to find a sculptor of established reputation secured to undertake the needed work.

In the final months of 1926, the committee began a public campaign in earnest towards raising funds for the project. By the end of November, nearly $40,000 had been secured from over 600 public donations. The statue's total cost had also been revised downwards from the original figure to $65,000.

In order to achieve such rapid success with the fundraising, the memorial committee looked especially to the many close friends Burke had in life to help offset the cost. Both Professor Edmond S. Meany and his wife received separate letters in the fall of 1926 asking for financial support of the statue. As the chairman of the memorial's finance committee, Haller plied the couple with eloquent descriptions of the finished memorial, calling it "both beautiful and impressive ... an inspiration to present and future generations and keep alive the memory of the man to whom Seattle and the world at large owes a debt of gratitude."[14] The chairman also confided that while the memorial was envisioned for placement in one of the city parks, the sculptor had not yet been selected.

The choice of Hermon MacNeil to undertake the Burke Memorial was decided upon by Haller and the other members of the memorial committee in 1927. In September, they invited the sculptor out to Seattle from New York for two weeks to meet with him and to hear how he conceptualized a sculpture that would adequately memorialize Burke. By this time, both the total project cost and the total amount raised through donations had finally come together and settled at an amount of $45,000. By securing these funds, the project had cleared a major hurdle that had thwarted many other public monument projects before it. Having the funds in place also assured the committee's successful enlistment of MacNeil, a sculptor who was already much in demand across the country.

In 1926 alone, MacNeil completed a medal for the American Numismatic Society, a major public Sculpture of monumental scale for a city, and another portrait bust in his home state of New York. The year he accepted the Burke commission, he completed another monument to the Civil War soldiers and sailors in Philadelphia. During the next two years that he worked to complete the Burke Memorial sculpture, he continued to accept other, new commissions as well, including two more portrait busts destined for the Hall of Fame at New York University.

Perhaps one of the greatest testimonials to MacNeil's abilities came from another sculptor of note, who had also contributed to the public historical statuary of Seattle. In his treatise on American sculpture of the early twentieth century, Lorado Taft described a group of young sculptors "equipped by nature and by training as in the past few Americans have been" and identified MacNeil as "one of the most promising of this number."[15] MacNeil was also distinctly an "American" sculptor in both his desire to recognize figures from American history as his statuary subjects, and in a stylistic approach that was American in his belonging to a group of like-minded sculptors who were working at this time to combine realistic presentation with expressive concepts and motifs unique to the country. In this last respect, MacNeil was very similar to James Wehn in that both sculptors made repeated visits to Native American reservations to study Indian life and portrait subjects. Yet in spite of their shared appreciation and outlook on sculpture as distinctly American in both subject and style, it was MacNeil who ultimately was selected for the Burke monument.

During his fall visit to Seattle, MacNeil was the guest of honor at a dinner hosted by Caroline Burke at the Sunset Club to the fanfare of the local press. It was a tacit acknowledgment on the widow's part, that she had given her blessing as to the final choice of the sculptor to undertake her late husband's memorial. MacNeil further established his work plan for the monument in the public eye by staging an interview at the prestigious Rainier Club in downtown Seattle. Given that any number of the memorial committee's twenty-eight members either had close associates of the Club or were members themselves, the setting for MacNeil's public recognition as the official Burke Memorial sculptor came as no surprise.

Another important revelation made by the sculptor was the desired final placement of the memorial, which called for its installation in Volunteer Park in Seattle.

The sculptor's general concept from the start was to create a sculpture that combined both allegorical figures with a representational portrait of Judge Burke in profile as the central element. Like many of his earlier public sculptures, it was both large scale in size and utilized a combination of sculpture materials (granite, marble and bronze). Most importantly, a key factor in its inspiration was how it drew upon the character of Burke himself as a source of inspiration that was reflected in all elements of the design. MacNeil truly had come up with a vision to match the one anticipated by the memorial's backers. His final memorial sculpture both justified their choice of him as the sculptor and exceeded their expectations.

The effort took the next two years for the sculptor to complete. The main part of the monument was designed twelve feet high and carved with vertical decorative reliefs that depicted a pair of lit lamps, an open book, and palm fronds on the front. The tops of the frond reliefs on both sides framed a two-foot diameter, bronze portrait medallion of Judge Burke shown in profile and facing to the left side. On opposite sides of the main central column, a full-sized figure was sculpted from the granite. MacNeil described the emphasis of these two figures as symbolic and allegorical in nature, yet also reflective of Burke's qualities as a man:

> The gigantic male figure on the right holding the implements of construction, typifies his power when he came into this young town, saw the things about him which needed to be done, and said "Let's begin, let's build," and led the work himself. The calm, sturdy female figure on the left typifies the higher, finer things he strove for. Justice, of which she holds the emblem: peace, culture and understanding. The dolphin at her feet represents the international relations with the Orient, for which he strove.[16]

In a nod to the sculptor's longstanding appreciation for the Native American form, the male figure in the final execution of the memorial's design offered a countenance with distinct Native American features. Long braided hair frames a strong looking face, with the head slightly lowered and gaze intended for making eye contact with the viewer from below. Meanwhile, the female figure on the left presents a sculpture with Nordic features, represented with delicate facial features and long hair.

In addition to the rationale for the Burke memorial's design aesthetic, the materials employed were impressive and made to last. The sculptor had all three sculpture parts carved out of granite obtained from a quarry in Bavaria reputed for its finest quality of stone for public monuments.

The center column of the memorial was carved from a single, nineteen-ton block of this granite. For the casting of the portrait medallion, MacNeil called upon the foundry services of the Roman Bronze Works in New York, considered a mainstay source of casting by many sculptors in America and worldwide. As a final detail, marble insets were added to the base of the sculpture—one representing the West Coast, the other the Orient—with a broken segment in between signifying the loss of Burke as a unifying figure of both worlds. MacNeil called upon carvers known to him from his days in Paris, to execute the designs of his figures and reliefs on site at the Bavarian quarry, and made several visits overseas in 1928 and 1929, to check on their progress.

MacNeil proved himself to be a resourceful artist with the site planning for the Burke Memorial and coordinating this with the memorial committee. He enlisted the aid of local architect and University of Washington Professor of Architecture, Carl F. Gould, to help design the pedestal-bench plaza where the memorial was finally placed in Volunteer Park. As the sculptor's work on the memorial neared completion, the Burke Memorial Committee contacted the Park Engineer to plan for the erection of the sculpture at Volunteer Park.

Nearly two years had passed since the previous group of Park Board Commissioners had agreed to the location of the Burke memorial inside the park. But at the regular board meeting held on May 16, 1929, to review the committee's request for assistance, the new roster of Park Board Commissioners decided to reopen the subject of where the memorial should be finally placed. Rather than Volunteer Park as previously agreed upon, the current Park Board was of the opinion that the "University Campus would be a more suitable place to place the statue, owing to the substantial contributions Judge Burke had made to the University during his lifetime."[17]

Gould replied via letter a week later, indicating the Burke Memorial Committee's preference to keep the site of the memorial unchanged. Debate over the issue continued at the meeting where Gould's letter was read, with the position of the Park Commissioners still fixed upon trying to find an alternative site for the memorial. It went even so far as to call for Park Board President Burnett to go visit Lowman, the Memorial Committee's chairman, to further discuss the matter in person.

Burke's friends were powerful and influential, and in the end, the question of changing the site at this late date was out of the question. With Gould and Lowman leading the Memorial Committee's efforts on the local front and MacNeil's portfolio of public monuments to support their case, further discussion of altering the placement of the statue was curtailed in short order. An official request was sent by the Burke Memorial Committee for the statue's placement in Volunteer Park to the Parks Board and summarily approved on June 6, 1929.[18]

On October 13, 1929, the granite carvings for the memorial had been completed and shipped from Hamburg, Germany, direct to Seattle. It would take several weeks by freighter to transport the pieces, until they arrived in late November. The sculptor had demonstrated forethought in this advanced planning, so that the granite carvings would not require reshipment twice (i.e., first from Paris to Hamburg, then once more to Seattle).

The final cost of the Burke Memorial came to $50,000 or approximately $5,000 over the original amount that had been raised for the project in 1927. Following the arrival of the shipment, McNeil spent the next three months coordinating its placement into Volunteer Park. The combined weight of the granite pieces together was over seventy tons. MacNeil, however, was upbeat at the prospect of moving it the final leg of its journey: "It is going to be some task to get this up to Volunteer Park but I am in hopes that a conveyance and a derrick that will be adequate can be found. If not we shall all have to lend a hand as they did in the old Egyptian days."[19]

The installation of the memorial was without incident, and set upon its base at the head of the plaza that Carl Gould had designed for the site. In consideration of a suggestion previously made by F.C. Harper, the former collector of customs, the center column with the Burke profile portrait in bronze was made to face to the east, towards the Orient, in honor of Burke's accomplishments as a U.S. emissary to the region. On March 27, 1930, MacNeil inspected the memorial to add his finishing touches: checking that the bronze medallion was securely affixed; sanding the fold of a garment on one of the side statues. Two days later, Edmond Meany received a letter from C.T. Conover, Secretary of the Burke Memorial Committee, inviting him, as one of the donors who had contributed funds, to the dedication ceremony for the memorial sculpture on Saturday, April 5, 1930, in Volunteer Park.

As public statuary dedications go, the one held for the Burke Memorial was spectacular in terms of attendees and notoriety. Unveilings of new public monuments were still a rarity at this time in Seattle. MacNeil's sculpture was only one of two completed for the city during the Depression Era decade of the 1930s (*The Doughboy* by Alonzo Victor Lewis being the other). The ceremony for the Burke Memorial dedication was hosted by

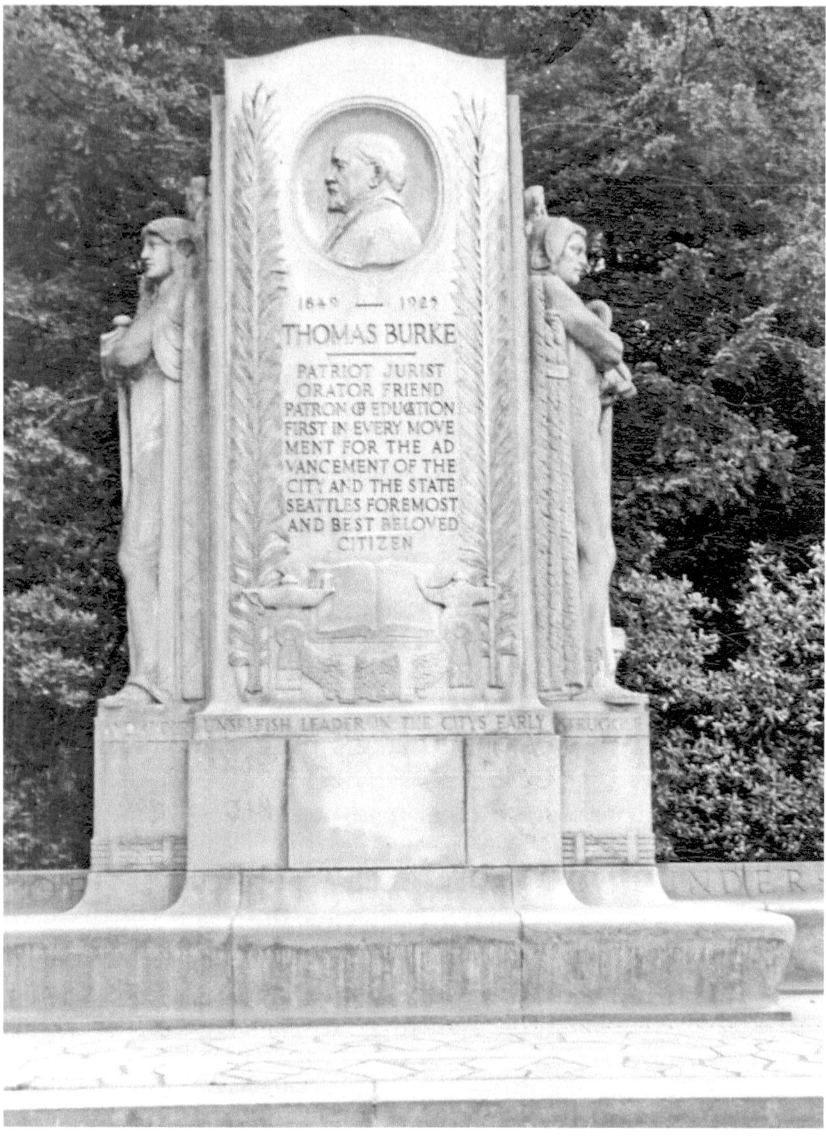

Judge Thomas Burke Memorial by Herman A. MacNeil. 1930. Gordon Newell, Photographer (1954). Seattle Municipal Archives.

L.C. Gilman, who was a longtime friend of the late judge. Among the guests of honor, these included MacNeil, Dr. Stephen Penrose of Whitman College, Judge George Donworth, J.D. Lowman as chairman of the Burke Memorial Committee, and Caroline Burke.

Several of those present remarked on the character and accomplishments of Judge Burke, and how these were now embodied in the sculpture before the assembled group. Dr. H. H. Gowen, another longtime friend, called the monument "a shrine to the great principles of international friendship."[20] Gilman also provided an eloquent description of Burke: "His friendship was like a sheltering tree ... he labored for the peace of the world. May our lives with this dedication be more fully devoted to the things for which he stood-patriotism, friendship and peace."[21]

Many of the same words Gilman used were also reflected in the memorial's inscription placed directly below the bronze portrait medallion: "Thomas Burke / Patriot Jurist Orator Friend / Patron of Education / First in Every Movement for the Advancement of the City and the State / Seattle's Foremost and Best Loved Citizen."

Even those not attending the Memorial's dedication acknowledged Judge Thomas Burke's role in having been a key leader to the development of Seattle. Clarence Bagley expanded on this sentiment and its reflections in tributes made to the man, saying "the city of Seattle is his monument, but the invisible flowers that adorn his last resting place are the love and honor enshrined in the hearts of people of every land and clime."[22]

As part of the official stewardship of the memorial going forward, the president of the Park Board, Simon Burnett, accepted the monument on behalf of the board while Mayor Frank Edwards accepted it on behalf of the city. In an interesting side note, the Seattle Park Board had voted unanimously to pass Resolution No. 152 the previous November, which called for the official designation of Roanoke Park as the city park designated for all future public memorials. In short order, this designation was put

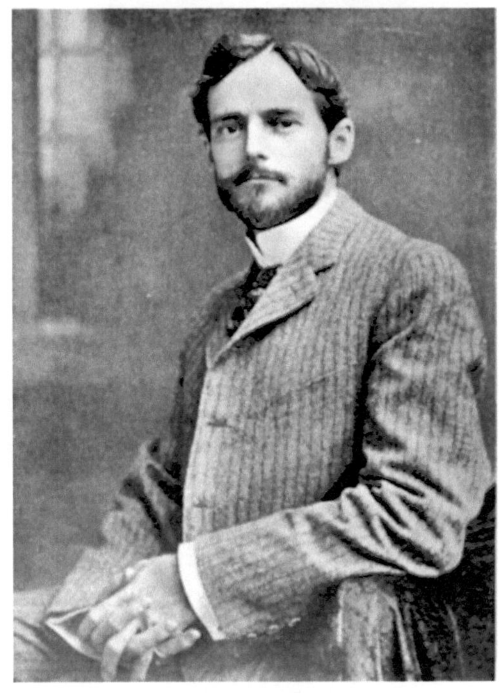

Photograph of Herman Atkins MacNeil. **Source: *The World's Work—A History of Our Time* by Walter Hines Page (1900).**

to the test again just two years later, with a new public statue by Alonzo Victor Lewis installed in central Seattle.

While the Burke Memorial proved to be the only public sculpture or monument that MacNeil contributed to Seattle, it serves as a lasting tes-

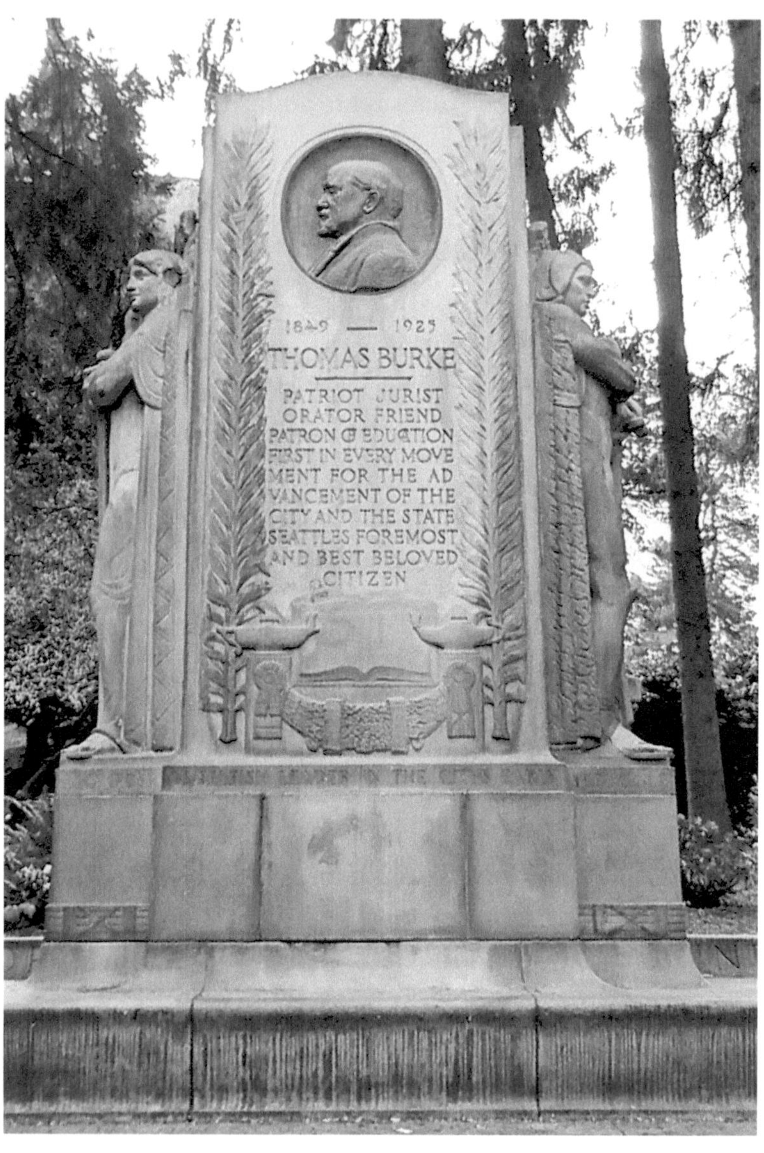

Judge Thomas Burke Memorial by Herman A. MacNeil. 1930. Fred F. Poyner IV, Photographer (2015).

timony to the sculptor's efforts to improve the early public art of the city. A year following the dedication in Volunteer Park, J.D. Lowman heralded MacNeil's latest triumph in the field when he learned of the sculptor's recent first prize award in a national medal design contest. The medal competition was sponsored by the Society of Medalists in New York, with MacNeil's winning design of a Hopi Indian dance (*Moqui Dance for Rain*) selected from more than 800 entries. Lowman's comments confirmed a widespread appreciation of the sculptor and the work done for Seattle amongst his achievements: "we who obtained the services of Mr. MacNeil to execute the Judge Burke Memorial are especially pleased to learn of his latest honor."[23]

Of his appreciation of the American ideal in sculpture, it can be said that MacNeil emulated the greatness of the American sculptor Augustus Saint-Gaudens, who throughout his career recognized the importance of historical figures and events which defined the country of equal merit in defining public sculpture for the current era. The Burke memorial sculpture certainly aspires to this definition.

Taken in a comprehensive view, the sculptures of MacNeil are found throughout the United States. A review of his sculpture titles found in the Smithsonian American Art Museum's database lists 111 monumental sculpture groups, statuary, portrait busts and reliefs, with many of these produced after 1900. MacNeil was (and is) a Seattle sculptor, but even in his day, was regarded as much more than only a "Seattle" sculptor. A fitting legacy, given that MacNeil's patrons believed Burke was much more than a Judge or that his memorial just another portrait on a bronze medallion.

8

Alonzo Victor Lewis
(1886–1946)

While some public monuments in Seattle were the result of just several years of planning and effort, others took considerably longer.

For one Seattle sculptor, the conclusion of World War I on November 11, 1918, led to his creation of three new memorial sculptures to those who served in uniform on behalf of the state of Washington and the nation. One of these war memorials in bronze combined characteristics of real soldiers and uniforms of the American military service, along with allegorical elements designed to foster feelings of patriotism, victory and identity for the viewer. While the monumental statue originally called *The American Doughboy Bringing Home the Bacon* proved to be an iconic memorial and tribute to the soldiers of World War I, it was also arguably one of the most challenging for sculptor Alonzo Victor Lewis to have permanently installed as a public sculpture in Seattle.

Born in Logan, Utah, on August 22, 1886, Lewis was one of three children of Marion and Lena Lewis. His younger brother, Warren, along with mother Lena Lewis, remained in close contact with Lewis in later years through correspondence often tinged with talk of bills and other financial troubles, concern over family, and desperation over living situations.

In many ways, Lewis did what he could to support his brother and mother, but had his own struggles to find a place in the world, with fine art always as his focus. At the age of fifteen, he lived briefly in Butte, Montana, studying under the western artist E.S. Paxson. However, the artist's stay was short lived. A letter of support sent by the mother of a female admirer, Credwyn Evans, to Lewis remarked on his move from Butte, saying "there is certainly not much there to develop an artistic temperament, but one cannot always find it convenient to leave even a disinteresting place at once."[1]

Lewis continued his studies in painting and sculpture at the Chicago Art Academy (today the Art Institute of Chicago). It was in this supportive environment where he first developed an approach that focused on a representation bordering on the classical, especially where this concerned historical statuary, portrait busts and full figure statues. He demonstrated both talent and leadership, receiving a gold medal in life drawing during the 1906–07 academic year, while also serving as secretary for the Art Academy League. Yet more distant horizons beckoned the young artist: first to New York, then continuing on to Cuba and Mexico. In the last location, he demonstrated an early command of realistic sculpting technique by modeling a portrait head of the Mexican President Diaz. By 1909, Lewis came to the Pacific Northwest and Portland, Oregon, where his brother Warren was working as a small-time editor.

The sculptor continued his travels around the Pacific Northwest, and moved away from the coast to the east side of Washington State in 1911. While living in Spokane, Lewis met Bessie Juanita Magee and married a year later, on August 31, 1912, in Kootenai, Idaho. Nine months later, they welcomed their first child, Dorian Lorraine ("Linnie") into the world.

However, the West Coast still beckoned to Lewis and in 1915 he made his return. In a letter addressed to his "darling wife and babies," he described his arrival to Tacoma by nightfall and awaking the next morning to "a mixture between a barn, a café, a storehouse, a brick yard, a carpenter shop, a painters studio, a flower nursery, a dog kennels—but I shan't worry."[2] Reports to his wife on work and other family members carried throughout: his mother now is living in Tacoma as well, his brother Warren has a new job in Portland, and the State History Museum owes him money for a death mask made of the museum's recently deceased curator, William Henry Gilstrap. Lewis further confided that the museum also reminded him of "a dew drop on a haystack, after a look at Los Angeles and San Francisco museums."[3] Bessie and the children joined him later that year, settling at 721 South "E" Street in the Stadium District.

Lewis enjoyed some early success as a sculptor in Tacoma, and in the process established connections with historians, educators and museum staff both in the city and further north, in Seattle. Several commissions were done for the Washington State Historical Society (WSHS) between 1915 and 1918, and even listed him as a Sculptor for the Ferry Museum in the latter year. He completed a monument at Point Defiance Park commemorating Captain Charles Wilkes, a project that was supported by the Daughters of the American Revolution (D.A.R.) in 1915. The sculptor confirmed the dedication placed on the Wilkes monument plaque as being authored by the late Thomas Prosch of Seattle in correspondence to Edmond Meany at the University of Washington, and that he had also made a death mask of Prosch for the WSHS collection. Ever the supportive brother, Lewis also requested that Meany mail a school curriculum or catalog to Warren, after his brother had expressed interest in attending the college in the "next term."[4]

For his brother's part, Warren was first a struggling student and then a writer, and barely able to take care of his own affairs, let alone those of an elderly mother. The boys' father, Marion ("Lon") Lewis, wrote to Alonzo during the years 1913 to 1917, but offered little in the way of support for the family, financial or otherwise. Warren keenly felt this as a burden, and wrote to Alonzo after his return to the Pacific Northwest to voice his concerns over the family's finances:

> I am trying hard to study and get along. However things sometimes worry me. Mother has only $50.00 left and we pay rent of $25.00 next April 4th. As I keep the accounts I realize how fast things are dwindling and with no income. Yes dear brother the world will someday doff her hat to you and talk of the struggle you have made.[5]

The sculptor also struggled to support himself and his work, despite a major commission begun in 1915 to model a monumental statue of Abraham Lincoln. The ten-foot-tall statue was supported by donations collected by Tacoma school children, but only after Lewis filed a lawsuit to collect $4,500 still owed for the work. In a letter dated February 9, 1917, to William Geiger, Superintendent of Tacoma School District no. 10, Lewis confirmed he would finish the statue but only if the funds were assured. Another full year passed until it was finally dedicated at Lincoln High School on February 12, 1918.

A second Lincoln statue that was begun in 1921 for Spokane dragged out for years due to a lack of funding while Lewis tried to collect on the original promise of $25,000 for his work. In 1925, members of the Grand Army of the Republic (G.A.R.) supported the commission and supplemented part of the cost from $6,000 again collected by local schoolchildren. It was finally unveiled in 1930, where it still stands today in downtown Spokane at the corner of Monroe Street and Main Avenue.

The Lincoln statues reflect an approach and style to sculpture that Lewis sought to emulate in the majority of his work throughout his career. He preferred to work in a monumental scale, such as that seen in the twelve-foot tall bronze casting for the Spokane Lincoln. As a rule, works produced by his studio were colossal in size. The sculptor preferred to model his subjects first in clay, with casting molds then made in plaster of Paris for shipment back east to the Roman Bronze Works foundry in Brooklyn, New York. An active correspondence between Lewis and the foundry between 1912 and 1922 demonstrate both his preference for them as a casting source and to produce final versions of his statues in bronze using the lost-wax casting method. Yet even his relationship with a favored foundry was not without financial complications. One invoice for $137.26 owed by Lewis to the foundry was received on September 17, 1918, for the bronze casting of an inscription tablet titled "Clark Way." The tablet—sent C.O.D. to the sculptor at the Washington State Historical Society—was not accepted by Lewis owing to a lack of funds. Nor was this the first time the foundry had been delayed payment for services charged by the sculptor for shipments of either plaster models to the foundry or completed castings back to the sculptor. In a cordially worded letter, the Roman Bronze Works stressed its desire to "avoid any misunderstandings with the express companies" and would further require New York Draft payments for foundry bills "on all future shipments."[6] Such was the reputation Lewis was generating with his patrons and service providers alike.

Lewis preferred to work with live models, even when his original subjects were long departed. For the Tacoma Lincoln statue, Lewis secured the services of a Mr. William Neilson to pose for him as a model. The sculptor paid the sitter three dollars for twenty-six consecutive days, to pose for three hours at a time.[7] The subjects for these commissions were by and large heroic in stature and steeped in history, ranging from those figures local to the Northwest (Ezra Meeker; Francis Cushman; Issac Stevens) others of national pride and prominence (Thomas Jefferson; Theodore Roosevelt; Chief Joseph of the Nez Perce Tribe) and those of international acclaim or notoriety (French military hero Marshal Foch; Norwegian polar explorer Roald Amundsen). Lewis was also equally skilled at portraying allegorical subjects for public sculpture commissions, such as the statue created to embody the spirit of the American cowboy in Pendleton, Oregon, or his *Prospector* statue destined for Sitka, Alaska, in memory of those who sought fortune in the frozen Klondike gold rush of 1898. Lewis used his son Max and another Seattle boy, Bill Schroder, to strike poses as live models for the "Sourdough" figure.

In spite of a steady demand for his services as both a painter and sculptor, the Tacoma years between 1915 and 1918 were marked by attorney bills, debt collections, quotations for casting order expenses and court complaints. In one such terse letter from a Tacoma attorney, both time and patience with the sculptor were clearly at an end. Adding to this mix were more letters from both Warren and Lena Lewis which highlighted the drama and interdependence between the family members.

Such was the case as seen in a poignant plea from the mother to son Warren in Portland, literally begging for help and at odds with a lack of support from either son:

> Why you treat me with such contempt I am grieved to know. I told you I was without money not one cent. For two days I never had one bite to eat. When you wrote me for money you got it. Now I haven't any. I am sick that is all. So here is a poor little hungry mother with two big boys—I'll have to have something soon or I'll starve. That is all.[8]

As if to capitalize on their mutual, dire situations, Warren wrote to Alonzo in the spring of 1916 to suggest a possible joining of forces and change of scenery that could benefit both men:

> For my part I am not making a large salary here and cannot see my way clear for increasing it materially for a year or so. I do not intend to make this business which I am now engaged in my life work and therefor it is to no advantage for me to stay where I am. I have mother to consider and college to hope for. For your part you are embarrassed with debt and lack of funds to properly engage in your choosen [*sic*] profession. Both of us are hampered with this handicap. If we could get on the circuit with your modelling act we would not only gain a great amount of valuable experience—but at the same time we would be making something with which we could clear up our debts.[9]

Alonzo did eventually take his brother up on one part of the suggestion, albeit without bringing him along. After a brief sojourn to Los Angeles, the sculptor relocated his studio to 2611 Eastlake Avenue, in Seattle. The timing coincided with a new offer from the University of Washington to serve as a Lecturer on Fine Arts for the UW Extension Program during the 1919 and 1920 academic years. This move to Seattle proved to be a permanent one for Lewis as a practicing sculptor. He professed a love of the Pacific Northwest and for his family, which now included three children: two daughters, Charmain (one year old) and Dorian Lorraine (age six), and a son, Max (age five). It was a time when his son Max recalled helping out in the new studio, doing some of the physical labor such as mixing plaster or applying clay to help create the oversized sculptures modeled by his father.

Seattle was now home for Lewis. The change of artistic venue to a newly adopted city also heralded the beginning of a monumental artwork that ultimately proved to be one of the most controversial and challenging sculptures of his career: a fourteen-foot-high statue of a soldier, the inspiration for which stretched back to a wartime era. The United States was getting ready to enter World War I.

In 1917, the U.S. Army formed the 91st Infantry Division comprised of young men primarily from Washington, Oregon, Alaska, and half a dozen other western states with the force stationed at Camp Lewis in Washington State. Training preparations continued for the next year and a half, with squads engaged in combat daily firing exercises that became known as "gunning for Huns." By October of the following year, men from the 91st were engaged in action in Europe.

During the final months of World War I, the soldiers of the 91st waged a hard campaign across battlefields in Flanders and France, and earned distinction for both their fighting ability and the highest average advance rate per month out of any front line unit. The 91st was known by several names: the "Pine Tree Division," the "Wild West Division" and the "Powder River Division," with the last name inspired by a passionate motto from the American homeland: "Powder river—Let-'er-buck—a mile wide, an inch deep and flows back to Texas."[10]

Infantry soldiers such as those of the 91st—known as "doughboys"—gained recognition in decisive actions such as the St. Mihiel Offensive in France and the Meuse-Argonne Offensive which succeeded in destroying the German enemy lines. The wartime diary entries of private First class Ervin Gahringer, who served with the Division's 347th Machine Gun Battalion, "B" Company, described firsthand the horrors of the war shortly after his arrival to the front:

> Oct 9 / Our company went on the line this a.m. up near hill 269. Forest full of barbed wire entanglements. The boys have been fighting hard—lots of casualties—both sides. Lots of H.E. [high explosive ordinance] today.
>
> Oct. 10 / Today we captured hill #269. Some fight. The boys are 'all in' for sure now. We have been on the front for a long time. They seem to pick on me for night runs. Rather keeps one on his nerves to go thru those woods anytime in the night with H.E. bursting all around you and star shells lighting your way. There are more Huns, dead ones, on this hill than on any we have taken yet.
>
> Oct. 13 / 7:00 and marched 20 kilos across the land which has been NoMans [*sic*] land for four years. Hard marching and we were all mighty tired.[11]

For his service, Private Gahringer along with the rest of the 91st was awarded both the Victory medal and the Silver Star medal, with the latter cited in General Orders no. 6 on January 27, 1919. Nor was his an isolated case of courage amongst the group. The Division's Headquarters included a list of those cited for bravery under fire as part of General Order no. 6, with the names and dates of action given for 85 enlisted men and officers. A sampling of the comments appearing beside all of these names described them as "efficient and courageous performance of duty under fire, Ypres-

Lys offensive," "cool and courageous performance of duty under heavy fire," and in like words of evocative praise.[12]

Newspaper accounts back in the states reported in dramatized detail the exploits of the men of the 91st, and with equal horrifying description, fates of those under the command: one story described scores of men blown to pieces during an hour-long shelling period of over 700 German artillery rounds per minute. The losses were staggering. In the second battle of the Argonne alone, the 91st lost 850 men over nine days of fighting, with another 3,500 wounded. Another 4,500 had perished in the first Argonne offensive in that September alone.

Following the conclusion of the war with the Armistice Day signing on November 11, 1918, and an extended period of post-war service in France, the 91st Division's members returned to the states. The group still numbered more than 15,000 members two years later. The close bonds formed by the group in wartime proved to extend into the peacetime era.

Lewis had never served in the military, and therefor wasn't a veteran of the war. But he was approached by the 91st Division Association in advance of the group's planned second reunion held at the Butler Hotel in Seattle on September 24 and 25, 1921. While unconfirmed, the timing for this meeting was most likely around April 1921, when the reunion's planners first met to discuss and plan for the event later that fall. In addition to the meeting's prominent veteran members such as Association president J.E. Markow and Washington State's Lieutenant Governor, W.J. ("Wee") Coyle, the Seattle contingent included support from the American Legion headquarters in the city, the Commercial Club, and the Elks Club.

For Lewis, the opportunity afforded by the 91st Division members to undertake a sculpture commission was the beginning of a larger effort to promote the statue as a new public monument for Seattle. The reunion group wanted a temporary, but large scale, statue of a doughboy soldier returning victorious from the field of battle to present as part of a display at the 91st Division Association reunion. This was only the second reunion held by the group since the war's end, and the addition of such a statue would serve as a great honor to the group's members in attendance.[13] Lewis was obliged to offer these assembled veterans a figure that they could identify with as victorious soldiers glad to be alive at war's end.

Members of the American Legion's La Societe des Quarante Hommes et Huit Chevaux—known by the moniker "40 & 8"–coordinated festivities for the 1921 reunion, which included a formal luncheon at the Butler Hotel, an afternoon baseball game at the Coast League Baseball Park, and a "Zero Hour" evening banquet culminating in the Masonic Club rooms of the

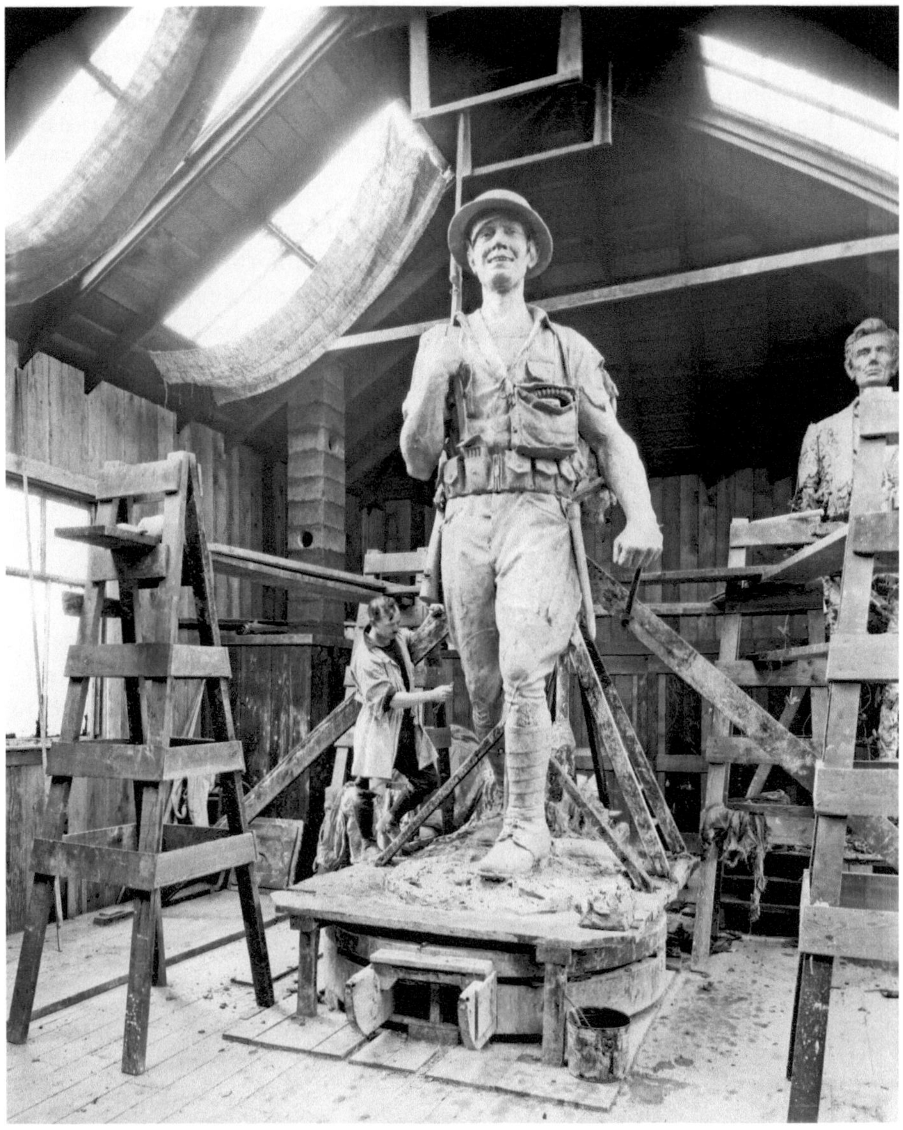

Clay model for the World War I memorial statue. **Photograph ca. 1922. Webster & Stevens, Photographers. Museum of History & Industry, Seattle.**

Butler. In publicized accounts describing the 91st reunions held in Seattle during 1921 and 1922, no mention was made of a "doughboy" statue by Lewis. Nonetheless, after a year of effort, he completed the modeling for a U.S. Army solider statue using three tons of clay in December 1922. Both a realistic presentation of the figure and its meaning as a national symbol were characterized by Lewis following the completion of the model:

> In America there is a demand for all to forget the war ... but I feel we don't want to forget the war. Rather, we want to forget the horrors of war. When I started on my American Doughboy I wanted to portray America's participation in the struggle, America's glorious victory and at the same time, do it with a smile.[14]

The statue Lewis produced showed a soldier grinning and with his left eye closed in a wink, wearing an infantryman's uniform—boots, leggings, belt and helmet—and carrying a Springfield M1903 rifle slung over the right shoulder and affixed with a bayonet. Also slung across his back right shoulder, were two German helmets taken as souvenirs from the European battlefields.

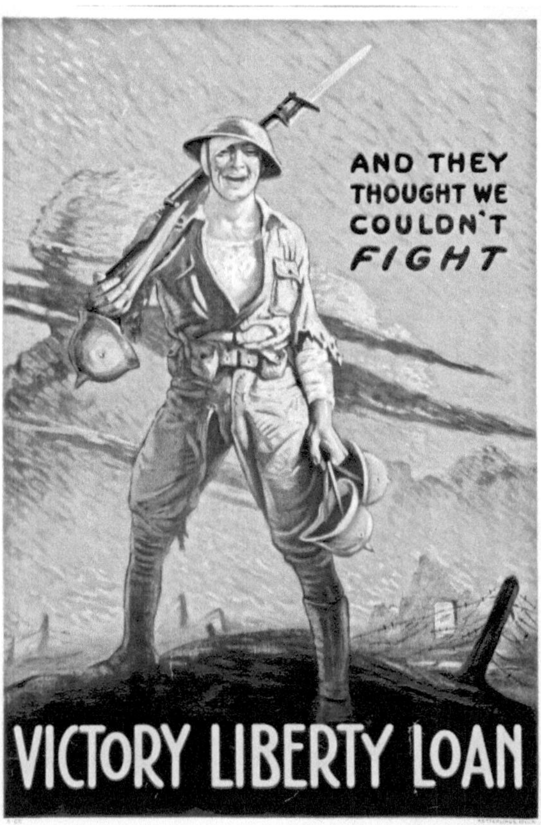

"And they thought we couldn't fight"—Victory Liberty Loan **poster by Clyde Forsythe. 1917. Library of Congress Prints and Photographs Division, Washington, D.C.**

The left hand is closed in a fist, and frozen in the action of the arm swinging forward, in tandem with the left foot forward, captured in mid-stride. On the figure's belt, a pouch flap rides open, revealing a clip of bullets within. Worn on the back, is a pack from which the handle of entrenching tool hangs down along the figure's spine. The scabbard for the bayonet hangs down on the soldier's left side from the belt, and parallel to the arm.

The sources Lewis used to model the doughboy statue were taken from real life. Three soldiers from the local Fort Lawton Army base reportedly served as models, while the sculptor had also studied "the faces, expressions and thoughts of dozens of men who left Seattle for France and who lived through the scene depicted by 'The American Doughboy.'"[15]

Lewis portrayed the soldier as part of a scene not unlike many of the World War I propaganda posters produced by other American artists between 1914 and 1919. Uniform details, weapons displayed, the posture of soldiers engaged in action, even the smiling visage and carrying of German helmets as war trophies were commonly depicted by artists such as Vincent Lynel's poster *Ammunition!* (1918), John W. Sheeres' poster *Regulars...* (1919), and notably, Vic Forsythe's poster *And They Thought We Couldn't Fight / Victory Liberty Loan* (1917) which featured both the smile and the helmets details. Even the 91st Division had depictions of its soldiers in other artworks, similar to what Lewis had created as a likeness both true to the nature and identity of the American soldier during World War I. Ross Carpenter's poster done for the *91st Division National Army Camp Lewis* (1917) showed three doughboy's racing across a battlefield, rifles in hand while an artillery shell bursts overhead.

A photograph by the *Seattle Daily Times* photographers, Webster and Stevens, pictured the finished clay model of the statue in the sculptor's studio, with Lewis shown working on the right knee area of the figure. A broad platform supported the base of the statue, while several wooden scaffolds were positioned around the studio. Curtained skylights illuminate the sculptor and his work.

While the original statue designed for the 91st Division's reunion was never intended to be more than a temporary decoration and reminder to those who had served in the war, it opened the door for Lewis to pursue other venues for the design as a permanent monument cast into bronze. His first proposal was to offer it to the University of Washington, for placement as a new World War I monumental sculpture on campus.[16] In anticipation of the statue being given approval, Lewis contacted the Roman Bronze Works, Inc. about the cost of casting a twelve-foot-high plaster mold of the figure into bronze using the lost-wax method. He received a reply on October 16, 1922, with the foundry noting it would cost approximately $3,630 for such a casting over a period of four to five months. The letter concludes in good will to the sculptor: "please keep us informed of how things are going, and we are counting on your old friendship."[17]

However, support for placement of the statue on the University of Washington campus was found wanting and a casting order was not placed. Over the next six years, Lewis continued his efforts to gain support for the monument through both local veteran groups such as the Rainier Nobel Post No. 1 of the American Legion, and in city government with the Board of Parks Commissioners and the Mayor's office. But progress on a publicly supported commission for the statue was slow going.

In November 1924, it appeared that Lewis had made a breakthrough by gaining the support of Mayor Brown, who called for a meeting of representatives from across Seattle to formulate a plan for the statue as a new public monument. Brown offered effusive praise for the work as a lasting tribute to those who had served, and one that was overdue:

> The people of Seattle owe it to our soldiers to erect this monument in City Hall Park. As the work of a Seattle man it deserves recognition from the people of Seattle, and it would be particularly fitting for this city to adopt the plan for placing where it will be a constant reminder of the part played by Seattle boys in the World War.[18]

Discussion of placement for the statue included another idea to place it near the south entrance of the County-City Building, opposite the park. However vocal Brown's support was at the time, it may have been spurred on by his need for voters in an upcoming election year, with the promise of the statue offering a convenient platform to stump as a fellow patriot and supporter of veteran's causes. Citywide support through veteran's groups also failed to materialize, leaving Lewis to continue efforts on his own to finance a statue cast in bronze and installed into a public venue.

The timing for the new interest in the *Doughboy* statue was likely related to another commission Lewis was successful in securing for Centralia, Washington. The effort was led by the American Legion's Rhodes Post No. 2 in Tacoma, a statue committee headed by C.D. Cunningham, and the Centralia Memorial Association to fund the creation of a ten-foot-high statue in bronze as a memorial to four veterans killed in the Centralia massacre on Armistice Day, November 11, 1919.

While the Centralia doughboy statue known as *The Sentinel* was comparable in some ways to the Seattle statue, such as the helmet worn and rifle held, its design was significantly different in most other respects. Rather than shown in motion, the figure of the soldier was stoic, standing on guard duty, with rifle clasped between hands and bayonet folded on the stock. The figure of the doughboy is serious (not smiling) with the collar of his uniform trench coat turned up against the elements. A simple engraving on the base of the statue signifies the identity of the soldier as "a sentry at his post" but makes no specific mention of World War I. Only on the back side of the base, is an engraved tribute to the memory of the four soldiers slain in Centralia in 1919, with bas-relief portraits on the sides of the base along with the names of the dead: Ben Casagranda, Warren O. Grimm, Earnest Dale Hubbard, and Arthur McElfresh.

Tensions were already high as far as the public effects of the Industrial Workers of the World (IWW) labor movement underway in Washington State. Several members of the IWW were convicted of the slaying of Warren O. Grimm, the Commander of American Legion Post No. 17 in Centralia, with the end result being a subdued memorial as far as its formal inscription and official dedication ceremony. Both in the general public and elements of left-wing media, there was the assertion that the Army soldiers had been the instigators of an attack on an IWW headquarters in Centralia, in spite of a trial record which demonstrated evidence to the contrary. The jury convicted nine members of the IWW who were charged with the shootings. The end result was a decision by the statue committee to omit mention of the word "murder" in the monument's formal inscription, as well as any role of complicity the IWW had as aggressors. In the mind of Cunningham and the other committee members, to do otherwise "would be an open invitation for a dynamiting."[19]

For his part, Lewis appeared as the sculptor for *The Sentinel* after the statue committee formed in 1922, but only after the group ran into trouble securing funds through statewide veteran's groups, notably the Legion posts. Estimates of upwards of a quarter million dollars were the initial target, but fell far short of the mark, with only $16,000 publicly collected. Faced with the need for a low cost solution, the group turned to Lewis in Seattle to complete the work. The statue was cast in bronze and dedicated on Armistice Day, November 11, 1924. Twelve days later, Lewis had Mayor Brown visit his studio in Seattle, to review the 91st Division's *Doughboy* statue in person.

That Brown was unable or unwilling to further his efforts to unite veterans groups in support of *Doughboy* as a new public sculpture and war memorial speaks to the lack of citywide support Lewis could expect after 1924. It also underscores how the American Legion posts in particular had fundamental difficulties in coming together for a common cause. In a letter sent by C.W. Ardery to the Adjutant at Rainer Post No. 1 in Seattle, the National Correspondent acknowledges the differences dividing the veterans in 1926:

> I agree with you that the Posts in Seattle are not united and I do not believe that any particular Post can be picked out as being to blame for this condition but I believe you will agree with me that there are certain individuals in all of the Posts who can be blamed for it and rightly are.[20]

In a less official capacity and tone, Ardery writes to his friend Steve Chadwick, who was the Chef de Gare of Voiture 75 with the American Legion in Seattle, about the Rainer Post No. 1 Adjutant being an "old obstructionist" and the need for "the Grande Voiture of Washington to do one solitary thing that would warrant and merit its existence as a Grande Voiture."[21] While Ardery's note conveyed frustration with the lack of action by the American Legion's leadership in the state, it left the door open to the future possibility that the organization could eventually aid Lewis in his efforts for the *Doughboy* statue to become that "one solitary thing," as a new war memorial with the Legion's backing.

New support for the statue finally materialized in early 1928. A delegation from University Post No. 11 led by Post Commander Harry Lewis came to the February 23, 1928, meeting of the Seattle Park Board of Commissioners to state their intentions of having the *Doughboy* statue installed in one of the city parks. As part of their request for support, the Post endorsed an offer from the City Council to provide $5,000 in funding for the statue "designed by Lewis" through the Park Board's budget, with the balance of the $50,000 total cost "to be paid for by contributions."[22] The proposal to have the statue serve as a public monument to those who participated in World War I was carried unanimously by the Park Board.

Harry Lewis continued to lead the Post's efforts to secure financial support through the city government. He wrote to the City Council three weeks after the Park Board meeting about the $5,000 commitment, and was successful in securing the aid of Councilman Philip Tindall in the preparation of Resolution No. 9529 by the city's Law Department. In a letter to Tindall confirming the Resolution was ready for Council adoption, legal counsel Thomas Kennedy identified the American Legion as the party offering "to donate to the City of Seattle a statue known as the 'Doughboy.'"[23] No mention was made of Alonzo Lewis as the sculptor, nor was he included anywhere in the language for the Resolution approved by the City Council on March 19, 1928. Passage of the Resolution authorized that the $5,000 was available in the Park Board's 1929 budget, while the furnishing and erection of the Doughboy statue for placement in a city park was the responsibility of University Post No. 11.

The backing of the Park Board had only secured a fraction of the funds promised to Lewis by the American Legion for *Doughboy*. The veterans group now focused on securing additional aid on the civic front, by enlisting Mayor Frank Edwards to the cause. In August, Edwards announced he was forming a committee of 173 prominent business and civic leaders in support of the Lewis statue—now renamed *Armistice*—as the first-ever memorial dedicated to Seattle's World War I dead. As had been the case four years earlier with Mayor Brown, the primary location envisioned for the new statue was at City Hall Park.

Edwards was clear in his mandate as to the fundraising purpose of the new committee, and its timing as a cause worthy of public support:

> Next November 11 will mark the passing of the tenth year since the signing of the Armistice. It is time Seattle did something tangible to honor the memory of those young men who died answering the call of their country. In these past ten years while governments, nations, states and cities have in one way or another honored their soldiers, Seattle has done nothing.[24]

The mayor's efforts drew new public attention—and scrutiny—to both the design of *Armistice* as a new public sculpture and to Lewis as a local sculptor. Literally the day after Edwards' announcement in local newspapers about the formation of the committee, other veterans groups came out in opposition to the statue. Among the objections voiced, was that the representation of only the Army service branch through the identity of the solider did a disservice to the other branches that had contributed to the war effort, namely the Navy and Marines. Other criticisms were that the doughboy soldier depicted was not an accurate presentation of the figure and that the German helmets shown carried over the shoulder—heralded in 1922 as an acceptable symbol of victory—were now inflammatory and "the seeds of future discord and misunderstanding."[25] News coverage confirmed that not all those who came to see the Mayor were in agreement on these points. Among those petitioning the mayor's office, were Commander John O'Brien of the Rainier Nobel Post No. 1 and Commander Harry Lewis of the University Post No. 11.

The opposition from the veterans was over as quickly as it had begun. The outcome of the conference with Edwards was a united front in support of the Lewis statue as the preferred choice as a new war memorial. What had begun in 1921 as a tribute to living veterans who were local to the western states and had lived through the World War, had now become fully transformed in the public's collective mind as a statue dedicated to the war's dead. The question remained of how the fundraising would be completed, with Lewis still expecting to collect on the full $50,000.

On September 13, the sculptor was joined by William Pitt Trimble and the Mayor's Committee Chairman, B.N. Hutchinson, at the regular Board of Park Commissioners meeting to show details of the planned memorial. In addition to the statue, the plan for the war memorial site included the placement of five trees from battlefields in France, provided by the French government. Of pressing concern to Lewis and the others was a need to secure the Park Board's reaffirmation of an earlier endorsement of the plans and to confirm a location for the statue's placement. Board President Kerry assured the group the Board's support for the project was unchanged and promised that the Board would cooperate in finding a suitable location.

By November, the new Civic Auditorium was selected as the site for *Armistice*. Park Board President Kerry and Mayor Edwards made a joint announcement that the statue would be placed near the auditorium's entrance, on a plot of ground designated as Memorial Park. Edwards added that the statue "had not been completed, as it is now being cast in bronze in New York City..."[26] Premature as the announcement was, Edwards held a public ground breaking and official dedication of the Civic Auditorium site for the new war memorial on November 11, 1928.

Following the dedication, the city continued to hold onto the promised $5,000 in spite of a pledge to include this in the Park Board's 1929 budget. Part of the delay may be attributed to the negative press the statue received that fall, as questions were raised about the statue's value as a public artwork. The press was even calling into question other public sculptures already in the city, such as the *Chief Seattle* statue by James Wehn. The role and motivations of Hutchinson as a primary advocate for the *Doughboy* were also called to task:

> Another point in question today was whether the statue was representative of a general community feeling or that of one or two persons. It was recalled that B.N. Hutchinson, chairman of the citizens' war memorial committee, had been prominently identified with its acceptance and plans for raising the fund for its purchase. Today, when plans for the dedicatory ceremonies were being whipped into final shape, there seemed to be some wonderment extant as to whether this community enterprise was turning out to be as communal as first intended or whether it migh't [*sic*] be a one-man job.[27]

As Lewis had experienced in the past with other monumental public sculpture projects, funding continued to be in short supply for his studio. A plaster cast from the clay model was ready to send on to a foundry but by the end of 1929, funds were still insufficient to proceed. A letter from the Chairman of the City's Finance Committee, E.L. Blaine, sent at the end of the year to a trustee of the Seattle "Doughboy" fund explicitly stated that any additional funds required for bills associated with the purchase and erection of the statue above the $5,000 amount needed to be in place before any city funds would be released.[28]

Despite the city's reluctance to release funds, the sculptor proceeded with sending his plaster model of the fourteen-foot-high statue back east to the Roman Bronze Works, Inc. for casting into bronze. Foundry records show the order was commissioned for the "Doughboy" on January 28, 1930, with a cost of $3,600 incurred for the statue cast using the lost-wax method. It was completed and shipped back to Seattle on July 3, 1930.[29] Upon arrival from New York the statue was stored in its shipping crate at the yard of the city's Water Department maintenance barn in Freemont. There it would sit.

The terms of the foundry had stipulated that payment was due before starting the casting work. To offset this cost, Lewis had relied on a sum of $4,000 collected by the committee from the community, primarily from those veterans groups such as the American Legion which had supported the memorial. Any monies that had been so far collected on the sculptor's behalf had been used for the project. While the realization of the statue was now achieved in its final bronze version, Lewis experienced more delay and renewed controversy over now having the statue finally installed at the Civic Auditorium.

By 1931, efforts to see the statue installed as a memorial had come to a standstill. No more public funding was forthcoming to Lewis to pay for the statue, including the $5,000 still held by the city Parks Board. The delay of payment marked a sad continuation of a practice Lewis had maintained throughout his career with commissions, and so he yet again turned to the law to seek recompense. He filed a plaintiff lawsuit with the King County Superior Court against the City of Seattle which sought restitution for the unpaid balance still owed for the statue. The city's position was that despite the fact the statue had already been cast in bronze, the funds Lewis was seeking were supposed to have come from a public fundraising campaign coordinated by other parties. The legal dispute dragged out over the next several months.

Whether spurred on by the legal action taken by Lewis, or by the prospect of the statue finally being installed as a dedicated war memorial, the City Council commissioned an independent art commission on November 5, 1931, to examine the value of *Doughboy* as a new public sculpture. The commission members representing the Art Institute of Seattle, the Parent Teachers Association of Seattle, the Commanders and Adjutants Association and the American Institute of Architects, recommended that given the previous city support offered by Resolution No. 9529, the statue was deemed acceptable as a piece of public sculpture but not in the context of being offered as part of any official war memorial.[30] The final report was submitted to City Council President Phillip Tindall on January 4, 1932.

Added to the mounting opposition against Lewis were voices both past and present decrying the aesthetics of the statue's figure and its ability to serve even as an allegorical model for patriotism, heroism, and honorable military service. Tindall, who had commissioned the independent study of the artwork, criticized the statue as "too exultant, too happy."[31] Another letter of protest sent by the Veterans of Foreign Wars Theodore Roosevelt Post No. 24 to the City Council (and later forwarded to the Parks Board) railed against the statue as not a fitting tribute to the men of the war or serving as a memorial to their service.

Even those acquainted with the sculptor on a more personal level were critical of the statue conceived as a war memorial. Carl Gould, who had worked with Lewis as a fellow instructor at the University of Washington in 1921, was one such example. Gould had made public comments against the statue back on November 11, 1928, which found renewed coverage in the local press three years later. One of the more damaging assertions from the University of Washington Architecture Professor characterized the statue as having an expression "completely animal and with no vestige of the heroic or of the purpose for which we sacrificed so many lives."[32] Lewis considered Gould's public comments damaging to his reputation as a sculptor and fuel for the continued delay by city government to see the statue installed. He initiated a lawsuit against the architect and asked the Superior Court for a $50,000 claim in both slander and loss of income from the *Doughboy* statue. Intense as it was between the architect and the sculptor, the lawsuit was short-lived. A demurrer filed by Gould's attorney was sustained and case no. 247743 was dismissed on December 30, 1931, with no damages awarded to Lewis.

As if the trials of getting one of his public commissioned sculptures installed were not enough, Lewis and his wife Bessie endured a personal tragedy in 1931. Their eldest daughter, Dorian, was killed in California at the age of seventeen. Tragic as the event was, the sculptor was not dissuaded from the ongoing controversy in Seattle over his artwork.

Over the course of the past three years, *Doughboy* had undergone yet another transformation as a public sculpture, now deemed unacceptable for use as a World War I memorial as endorsed by the City of Seattle. While the monumental bronze soldier waited in storage, the King County Superior Court forced the City to come to terms with Lewis on the question of any remaining compensation still owed to the sculptor. On February 29, 1932, the City Council passed Ordinance No. 62319, which called for the city to complete the furnishing and erection of the statue known as the *Doughboy* as a new public sculpture and authorized a final payment to the American Legion University Post No. 11 in the amount of $5,000. The Ordinance was granted final approval by Mayor Robert Harlin on March 1, 1932.

While Lewis was finally able to collect from the American Legion the City-released funds, the $5,000 payment represented only a fraction of the original $50,000 cost that had been promised to him for the *Doughboy*. No further compensation for his work was forthcoming from either the city or the veteran groups. The process had taken more than a decade to see the sculpture come to fruition, and in the minds of many viewers, the sculptor's claim that it depicted "the supreme moment of victory" was unfounded.[33] The public debate between Lewis and Gould in particular had an alienating effect for the sculptor, impacting future relationships with the city on other public sculpture projects. While a hard won victory for the sculptor, it also served as one more prominent example of his difficulties to successfully promote himself as an artist and clearly set terms of payment for commissioned works of art.

Even the news media, which had once appeared to support the prospect of the statue as a war memorial as late as 1928, referred to the statue in negative terms once the sculptor's remediation with the city proved successful. Among the chief objections still given voice was the expression of the soldier figure:

> A place has at last been found for that doughboy statue, which the City Council, in a fit of generosity, bought for Seattle without any idea what to do with it. The statue will be raised at the Civic Auditorium, a center of public amusement. That sardonic grin on the doughboy's face, to which some critics have objected, will be appropriate enough when wrestling "matches" are held.[34]

Nor were certain elements on the City Council content to have the statue installed as Lewis had originally designed it. Both Tindall and fellow councilman James Scavotto were vehemently opposed to the two German helmets shown carried as war trophies, and objected to the statue's installation with this detail left unchanged. The shared opinion of the two men was that to leave the helmets intact would perpetuate war animosities, so further discussion about their removal was deemed necessary with Park Board engineer E.R. Hoffman.

On May 30, 1932, the statue was finally unveiled in front of Civic Auditorium. Now called *The American Doughboy—Bringing Home Victory*, it was officially dedicated six months later on Armistice Day, November 11, 1932. In the interim period between the unveiling and the dedication, the offending German helmets slung across the soldier's shoulder were removed. The dedication ceremony was marred further when a twenty-one-gun salute shattered several apartment windows across the street from the statue.

For the next three decades, *The American Doughboy* remained a de facto memorial and visual reminder for those who had both served in World War I and given their lives in that conflict. Its placement during this time was a prominent one, and encouraged public recognition of the statue as a war memorial and not just another piece of public sculpture. During this time, the statue often served as a gathering location for various Veteran groups who publicly observed Memorial Day on May 29 and Armistice Day (officially renamed Veterans Day in 1954) on November 11 each year.

With the coming of the 1962 World's Fair to Seattle, the city made an attempt to surplus the Lewis memorial but through efforts of local businessmen and veterans, the statue was merely relocated to a new place in front of Veterans Hall, but behind the Opera House.[35] This removal of *The American Doughboy* from immediate public view was a compromise of sorts for the planners of the Exposition, who were allied with the Mayor's Office and the Parks Board in a shared vision of offering new cultural centers, public fountains and sculpture done in a modern vein as preferred over new (and existing) historical monuments, memorial sculptures and statuary.

In the years that followed the statue's relocation, details concerning its original purpose faded along with the memories of those who first bore witness to its dedication in 1932. By this time, the number of living World War I veterans as well had significantly declined. Public interest in the statue as a site for public observances of Veteran holidays waned as a result.

Even as it remained sequestered out of the mainstream traffic of visitors to the Seattle Center, the statue continued to attract periodic attention. Earl Laymen, a historic preservation officer for the city, observed:

> I think it's kind of disgraceful the way that doughboy statue was removed from a prominent spot and hidden in a dark corner ... it was erected at a time when we were more sentimental about our war dead, and about our veterans. But I still think that statue has been terribly neglected.[36]

The decade leading up to and immediately after the turn of the century saw many changes at the Seattle Center, including a major renovation of the Center House/Armory Building in 1995 and the demolition of the Flag Pavilion Building in 2001 to construct the new Fisher Pavilion. The time had also come for *Doughboy* to be removed from the site. Under the sponsorship of Councilman Nick Licata, the City Council declared the statue surplus city artwork and unanimously passed Ordinance No. 119115 on August 17, 1998, which both repealed the earlier Ordinance No. 62319 and allowed for the Director of the Seattle Center to enter into an agreement to move the statue to another location. The Mayor's office approved the transfer of *Doughboy* on August 19, 1998.

A new site for the Lewis statue was found at the Veteran's Memorial Cemetery at Evergreen Washelli in Seattle. The city donated the statue to the cemetery, and it was installed and re-dedicated on November 11, 1998, as *The American Doughboy*. The bronze figure was shorter than the original version—only twelve feet, eight inches high—owing to the removal of the bronze rifle bayonet from the statue in 1970. Another change from the original 1922 design was the wording for the statue's title on its bronze base. The second half of the title no longer read "Bringing Home the Bacon" but instead reflected the renamed statue title with "Bringing Home Victory" on the left side of the base edge.

This second relocation of *The American Doughboy* marked a final transition of the sculpture back to representing a general memorial to U.S. military servicemen who had served in World War I and other wars. Washelli's Veterans Memorial Cemetery was a logical pairing in this regard, established in 1927 as a site for the burial of both veterans and their spouses. In its new position, the statue stands against the park like backdrop of Washelli, with its immaculate green lawns, rolling hills, trees, and stonework. Nor was the *Doughboy* the only memorial sculpture installed here. Sculptor James Wehn contributed a portrait medallion of Edmond S. Meany for a memorial reflecting fountain and pool, along with another medallion to G.A.R. Commander Hiram Gale placed on the hill overlooking the location of the Lewis statue.

By moving the statue to the cemetery, the city's action in 1998 served as an affirmation of Mayor Edward's original vision seventy years earlier to have the Lewis statue as part of a larger war memorial for the city. While the reality of the statue's move did provide a more tangible connection to a site dedicated to the war dead, it also resulted in it being far removed from the heart of the city, to its very outskirts.

Despite the prolonged saga of the Lewis soldier statue, its resolution did not mark an ending to the sculptor's contributions of public statuary to Seattle and the greater Pacific Northwest. He successfully completed his third major World War I statue (*Winged Victory*) a grouping of four monumental figures with the winged figure of Nike, Greek goddess of Victory in bronze for the State Legislature in 1938. Following the monument's dedication on the grounds of the State Capitol campus in Olympia, Lewis was named Washington Sculptor Laureate by the Legislature.[37]

Besides *The Doughboy*, the Lewis studio produced four other major public sculptures in Seattle: the "First Around-the-World Flight" monument for the Sand Point Naval Air Station that featured a pillar surmounted by a bronze wings sculpture and plaque (1924); a dual portrait medallion in bronze dedicated to both Will Rogers and Wiley Post (circa 1936); a second profile medallion as a memorial to Will Rogers, placed at the Will Rogers baseball field (1936); and a bronze bust of Reverend Mark A. Matthews installed in Denny Park (1941).

While the United States engaged in another world war, Alonzo Victor Lewis—or, Victor Alonzo Lewis, as he was known to go by at different times in his career—experienced new, financial hardships and personal upheavals in his life. He divorced Bessie in the late 1930s, and was remarried to second wife Betty in 1941. That same year his new young wife gave birth to their first son, Victor Hugo.

Early in 1943, Lewis petitioned the aid of the Seattle City Council to forestall the public sale of his studio to a former patron, Alaska-Yukon Pioneers, after Lewis lost the property for failing to keep up tax payments. The Pioneers claimed to hold a mortgage on the studio dating back to 1937, and had asked the city to sell the property to their organization after dealings with Lewis over a commission had turned sour. For its part, Councilman Frank Laube refused to have the city embroiled in yet another Lewis controversy, which allowed Lewis to get his home back.[38]

As a coda to the Lewis statue debate, a postwar planning commission met with the City Council on April 19, 1945, to discuss postwar projects and a new policy that favored civic improvements over the creation of new statues and monuments as war memorials. The Chairman of the planning commission, Walter Wyckoff, explained the need for such policy in light of past public disputes over such sculptures:

> There have recently been newspaper stories about proposed war memorials for Seattle ... we have observed that in the past, the location and the design of such memorials has often been the subject of bitter and unpleasant public controversy. These disputes leave the public in doubt as to the quality of the finished project and somewhat unappreciative of it. There is a growing feeling that the public memory of men and events might be better preserved by building needed buildings, parks, playgrounds and other usable civic improvements instead of erecting statues and monuments.[39]

As enlightening a prospect as such a policy promised, the city's validation process for new public sculptures, including memorials, monuments and statuary, continued to remain the purview of the city's Parks Board. It would be another ten years before a major shift to this policy, when additional input was finally solicited on public artworks from the first Municipal Art Commission formed in 1955.

Lewis looked to begin a new enterprise involving the mass production of sculpture busts featuring the portrait of wartime President Franklin

D. Roosevelt (FDR) in 1944. Self-professed as a lifelong Republican, the sculptor cast each bust in "dealstone" a synthetic stone that could be easily used to produce a large number of busts at Lewis' Eastlake studio. Lewis partnered with two other men—former newspaper man, A.J. Richie, and an oilman from California, A.E. McCroskey—to form Alonzo Victor Lewis Associates as the company for selling the busts.

While the FDR busts proved to be a popular item among collectors and the general public alike (Lewis produced 100 casts in the first batch released in 1944) the endeavor, like many of the commissions and other business deals Lewis had engaged with in the past, soon became mired in legal dispute. In March 1946, Lewis was called to testify as part of a lawsuit brought against his two partners by H.P. Mears, who claimed he was defrauded out of $1,250 by the Associates. While the attorney for Mears called the lost funds the result of an unsecured investment by his client spurred by false pretense of the partners, Lewis himself countered that Mears has been taken into the studio as an apprentice, and that the funds had paid for his instruction to help produce the busts.[40] After a week of deliberations, a jury awarded Mears the full amount in damages.

As the Mears lawsuit concluded, Betty and Alonzo had their second son, Sigmond Marion. It would serve as a final joy to the sculptor, now at the age 60, with a new family to support. Whether the result of new stress from family obligations, accumulated tribulations over a lifetime, or from just plain tiredness, Lewis died from a heart attack on November 7, 1946. He was survived by both his mother and brother, four children and one monument in the form of a smiling American soldier that has finally found its place in Seattle.

9

John Carl Ely (1897–1929)

Does the absence, or loss, of any one particular twentieth century sculptor have an impact on the record of historical public art monuments and sculptures made for Seattle? One might be tempted to say that if a sculptor makes only one or two such contributions of artwork, then they should be counted amongst those credited with helping to establish public sculpture in the city.

John Carl Ely was one such sculptor. His legacy of work in the sculpture medium shines through to the current era, despite his brief time in the sun.

At the tender age of five, Ely came to Seattle with his family from Mason City, West Virginia, in 1902. Ely's father, John Henry, was a motorman by profession, and may have been drawn west with the promise of steady employment offered by Seattle's building boom underway at this time. Ely's mother, Alice, was a homemaker, and took care of John along with the two younger children, Alan and Inez.

By the time he finished high school at West Seattle High School in 1915, Ely already had shown a passion for the arts, where "his deep sympathy with all forms of beauty, linked with a desire for their expression, was ever apparent."[1] Ely first entered the University of Washington in the fall of the following year, and also briefly worked for the Pacific Coast Steel Company while continuing to live at home with his parents. Records show that while he registered for the draft in August 1918, he wasn't required to serve in the U.S. military during World War I.

Ely's formal instruction in the fine arts was through the University of Washington, starting in 1917. By fortuitous timing, the University of Washington began its first School of Sculpture under the direction of local sculptor James A. Wehn in the fall of 1919. For the next two years, Ely took Wehn's sculpture courses in life modeling, working with clay and plaster to form reliefs, portrait medallions and sculpture busts. This coursework offered by Wehn ranged from media techniques to modeling subjects such as body parts (ears, lips, noses) or copies of neoclassical statuary offered as still-life studies.

Wehn, an accomplished sculptor in his own right, recognized early on the potential in Ely and encouraged the young sculptor by providing Ely with a key to access Denny Hall's room 408 in the spring of 1920 "for the purpose of completing special work."[2] He also had Ely demonstrate modeling techniques in clay as part of classroom demonstrations. Ely graduated from the University with a Bachelor of Fine Arts in August 1921—but the ceremony was not officially held until the following year, when the University could boast its largest recorded class in history with 648 graduates.[3]

Photographs of Ely at this time often showed him smiling for the camera, a sharply dressed man and clean-shaven, and the picture of flamboyant youth and health. In one image, which shows him teaching a sculpture class to students in the Denny Hall fourth floor studio, Ely intently scrutinizes a medallion design being shaped for the class. Another picture has him grinning into the camera lens, his hair closely parted in the middle and a Model-T Ford parked behind him. Even newspaper photographs captured Ely's good nature and personality, such as a view of him grinning and posing with one of his sculpture heads done in marble.

Following graduation, Ely was offered and accepted an instructor position with the University's Art Department, teaching design, sculpture and freshman drawing for the 1921–1922 academic year. Ely continued to produce his own sculpture as well, with a life-sized plaster head of his father, John Henry, one among several portrait-style works he made that year. Following the June 17 meeting of the University's Board of Regents, he was again offered an Assistant in Fine Arts position with the University of Washington. The new role was scheduled to begin on October 1, 1922, and extended through the academic year to June 30, 1923. However, Ely's desire to excel at his own work in sculpture took precedent over teaching others. Opportunities for receiving advanced instruction in the medium were found wanting at the University at this time, given both a lack in student demand and a reluctance on the administration's part to expand the Sculpture Department beyond basic coursework.

Partly on Wehn's written recommendation and association with W. Frank Purdy, Ely applied for and was accepted into the School of American Sculpture (SAS) in New York for the fall, 1922 session. Purdy confirmed the choice of Ely as a good one, calling him "a splendid fellow and I am looking forward to a happy winter with him."[4] The decision to attend the school proved to be a critical one in how Ely would refine both his technique and style in the medium.

While at the SAS, Ely studied under Ralph Laurent, another relative newcomer to New York. Laurent was a Frenchman who had immigrated to the United States and was also a World War I veteran. At the time he met Ely, he was 32 years old, yet already an accomplished sculptor who worked in woodcarving, alabaster, and limestone. Ely described the influence of this initial time spent on the East Coast: "I use a somewhat different method than most sculptors. I cut directly into the marble, without making a clay model first. To learn this stone cutting, I have been studying with Robert Laurent of Brooklyn, one of the few sculptors using this method."[5]

During the first two years he spent in New York, Ely produced two marble sculptures that clearly defined his shift away from a purely representational treatment of subjects, to a more expressionist and interpretive style. These sculptures were two variations on female portraiture, one titled *La Passante* (The Passerby); the other called *The Head of a Woman.* Both were also carved out of solid blocks of marble per the approach learned from Laurent. In each version, Ely employed minimal lines and curves to denote both the hair and facial features. In the first sculpture, an ovoid face has framed the blade of a nose with two slightly olive-shaped eyes, and a pursed mouth below. It presented a harsh look almost puritanical in the effect of the hairline defining the head. The second portrait was softer in appearance: one hand raised to brush back her hair, with eyes closed in the act. She could almost be pictured as sleeping, her lips curved slightly upward in a happy dream.

From the time these works were completed, Ely's outlook on sculpture rejected any labels concurrent with the art scene of his day and in fashion with the public: "I never was an expressionist; or any other 'ist.'"[6] When pressed for an explanation of how *La Passante* was conceptualized, he observed that "the passerby ... it is just a fanciful face, very, very fleeting, all that you might catch or recall of the face of a chance passerby."[7] His subjects were still identifiable as both from real life and mythology, but the results were now a result of Ely's artistic interpretation.

Ely's success with this new approach to his sculpture found acceptance both in New York and Seattle, keeping him moving back and forth between coasts for the next several years. He exhibited *The Head of a Woman* at the Andersen Galleries *Salons of America* exhibition in spring, 1923. The fall of that same year, Ely returned to Seattle to and spent the next several months working out of a studio in his parent's home on 44th

Avenue Southwest. This time marked a continuation of Ely's productivity in sculpture, with the production of expressionist works in materials other than marble. One such sculpture was a dryad figure carved from a Madrone (a tree specifically found in the Pacific Northwest) cut down by his family's house. This period of work culminated with another public exhibition of work in February 1924, where he featured several sculptures including *The Head of a Woman, La Passante,* and another sculpture, *The Man in the Derby Hat,* at the Seattle Fine Arts Society gallery on Third Avenue.

In the fall of 1924, he was again back in New York and resumed working with Laurent. As a token of their friendship, Ely gave the elder sculptor his rose-pink marble torso of *The Man in the Derby Hat.* The timing of his return to New York also marked Ely's first commission for an art museum, with the sale of *The Head of a Woman* sculpture to the Roerich Museum and its Riverside Collection of art. As evidence of his growing reputation on the East Coast, the sale of the sculpture coincided with notification of a Walt Whitman scholarship award on October 7, 1924, from the Master Institute of United Arts. In her congratulatory letter, the Executive Director, Frances Grant, called Ely's work "of exceptional merit."[8]

According to a catalog of Ely's artworks developed by David Plummer, Ely's nephew, the last sculpture identified by date was a second *Head of a Woman* portrait head in black marble, modeled in June 1924. The sculptor's record of work in the medium, including a later exhibition of sculptures done in terra cotta and walnut for the College of Puget Sound in Tacoma around 1927 suggests that Ely continued to emphasize sculpture as his primary medium of choice. To further his academic instruction in the arts, Ely's last period of time spent in Seattle culminated with his earning an MFA degree from his alma-matter, the University of Washington, in 1927.

Ely's return to New York coincided with his securing a part-time job as a Preparator for the American Museum of Natural History starting on October 31, 1928. While not specific to sculpture, this choice of work was no doubt of interest for Ely, since it involved the hands-on physical installation of artifacts and objects from natural history collections to help create public displays. An undated photograph taken by M.D. Burch shows Ely "preparing" a new museum display with another museum employee: both men look calmly into the camera, while carrying leafy branches to place into a wall display behind them. The new position also afforded Ely the chance to continue his professional relationship with Laurent once he had relocated back to the East Coast. Just as his earlier time working with

Laurent had helped to define his outlook on sculpture as an expressive medium, the association proved beneficial in other ways. In the fall quarter of 1929, he was invited to teach sculpture with Laurent at the Master Institute of United Artists in New York.

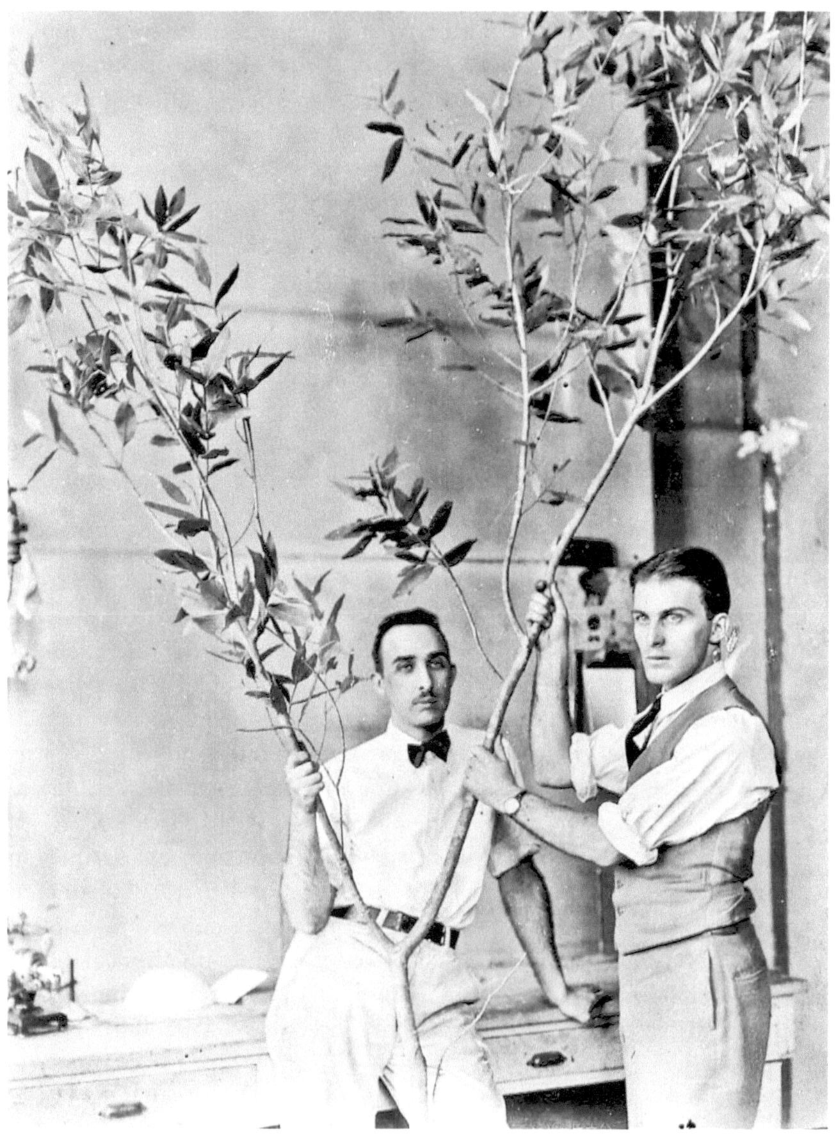

John Carl Ely (left). Ca. 1928. M.D. Burch, Photographer. Courtesy David Plummer.

In a 1929 photograph taken by M.D. Burch for the museum, Ely is shown with ten other men sitting on the steps of the Museum's 77th Street entrance, which served as the staff entrance and exit at the time. Ely had grown a moustache since his last exhibition held in Seattle in 1924; and distinctive amongst his assembled peers, he was the only one to wear a bow-tie for the group portrait. The image would be one of the last taken of the sculptor, before his untimely death on August 4, 1929, in a drowning accident off a Cape Cod beach. Ely had been vacationing with some friends at Dennis, Massachusetts, and was caught in an undertow while swimming off the beach. He was thirty-two years old.

As a total summation of his efforts, Ely's portfolio over a ten-year period, numbering forty reliefs, medallions, busts, heads and other sculptures "in the round," has helped to illustrate two distinct phases of his progression as a sculptor.[9] From about 1919 to the summer of 1922, Ely's

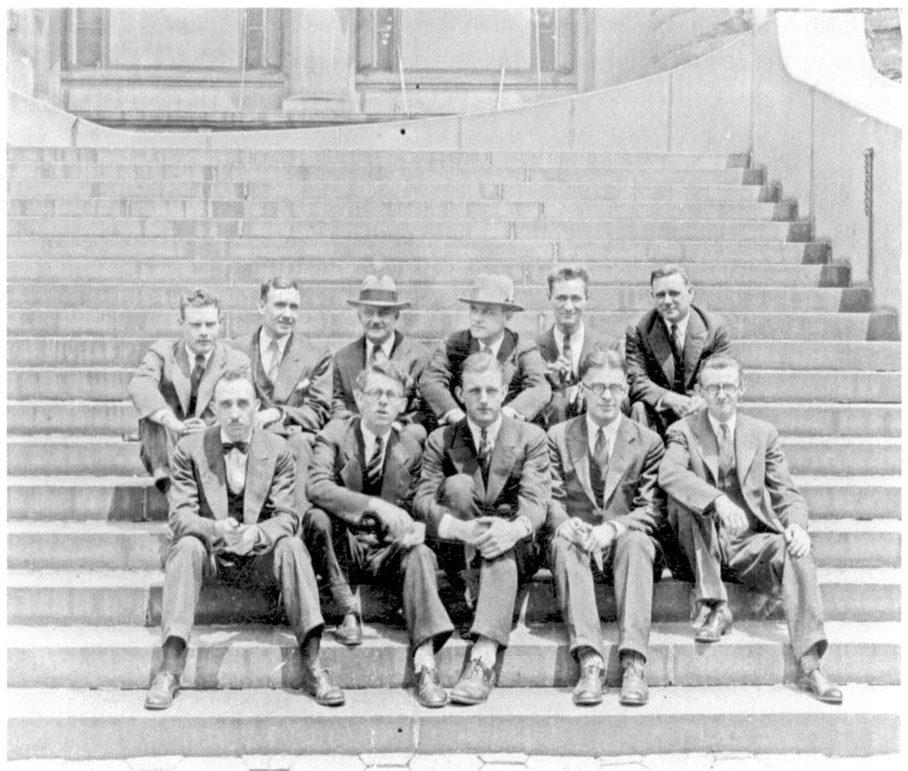

John Carl Ely (front row, left) *on steps of American Museum of Natural History.* 1929. Courtesy David Plummer.

early work was defined as representational and emulated his initial instruction in the medium under James Wehn. This was seen in the choices made by Ely to model specific individuals for his portrait busts and heads: one of them of his father, John H. Ely, with others of Jerry McGill and Carl Pitzer in low relief plaster similar in both style and technique to those being taught and produced by Wehn himself during this same period.

Ironically, it was two of Ely's earliest attempts at relief sculpture which are perhaps most notable as his lasting contributions to the historical, or "representational," public art of Seattle. In 1919, he produced a two-panel memorial plaque in bronze for the students of West Seattle High School who had served in the Great War. On one panel were the alphabetized names of the students, with the opposite panel reprising the poem *The Peacemaker* by Joyce Kilmer. Three names honoring those who died were inscribed on the bottom of the first plaque, in slightly larger text. The text in both panels was surrounded by plant motifs at the borders: the names plaque bearing a border decorated with Evergreen tree cones and boughs from the Pacific Northwest, while the poem plaque offered Acanthus-type leaves. Both plates were installed in the portico of the West Seattle High School as a war memorial.

The second relief by Ely followed just a year later, with another memorial plaque to those students from Queen Anne High School between 1917 and 1919 who served in World War I. Similar to the diptych the majority of this new plaque's copper relief surface was devoted to columns of student names. At thirty inches wide and fifty-one inches high, it made for an impressive memorial in terms of sheer scale. A symbolic American eagle surmounted the top of the plaque, with laurel wreathes on either side of the caption "Our Boys" and rosettes placed at all four corners as decorative elements. In one of the plaque's finer details, an inset box included the names of nine additional boys, with the caption "in memoriam" and year date of "1920"—as a special memorial to those students who perished in war. The historian for the Queen Anne High School Alumni Association, John Hennes, recalled the placement of the memorial from 1946 to 1951: "the plaque, as I recall, was mounted on the wall on the left at the top of the front stairs coming in the main (north) entrance."[10]

Today, the memorial plaques done for the Seattle high schools are the only known commissions for public institutions that Ely completed in his career. However, two other plaques were done in 1921 as private commissions to memorialize figures from the community. These plaster reliefs showed the portraits of the recently deceased and traditionally were cast into bronze in order to serve as cemetery markers at the gravesites

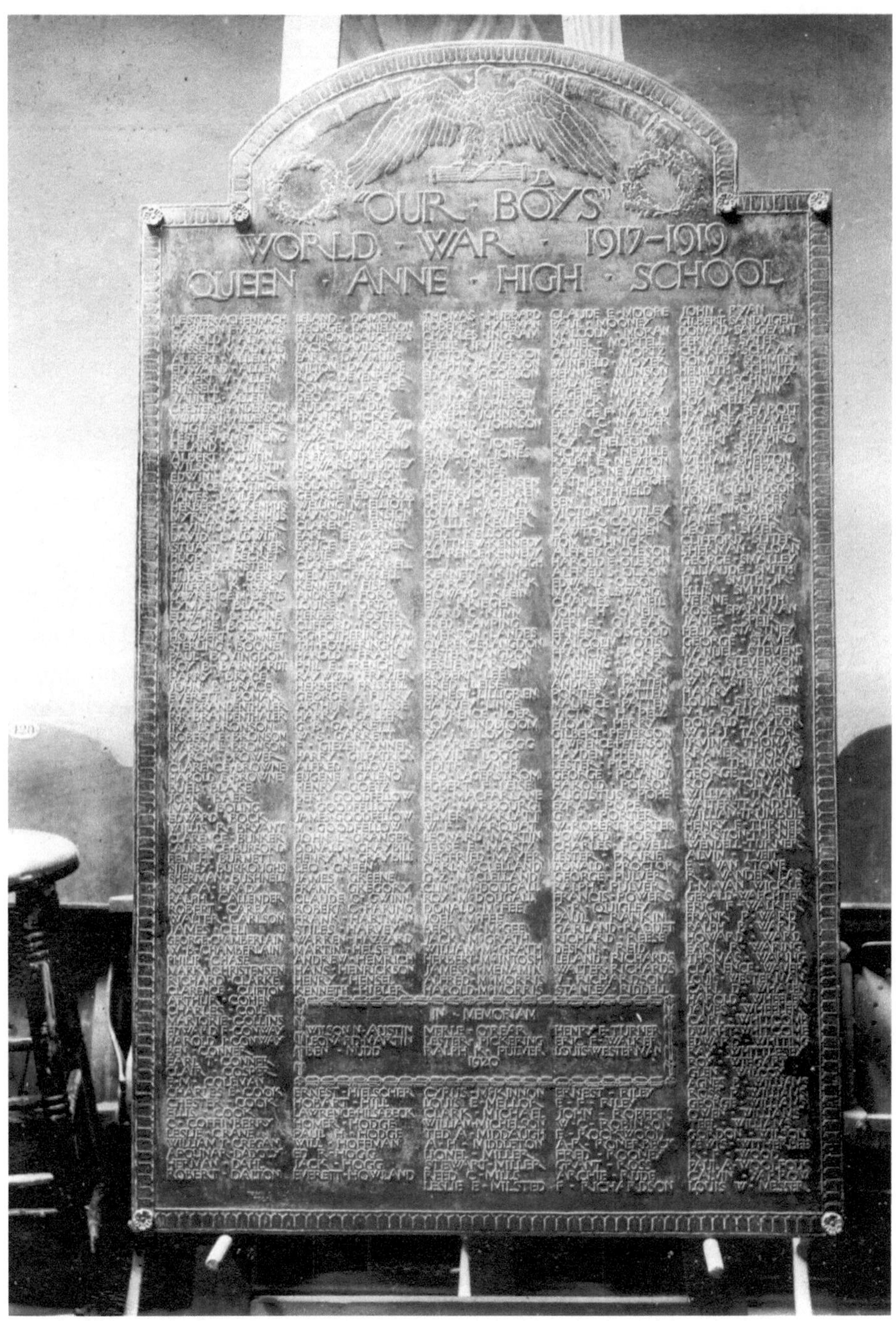

Queen Anne High School Memorial Tablet by John Carl Ely. Ca. 1920. Seattle Public Schools Collection. Undated photograph. Courtesy David Plummer and Seattle Public Schools.

of the interred. This kind of memorial relief was common for the 1920s and into the early 1930s in Seattle, and utilized the same modeling techniques taught by James Wehn in his sculpture classes at the University of Washington.

Several of the other documented sculptures by Ely have unknown creation dates, yet their subjects, style and choice of media all demonstrate a similar approach towards realism seen in the sculptor's early period. These included two portraits in cast plaster of Amos Hiatt; a relief also in cast plaster of Gulley Foster; and a third relief profile of the Suquamish Chief Seattle done as a medallion portrait. Much of this realism may be attributed to the early teachings of Wehn, and the elder sculptor's preference for precise anatomical detail seen in portrait subjects.

Ely's shift in a new direction for his art clearly coincides with the beginning of his first trip to New York and influence from Robert Laurent. The motivation for this change was primarily from a desire to grow as a sculptor in both vision and technique, and to embrace the "expressionist" view of the world and its inhabitants. The sculptures from 1923 and on demonstrate this dramatic shift in his emphasis as a sculptor, from one governed by anatomical detail to one guided by the inner eye's perception of form. For Ely, this view trended towards a primitive representation of the human form, so that lines used to convey basic shape also provided details in appearance. In one of his last sculptures, a relief carved from teak wood, the figure of a man is shown carrying a calf over his shoulders. The appearance is archaic, with the legs of the animal forming the outline of the man's torso, while the top of the man's head completed the arch of the calf's supported back. The eyes of both man and beast recall those seen in *Head of a Woman*, ovoid in shape and devoid of emotion or personality.

After 1922, Laurent's influence on Ely was a key to his new outlook on the medium. The approach to carving both human and animal figures directly from stone, marble and wood was a practice readily adopted by Ely as a sculpting technique of choice. Several of Ely's sculptures, including *Wag* (a sleeping dog sculpted from teak wood), *Fighting Birds* (two opposing cocks sculpted from walnut) and *Being and Becoming* (fern fronds sculpted from walnut) all have design elements comparable to Laurent's series of five fish surrounding a nude reclining female for the Showalter Fountain sculpture at the Fine Arts Plaza of Indiana University. Laurent's style continued over the years since his association with Ely, finding endorsement as a public art piece at the University where it was unveiled on October 22, 1961.

The appeal of Ely's new work in sculpture had also encouraged the artist on both coasts. The Himebauch & Brown Gallery in New York offered three of his new sculptures for review in 1925, while an art review from that same year called him "the latest North-westerner to receive recognition in the metropolis."[11] His next trip back to Seattle yielded not only his MFA, but also a one-man show of work at the Henry Art Gallery in the spring of 1927 which included "11 sculptures in terra cotta, five wood sculptures and 19 paintings."[12] This public recognition continued to keep Ely rooted firmly on the path of modernism over any possible return to practicing historical representation in sculpture.

Following Ely's demise, his reputation as an accomplished modernist sculptor endured amongst the art world. This was especially true in the first few years following his tragic accident. In 1930, the Henry Art Gallery accepted the gift of *La Passante* from the Ely family for its permanent collection of art at the University of Washington. A memorial exhibition held at the Seattle Fine Arts Gallery in April 1930, featured forty-one assorted paintings and sculptures, and went as far as to mistakenly cite the artist's work as being in the permanent collection of the Museum of Modern Art in New York. Decades later, the Rose Art Museum at Brandeis University acquired the marble sculpture *Head of a Woman* with the transfer of the entire Riverside Collection to the museum in June 1971.

Of Ely's original two war memorial commissions for the Seattle Public Schools, their visual prominence faded over time as a result of both loss and renovation. The right half of the diptych relief set with the "Peacemaker" poem disappeared from West Seattle High School, with no record of its whereabouts today. The memorial plaque for the Queen Anne school was permanently removed when the high school closed its doors in 1981. It remains on view today at the John Stanford Center for Educational Excellence at Seattle Public Schools District Headquarters.

Ely was a sculptor before his time, more suited to the modernist era of public art in the 1950s that swept the globe and encompassed Seattle, as exemplified by new installations of abstract and expressionist sculptures such as those that were publically exhibited at the 1962 World's Fair in Seattle. In the final analysis, he chose to pursue an approach to sculpture as a medium for artistic expression, rather than the historic representation seen in traditional monuments, memorials and statuary devoted to individuals and events. This was his lasting legacy as a sculptor of Seattle, as one of those active sculptors who were part of the city's changing face of public art over the past century.

10

Alice Robertson Carr (de Creeft) (1899–1996)

In the best light, the achievements of Alice Robertson Carr in sculpture for Seattle can be summarized as a mixed triumph. The two major sculptures she produced for the city between 1923 and 1925 offer a cautionary tale in how the perceived value of public artwork from one era may transition into something else altogether over time.

Originally from Roanoke, Virginia, Carr grew up on a homestead in Sun River Valley, Montana. The sculptor recalled this time as being close to nature, and horses in particular, as well as one of her earliest memories of working in the sculpture medium:

> We rode Indian ponies to school, and in the winter we turned out the ones we didn't need to winter on the range, so that in spring, we rode, my brother and I, for immense distances, from band to band of range horses, until we found our ponies. We rode up Square Butte and Shaw Butte (Charley Russell country-when I was modeling horses in clay from the bank of a pond, I was taken to call, as a child prodigy, on Charley Russell in his studio in Great Falls—I remember only the little bear in beeswax he had just finished, not the great man himself!)[1]

Later as a teenager, she moved to Seattle with her parents, older sister, slightly older twin brother, and younger brother. Carr finished high school, and then attended the Arts Students League in New York between 1919 and 1920, where she studied life drawing under George Bridgman and sculpture with A. Sterling Calder. Her first art exhibition was held at the Studio Club of New York in 1920, where she won an honorary award for one of her sculptures.

Carr continued her formal instruction as an art student with Albin Polascek at the Art Institute of Chicago in 1922 and 1923, after which time she relocated back to Seattle and was listed as a sculptor with a studio on Madison Street. Her timing was fortuitous, as projects and events were unfolding both in local government and the development of Woodland

Park. It would prove to be a major period of opportunity for the young sculptor.

The genesis of Carr's first public sculpture commission, titled *The Fountain*, was partly the result of two separate public works efforts which culminated in 1924. The first effort was to construct a public fountain from a $5,000 donation made by the estate of the late Father F. Xavier Prefontaine.

The initial offer of a fountain dates back to the Seattle Chamber of Commerce meeting on February 14, 1906. B.J. Barrett, writing "under authority" of Father Prefontaine, asked the Chamber to urge the City Council "to designate the middle of the thoroughfare known as Prefontaine Place as a suitable location for the erection of a fountain."[2] A report issued a month later by the Committee on City Affairs, which had reviewed the offer, suggested a new fountain could potentially be placed on the triangle strip bounded by Third Avenue, Yesler Way and Jefferson Street. Despite the recommendation, it was many years before discussion of a fountain at Prefontaine Place was renewed.

At their February 23, 1922, meeting, the Board of Park Commissioners reviewed another letter sent by Prefontaine estate trustee Daniel Kelleher to Acting Mayor of Seattle, Robert Hesketh, which stated "a preference that the fountain be located if possible, in the immediate vicinity of Prefontaine Place."[3] This was for the same triangle of land bounded by Yesler Way, Third Avenue and Jefferson Street identified in 1906.

Despite the generosity of Prefontaine, the question about where a fountain in his name would go remained unresolved for years after his death. One delay was that the $5,000 designated in the will was not transferred to the City of Seattle until 1922. Another factor was that the Yesler triangle plot of land had been originally deeded to the city's Library Board by Henry Yesler on April 9, 1909, with the stipulation it be used only as a site for a public library. Deemed "too small for its purpose" the land was transferred in a quit claim deed from the Library Board to the city on March 29, 1912.[4] In spite of the transfer, there continued to be public opposition to the memorial at this site from a vocal citizenry that included several of Seattle's original pioneers.

The legality of the Parks Board to use the site for its planning purposes still remained in question as late as October 10, 1923. In its meeting minutes, the Board of Park Commissioners recognized the legal constraints placed on the deed of property, one of which stated: "A library be constructed at Twenty-Third Avenue and Yesler Way, to be known as the Henry L. Yesler Memorial Library ... and that the location of the library had been by consent of the trustees transferred to Twenty-Third Avenue and Yesler Way."[5]

With the controversy over placement of the Prefontaine fountain in the Yesler triangle an ongoing concern for the City of Seattle and the Prefontaine estate, efforts towards another public works project were coming to fruition in the early 1920s. The Civic Rose Garden at Woodland Park was nearing completion after a year of coordinated efforts between the Park Department's head gardener, Jacob Umlauff, the Seattle Rose Society, and the Lions' Club of Seattle.

The origin of Woodland Park as a city-run park dates back to 1900, when it was first purchased by the city from the estate of Guy Phinney for $10,000.[6] Following the acquisition, the Seattle Parks Department moved a private zoological collection maintained by the Seattle Electric Company from Leschi Park to Woodland Park. An early history of the zoo suggests that the location was used by a wide variety of visitors, ranging from "big government officials" to "sportsmen, big-game hunters, sculptors, artists … people from all walks of life."[7]

Over the next two decades, several organizations and civic clubs maintained an active interest in the park, its assorted zoological collections, and its other amenities as a community center. Just as Woodland Park had benefited from the support of these civic clubs over time, so too Carr came to benefit from their support as a sculptor.

The Parks Department had given its approval of the Seattle Rose Society's development of a two-acre parcel of land in Woodland Park, on October 4, 1922. While the Society did not have the funds to build or maintain the garden, the support of the Parks Board of Commissioners guaranteed that a new garden would come under the jurisdiction of the Superintendent of Parks, which could authorize the construction of the garden to proceed. The new rose garden promised a multitude of rose species and other flora accompanied by a number of circular pools in the center, north and south to accommodate aquatic plants such as lilies and papyri. Garden furniture, bird baths, a sun dial, and small pieces of sculpture were also incorporated into the landscape.

Park Department Board Commissioner Robert Fisher was especially proud of the Park's role in securing federal permission for the Seattle Rose Society to import and plant several species of rose from outside the country. On April 25, 1923, he made a motion that the Board of Commissioners should accept community support for the project so that it might move forward:

> Mr. Fisher reported that the Rose Society and Lions' Club had agreed to finance the completion of the Rose Garden, with the understanding that all plans be submitted to the Board for their approval, and that the work [would] be done under the supervision of the Parks Department.[8]

Besides authorizing the land for the project, the Park Department also contributed $1,200 to offset the $10,000 project's total cost. The Lions' Club contributed another $5,000, with $1,300 raised by the Seattle Rose Society and several other rose clubs. By June 3, 1923, a total amount of $7,500 had been raised, along with donations of many rose plantings to fill the grounds.

While Father Prefontaine's estate had expressed a preference for having its memorial fountain located in downtown Seattle, the $5,000 was not legally tied to any specific named location as a condition of the gift. This afforded a possible alternative site for the fountain as a part of the new rose garden, with the additional funds helpful in seeing the garden to completion. Such a fountain would serve as "the focal point in Seattle's great public rose garden."[9] Not only would this become Carr's first public art commission, it would also be the first ever commission for a public sculpture in Seattle awarded to a female sculptor.

The plan for this fountain was for it to be located at the north end of the garden, and dedicated to Father Prefontaine with all of its elements sculpted by Carr. A semicircular basin would front a bas-relief frieze twenty-four feet long and six feet high. The model Carr had designed over several weeks depicted seven life-sized figures in various poses: two figures appeared to be crowning a central figure with a laurel wreath, while those on either side danced and cavorted. On opposite ends of the pool's basin two robed female sculptures were poised: the figure on the left bent over and gazing into the pool, while the figure on the right sat on a set of stairs fronting the frieze, both feet draped over the edge into the water.

The origins of this relief design can be traced back to a sketch Carr had made for an architects show in Seattle, done prior to her arrival at the Chicago Art Institute. The final scene was complimented by two memorial panels to Prefontaine placed on either end of the frieze relief.

The vision of both a memorial to Prefontaine in the Civic Rose Garden and Carr's inspired design for this fountain did not come to pass. On August 27, 1924, Park Board Resolution No. 45 was introduced by Board President J.C. Dutton, to establish "Memorial Park" from the Yesler Triangle land and allow for the site's development as a park to include the "erection of tablets, etc."[10] The Resolution was passed at the next Park Board Commissioner's meeting held on September 10, 1924. Further discussions in

1925 between Mayor Brown's office, the Park Board and the Yesler estate resulted in the Yesler triangle site being finally agreed to by all parties as the lone location of a memorial fountain to Father Prefontaine. The Park Board meeting minutes for March 4, 1925, noted that estate trustee Kelleher had submitted for approval plans for a proposed fountain in Yesler Memorial Park, and furthermore "that the money being available he was ready to let a contract and proceed at once."[11] The Park Board commissioners endorsed the plan, and authorized Kelleher to proceed with the understanding that no expense for the construction of the fountain would be incurred by the Park Department.

The development was not altogether a surprise, especially given the shared history between Yesler and Prefontaine. Yesler claimed that his mill had supplied the lumber to build Prefontaine's Lady of Good Hope, the first Catholic Church for Seattle in 1870.[12] A new fountain was designed by local architect Carl Gould, with a concrete pool and memorial tablet. As a finishing touch, Gould secured the services of Seattle sculptor James Wehn to model and cast in concrete two tortoises which were placed on opposite ends of the pool's rim. The completed fountain was dedicated in 1926, and thereafter the site was known to locals as "Prefontaine Place."

However, Carr was not left without something to show for her time spent on the rose garden project. The Rose Garden Society saw the grounds of the garden planted with the last of its roses in the autumn of 1923. Carr's panoramic relief was cast into concrete, painted white and set behind a semi-circular fountain pool as planned. It was finally installed in 1924.

Carr's design had changed in several ways over just a few short months. The central trio of figures now appeared as a gathering of Three Muses, accompanied by women and children on either side with a pair of deer and a roaring lion. The number of figures had also been expanded from seven to eleven, with all of the adult figures portrayed as women. Gone from the original design were the two statues of the women perched on the basin's edge.

The sculptor's choice of presentation for the figures recalls similar works seen in Greek and Roman classical friezes of antiquity. They are seen nude or semi-nude; the Muses embrace arms, while the dancers sway to the sound of unheard panpipes. It is a work of beauty and grace, alluding to harmony with nature and at one with its surrounding environment. The flow of water below the relief only enhanced the sensual quality of the artwork. One wonders if the omission of the two end statues was done on purpose by the sculptor to help maximize the natural element's interaction with the relief, or if the missing statues were merely the result of a cost savings measure for the project. The two statues had also been rendered by Carr in more of an Art Deco style, and therefore presented a clash with the main frieze done in a neoclassical relief style.

The ends of the relief still offered plaques with text, dedicating the fountain on behalf of the Seattle Rose Society in 1924. Neither Prefontaine nor Carr was included by name anywhere on either panel. Regardless of inspiration or credit, the relief in the rose garden has retained its original beauty to the present day, and perhaps just as important for the sculptor, helped to pave the way for her next sculpture commission. Similar to the rose garden relief, the source for that commission would again come from a local sponsor, and from its inception again take the form of a memorial.

The Benevolent and Protective Order of Elks (B.P.O.E.) was founded on February 16, 1868, with the group's first lodger charter established in New York on March 10, 1871. As word of the club spread west across the United States by Elks members, new lodges were established in other American cities. Seattle was counted among these cities with the founding of its Queen Anne neighborhood Lodge No. 92 in 1888. By 1900, the lodge boasted a membership of 2,043 active members and in 1914 relocated to a ten-story building downtown at Fourth Avenue and Spring Street.

As a local civic group, the Elks of Lodge No. 92 were responsible for contributing several American elk to the newly founded Woodland Park Zoo. The club was not alone in this practice, with other groups contributing other animals: the Fraternal Order of Eagles with bald eagles; the Seattle Nile Temple giving Bactrian camels. Not only did these animals help the lodges attract out-of-town members to the zoo, but it was also believed that the placement of such animals benefited younger audiences or "smaller brothers who may be members of the Lodge."[13]

Among the founder's criteria for membership in the Elks, was both a belief in God and admission restricted to men only. These attitudes were commonly shared by the Boy Scouts of America and together these two groups played key roles in one President's visit to Woodland Park.

President Warren G. Harding was both a fraternal Brother of the Elks, through Lodge No. 32 in Marion, Ohio, and was appointed Honorary President of the Boy Scouts on March 7, 1921, shortly after he became the 29th sitting President of the United States. In June 1923, Harding embarked on a tour westward across the United States, giving speeches along the way to business groups, Veterans' hospitals, historic sites, and community clubs, sometimes as many as eleven in one day.[14] The tour was referred to by the President as his "Voyage of Understanding." On June 29, he presented medals to Boy Scouts in Butte, Montana, arriving four days later to speak at three other locations in Washington State. After giving speeches in Cheney, Vancouver, and two in Tacoma, Harding continued heading north to Alaska aboard the transport ship USS *Henderson*.

Harding was accompanied on the trip by his wife, Florence, and a contingent of newspaper reporters. One of the latter, Robert Barry, wrote to his wife Menne, from Juneau, Alaska, on July 10 with a pessimistic assessment of the region:

> It is rainy and cold and I wonder to God how people can live here. We are sick of it already but have 16 more days yet before reaching Vancouver, B.C. and 17 to Seattle. We go from Seward to Fairbanks by railroad, over the Government line, and then start on a three day trip in Fords. Many members of the party, especially the women are beginning to get cold feet on the trip, and so is the President, but Mrs. Harding is determined to go and she is running the show.[15]

Preparations for Harding's arrival to Seattle had been underway for weeks with the office of Seattle Mayor Edwin Brown. In addition to coordinating plans for the President to speak at Woodland Park and two other locations on July 27, 1923, Brown invited Washington Governor Louis Hart and his wife to be available in the city during the visit. That Hart came to the Washington Hotel on July 26 to lend support was all the more valued, given that past communications between Harding and Hart were strained.

The previous year on January 27, saw Hart offer a written invitation to Harding to come out to Washington State on April 11, to attend a dinner with "a group of prominent Washington state business and professional men."[16] Harding's reply on February 6 was mystifying to Hart, and moreover, clearly left an impression that Harding had no interest in such an invitation. The Governor ended up cancelling the dinner, to avoid any confusion or embarrassment. Regardless, Hart supported the party line, and when Harding visited a year later to give a speech in Tacoma, Hart and his family were on hand to receive the President. A letter from the Republican National Committee expressed thanks for Hart's public show of support for the President at the Tacoma speech on July 5, 1923.

After a brief stop in Vancouver, BC, Harding traveled south to Seattle. On July 27, 1923, Harding gave a speech at Woodland Park Zoo as the guest speaker for the annual Elks' Picnic to Boys of the State. President Harding's words of encouragement to the 30,000 assembled boys, Boy Scout Masters, Elk Lodge members and their families, would leave a lasting impression to the assembled throng that day:

> I want our Republic, this wonderful America of ours, this free America, beckoning with equal opportunity to all its children, to be a land of homes.... I wish for such a state in America, and I wish for the boys and girls in Washington a continuation of the careers which are suggested by this splendid meeting today.[17]

While many of the boys present that day were Boy Scouts, not all of those that attended belonged to the Boy Scouts of America organization. The Elks were sponsors for many "Boy Day" events around the country, as a day dedicated to boys in general. The program was an annual event in some communities and offered parades, athletic contests for prizes, baseball games, music and goodwill from mentors. In the same month as the Woodland Park celebration, hundreds of boys attended a similar day sponsored by Elks Lodge No. 1072, in Goldfield, Nevada; another a month later offered by lodge No. 85 in Salt Lake City, Utah.

For the Boy Scouts at the Seattle picnic, the chance to see the President was a once-in-a-lifetime opportunity. The timing for the President's visit also coincided with the Scouts National Jamboree being held in the city, which may account for the large number of Scouts in attendance that day. The presence of the Scouts was also viewed as a protective measure, and proactively planned prior to the President's arrival:

> Mrs. Harding paid Boy Scouts a very high compliment by requesting the official reception committees at various points where the Presidential party was to stop on its way to Alaska, to have Boy Scouts among the President's guards, as she felt safer for the President when scouts were present, as she and President Harding had noted that Boy Scouts have a humanizing effect upon crowds.[18]

Byron Fish, who attended the event that day, recalled that the Boy Scouts were ranked in front of Harding "as protection."[19] It was Harding's last such public appearance with the Scouts.

The President continued his tour at a whirlwind pace, in spite of consultation with his physician following the Woodland Park visit over pains in his abdomen. Upon arriving to San Francisco, his doctors confirmed he had pneumonia, a condition further exacerbated by a recurrent heart problem. After his speech on Foreign Relations had been released to the press, Harding was convalescing at his hotel on the evening of August 2, 1923, when he suffered a massive cerebral hemorrhage and died.

It was a testimony to Harding that the call for memorials in the wake of his death was both numerous and widespread across the nation. The Elks instructed all subordinate lodges that they include in their order of business the service announcing the death of "Brother Harding."[20] Churches throughout Seattle paid tribute to Harding in services the week following his death. The Seattle Park Board sent Mrs. Harding flowers, and acknowledged her thank you letter at its meeting on September 12, 1923. The Boy Scouts put out a nationwide call for support in the December 1923 issue of *Scouting* magazine, so that scouts might have an opportunity to help make contributions to the Harding Memorial Association. Memorials were proposed and planning begun for sites in Milton, Ohio, Vancouver, BC, Canada, and in Woodland Park, Seattle.

Leading the effort for the Woodland Park memorial was a committee from Elks Lodge No. 92 in Seattle. They wasted no time, with a concept of the memorial envisioning a bronze statue of Harding at the site where he had delivered his speech and the Oath of Allegiance to the assembled boys only a month before. Just six days after the death of the President, the Elks filed a petition for the erection of the statue at Woodland Park, which Parks Board Commissioner George C. Wheeler granted.

Secretary of Agriculture Henry C. Wallace, who was one of three cabinet members with Harding on July 27, publicly endorsed the project with a telegram to the Elks, saying the "statue of Harding in posture of administering the oath would perpetuate a thrilling incident of national importance and be a constant inspiration to youth of [the] great Northwest ... wish you success."[21]

A fundraising campaign by the Elks began in August and secured many donations from businesses in downtown Seattle as well as a pledge of support from Mayor Brown's office. Elks helped to organize other support from across the state as well. Over 1,100 boys from Everett and Snohomish county met on August 30 at the Everett Elks Lodge No. 479 to lend aid to the memorial effort.

By the time of Harding's passing, Alice Robertson Carr had already completed her preliminary design for the fountain relief in Woodland Park's new rose garden. She was a sculptor familiar to both the Seattle Parks Board and another local group, the Lions' Club, for her work on that project. Yet the Elks of Lodge No. 92 were still looking for a suitable sculptor to undertake the Harding Memorial and its statuary, as evidenced by a letter sent to the Elks Committee from Lillian Hocking in late August. Hocking was a student of the sculptor James Wehn while attending the University of Washington, and wrote the letter on behalf of her father W.R. Hocking. In it she extolled the experience and artistic abilities of Wehn, noting in particular his ties to the local Boy Scouts as their "Examiner of the Department of Sculpturing" and advising the committee to secure Wehn's services for the Harding statue.[22]

The Elks made progress on plans for the memorial with the assistance of the Parks Board on October 15, 1924. During the meeting of the Board's

Commissioners, it was moved that Commissioner Hill be appointed as a committee of one to work with Elks Lodge No. 92 on a suitable plan for the memorial. Owing to a desire to make the memorial "more utilitarian" and serve as a functional bandstand, the final design agreed upon by the Elks and the Park Board omitted any statue to Harding, but instead rendered his portrait in bas-relief as part of a panoramic scene recalling his administering the Pledge of Allegiance to an assembly of boys. Seattle architect Daniel Huntington was confirmed as the designer by the Park Board of Commissioners on November 26, 1924, with the understanding he would be paid ten percent of the memorial's total cost or $850, for whichever amount was less.[23] Alice Robertson Carr, not Wehn, was selected as the sculptor for all of the memorial's sculptural elements.

Between December 1924 and January 1925, Carr modeled the twenty-two foot panoramic relief in clay at her studio. It showed a life-sized figure of Harding in profile with his right hand raised to a group of twenty-seven

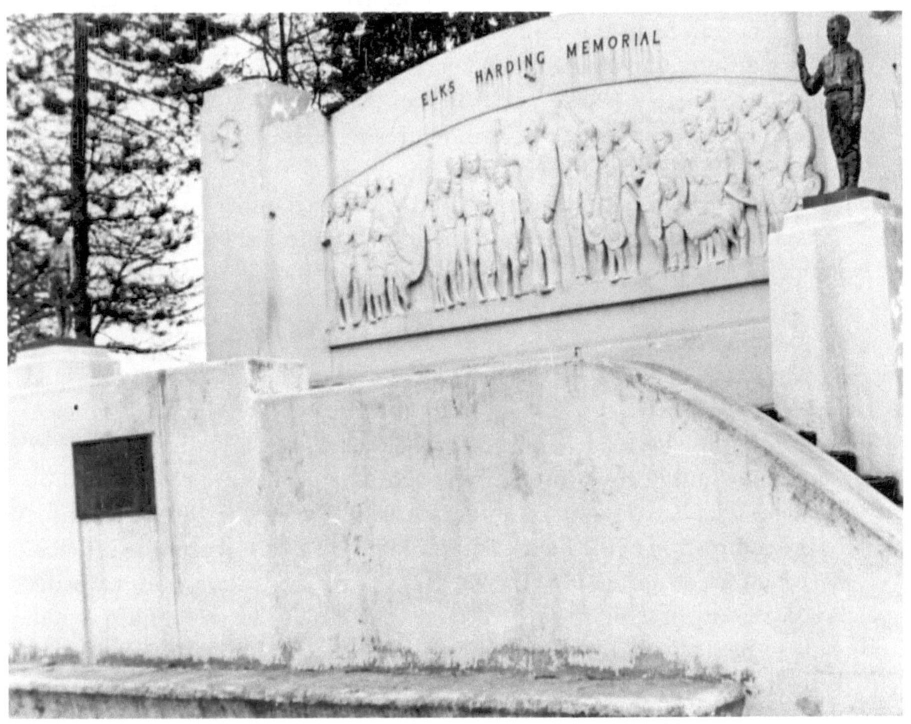

Elks Harding Memorial by Alice Robertson Carr. 1925. Woodland Park. Undated photograph. Werner Lenggenhager, Photographer. Seattle Public Library.

Boy Scout figures flanking him on either side. Details of the relief recalled the day of Harding's visit to Woodland Park, and the moment of pride he must have felt for the group as one with them, their shared love of country and sense of duty. Most of the figures are Scouts are shown in uniform, with a handful of boys described as younger brothers visible in the ranks. One Boy Scout held aloft an American flag, another a dog by its collar. The majority of figures are seen holding right hand aloft, in the taking of an oath of allegiance. This relief was considerably larger than the one Carr had done for the rose garden, measuring twenty-five feet long and seven feet high when fully cast into concrete.

While the size of the relief was enough to nearly fill Carr's studio on Madison Street, it was not the sole element of the memorial the sculptor created as part of the Elks commission. In November 1924, the Park Board conveyed its preference for having two Boy Scout statues also included as part of the memorial, and that these should be cast in bronze, not concrete. Carr modeled both of these two statues, each approximately four feet tall and which portrayed Boy Scouts in uniform standing at attention with right hand raised in the three-finger, Boy Scout salute. The two figures showed different boys, lifelike in every detail. One depicted a thin-faced boy, approximately twelve years of age; the other boy was shown with more rounded facial features. Both figures were dressed in the Boy Scout uniform of the 1920s: knee leggings, shorts, long-sleeve shirt with breast pockets, belt, and neckerchief secured with a neck-tie. The cast bronze statues found placement on either end of the finished relief, on raised platforms that had them level and in front of the relief's figures.

A dedication in bronze lettering to the late President was inset into the front façade of the concrete memorial, noting details of the Harding's visit on July 27, 1923. Even the placement of the memorial was by design, located on the same spot as Harding's previous speech, in the northeast quadrant of the Park's grounds. By early March 1925, all but the finishing touches, including covering the memorial in stucco, were completed.

The Elks had sought assurances from the sculptor, that the timing for the completion of the memorial would be assured. Carr recalled "being placed under a liquidating damage clause in a contract, where I was to pay $50 a day for every day on or after the 29th of March that it was not ready to be dedicated."[24]

The Elks presented the Harding memorial to the city on March 29, 1925. Present were over 2,000 citizens including many Boy Scouts from local troops, who recited the Pledge of Allegiance as part of the memorial's commemorating ceremony. Leading the pledge was Theo Johnson, Exalted

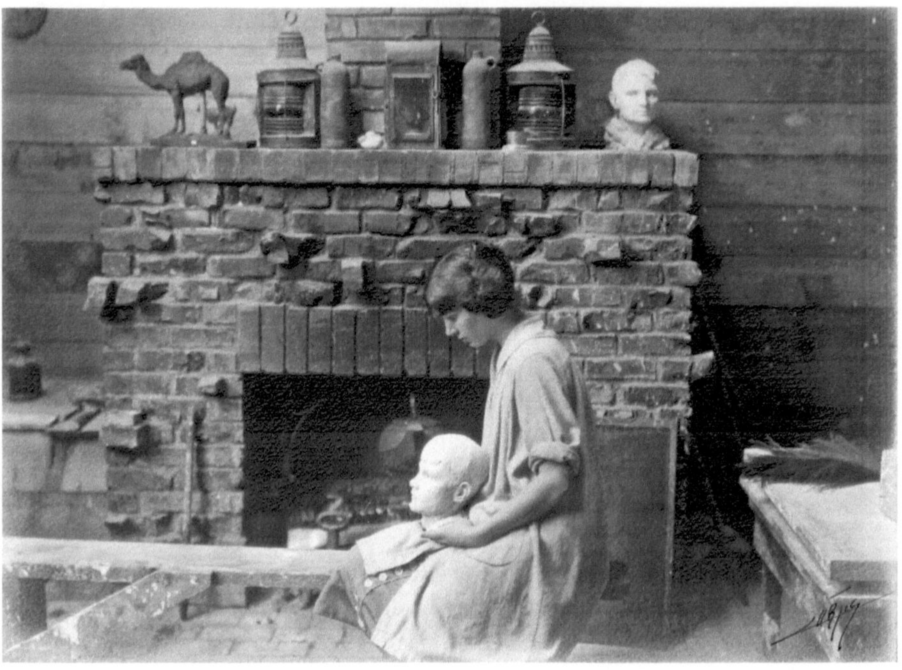

Alice Robertson Carr with Boy Scout Portrait. Ca. 1925. Courtesy Nina Ward (nee Carr).

Ruler of the Seattle Lodge No. 92 B.P.O.E., followed by Park Board President O.J.C. Dutton's acceptance of the memorial from Johnson for the City of Seattle. Many of those present remarked on how the event was similar to the day when Harding gave his speech in 1923. Bands from both the Queen Anne and Ballard Elks lodges provided music to add to the celebrations.

The year 1925 marked the completion of a second memorial to Harding in the Pacific Northwest, located in Stanley Park, Vancouver, British Columbia. Similar to the Woodland Park memorial, the Vancouver memorial also marks the place where Harding gave a speech on his public tour of the West Coast. So too, this memorial was sponsored by a local civic club, the Kiwanis Club, with one of the group's members, Charles Marega, as the sculptor. A third memorial was completed a year later in Marion, Ohio, and served as a tomb for both Harding and his wife, yet had its formal dedication delayed until 1931 by President Hoover.

The fate of the Harding memorial in Woodland Park may be tied to its namesake's reputation in the decades that followed its dedication. Scandals affected members of Harding's administration both before and after the President's death: the Veterans Bureau, the Justice Department, Secretary of the Navy. The last one later became known as the Teapot Dome scandal, involving oil reserves in Wyoming which Harding signed over to the Interior Department by Executive order. Revelations by an alleged mistress further added to tarnishing of the President's legacy. In the years that followed these events, Harding's public reputation as a President plummeted and was reflected in the upkeep and ultimate fate of the Harding memorial in Seattle.

Park records show that an awning was authorized on June 24, 1925, but took four years to install and then was problematic in that it would not drain during rainfall. Another inspection in 1939 showed wear on the memorial's lettering, but that sandblasting was "unadvisable" due to the stucco covering.[25] The Park Board indicated the cost of replacing missing letters on the memorial was exorbitant and therefore would not be done. Only after further prompting by the Elks was a new dedication plaque in bronze added by the Park Department in December 1939.

A letter from a concerned citizen to the Seattle Chamber of Commerce in 1939 summed up the memorial's condition at that time:

> This memorial is a disgrace to the city. If you will take a look at it, you will find it in such a deplorable condition that you will be ashamed. Letters are gone from the name—marks of blemish and disfigurement are everywhere visible. If you go to Vancouver, B.C. and visit the "Harding Memorial" in Stanley Park, you will feel more ashamed for our own memorial. There the memorial is respected—children are not allowed to deface it—chase each other over it, and the grounds around it are kept neat and clean. It is sacred.[26]

In a letter to the Board of Park Commissioners that same year, Theo Johnson of Elks Lodge No. 92 put the city on notice as well about the condition of the memorial and that further assistance by their organization in its upkeep would be soon discontinued:

> Inasmuch as this memorial was presented to the City of Seattle with the idea in mind and the understanding that all maintenance would be handled by the Park Department, we feel that this should be carried out and that the monument, which is at this time badly in need of paint and relettering, should be immediately taken care of by your honorable body, without any further assistance from the Elks.[27]

Over the years, the Harding memorial was still used by various groups for programs commemorating Independence Day and Flag Day observances, such as those done by the American Legion and Veterans of Foreign Wars. Public use of the memorial for these observances declined after 1948. As memories of those who originally attended the Harding speech faded into history, so too did the memorial's revered status as a public monument and sculpture.

By 1971, there were public calls for the Harding memorial to go. The final report of a Citizen's Advisory Committee for the Seattle Zoo released in July 1971, unequivocally stated "that structures not related to the Zoo such as the Harding Memorial, Cannons, Locomotive, be removed from the grounds."[28] A follow-up article by the *Seattle Times* identified the once noble sculpture as one of several "un-zoo like objects" that must go.[29] The Parks Department now identified the Harding memorial as one of several features that were not in keeping with the zoo atmosphere and also in the way of zoo expansion. In the same year, the Municipal Art Commission was abolished to create a new Seattle Arts Commission, under Ordinance No. 99982. The mandate for the commission to serve as in an advisory capacity on all matters related to public art was unchanged.

Zoo Director David Hancocks offered a new vision for the park in 1976, which in essence called for new bio-climatic areas with groupings of animals into near natural settings. Plans for a revitalized zoo soon crystalized, involving both the city's Department of Parks & Recreation and the Federal Government's Economic Development Administration (EDA) Local Public Works Program. The program was a result of the Local Public Works Capital Development and Investment Act of 1976, as amended by the Public Works Employment Act of 1977. Through this program, the City of Seattle saw an opportunity to fund the new construction of an African Savanna exhibit at Woodland Park Zoo. The city grant application described the new exhibit as "literally and figuratively … at the heart of the new Zoo plan."[30] The only mention of the Harding memorial in the city's application was a budget line item for "site preparation" cited in a report by the Architect/Engineer, which allocated $1,600 for "monument demolition" and another $1,000 for the "load/haul" of said pieces.[31]

In terms of advocacy, the Elks Lodge No. 92 had been opposed to the Harding memorial's removal since 1971. Officially, however, they were alone in this respect. The State of Washington's Historic Preservation Office wrote to the city's project manager's in October 1976, indicating that of the twenty-one projects the city had submitted for review—including the "African Savanna Exhibit Zone"—there were "no properties on the State or National Registers of Historic Places or in the Washington State Inventory of Historic places in the project area … the project has been cleared relative to archaeological/historic resources."[32]

The city's Department of Public Works submitted its application for

$1,911,653 to fund the effort, which was received by the Economic Development Administration on July 11, 1977. The city received word that the project was awarded funding for the full amount requested, on September 12, 1977.

The African Savanna exhibit was divided into two phases of work. Local contractor Sun-Up Construction was hired for Phase I, site preparation, beginning on November 28, 1977. This work primarily involved site survey, clearing, grading, and excavation work for utilities, and included the removal of the Harding Memorial as part of the site clearing. On June 28, 1978, the Sun-Up Construction Company received the contract to undertake the construction work for Phase II, after submitting a low bid to the city of $1,687,152. Greg Nickels, the EDA Projects Coordinator for the city, sent a notice to proceed to Sun-Up on August 17, 1978, with a total of 300 days allotted for this next phase of the project.

Between August 1978 and September 1980, the African Savanna exhibit took form in its new centralized space in the Woodland Park Zoo. Former Seattle Parks Superintendent David Towne recalled discussion about the Harding memorial during the African Savanna exhibit project, and how it came to fit into the project's construction scope. Through Towne, the zoo attempted to find a new home for the memorial, but the efforts fell on deaf ears: "nobody cared ... nobody wanted anything to do with Harding."[33]

However, the Zoo was successful in preserving one sculptural aspect of the memorial: Carr's two bronze statues of the Boy Scouts standing at attention were transferred to the Boy Scouts' Chief Seattle Council Office. One of the statues would remain at the Seattle council office site, while the second statue was eventually placed on display at the Camp Parsons Museum for the Boy Scouts at Hood Canal, Washington.

Carr's daughter, Nina, has suggested that the final outcome for the two statues might have been irrelevant to the sculptor: "my mother wasn't happy with the casting of the group of Boy Scouts. She said the eyes were not right, and they were not what she had in her model. I don't think she would have minded that they were buried."[34]

The rest of the Harding Memorial, including the bas-relief panel by Carr, would not be so fortunate. According to Towne, the concrete memorial was broken up and had its sections placed as fill to support the central overlook constructed in the African Savanna's landscape.[35]

A budget line item cost of $9,052 was reported for "demolition and removal" although this expense was not detailed further in the project's Quarterly Performance Report No. 12 released on September 30, 1980.

None of the Phase II performance reports between 1978 and 1980 reference the Harding memorial, or its use as landfill for the exhibit's landscaping.

When finally completed, the new exhibit encompassed a five-acre area of rolling grasslands, streambeds, moats and rocky outcroppings. No

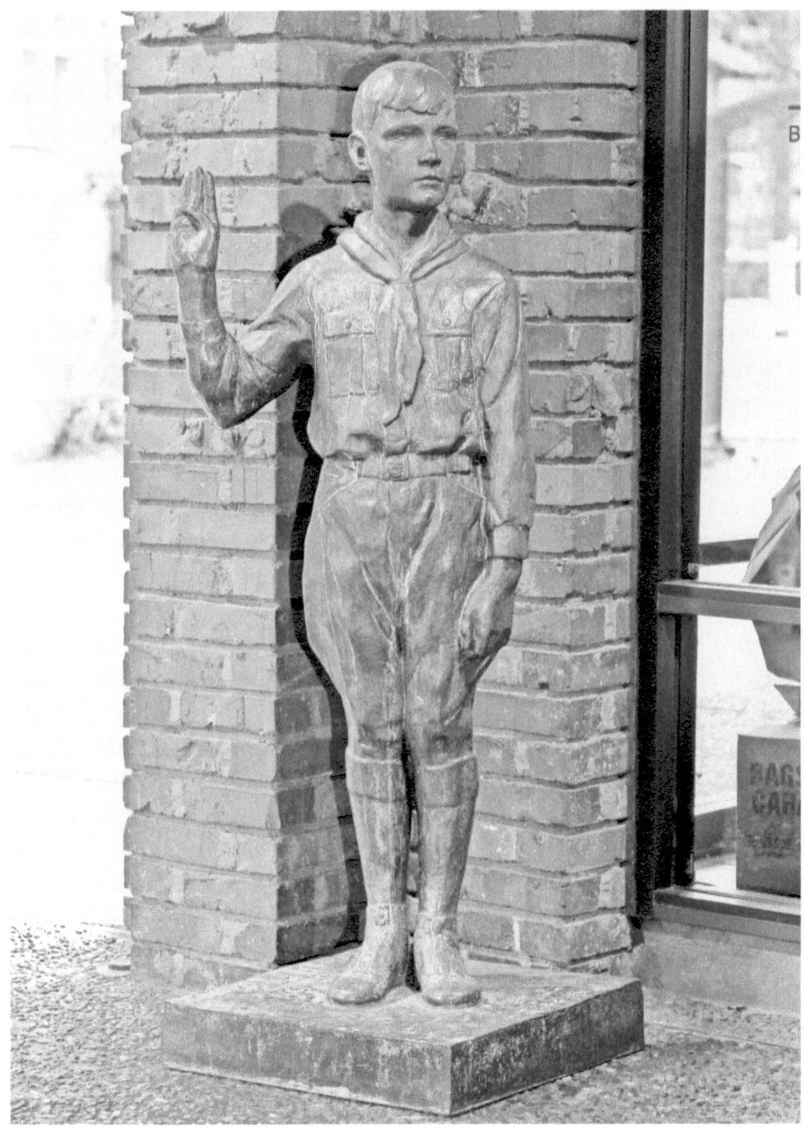

Boy Scout bronze statue from Elks Harding Memorial **by Alice Robertson Carr. Chris Dysart, Photographer (2016).**

visible trace of the Harding Memorial relief remained to be seen. The African Savanna exhibit was opened to the public on July 16, 1980, with Seattle Mayor Charles Royer presiding over the commemoration ceremony.

Reviews of Carr's two public sculptures for Seattle and the circumstances of their origins, and the demise of one of them, the Harding memorial, invariably raises the question of gender equality with respect to women in the profession of sculpture during the first half of the twentieth century. The same could also be said about the portrayal of real women (not allegorical subjects) in historical statuary during this same time period. It was not until 1905, when Alice Cooper's thirty-four-foot bronze memorial *Sacajawea* was unveiled at the Lewis and Clark Centennial in Oregon, that the United States had its first female statue of a historical figure.

Washington State's second statue for the National Statuary Hall Collection—*Mother Joseph* by Felix de Weldon—wasn't added until 1980, a full twenty-seven years after the state's first statue of *Marcus Whitman* had been placed on public display with the same collection.[36] Across the Seattle landscape, women sculptors were practically non-existent during Carr's era. Of the twenty-nine artists listed in the city directory for 1923, only five of these were women, with none of them listed specifically as "sculptors" or "sculptresses" by profession, with the exception of Carr.

A list of public statuary published in 1956 is equally telling. Out of 114 public sculptures identified, only six of these were done by women: Carr's memorial relief to President Warren Harding in Woodland Park; a relief group, *The Healing Arts*, by the instructor/student duo of Dudley Pratt and Jean Johanson for the University of Washington Health Sciences Building; another work by Johanson, a wood sculpture door panel for the chapel of the Children's Orthopedic Hospital; a bronze medallion of James D. Hoge by Jessie Phillips; a terra cotta, *Lily Madonna*, by Frieda Portmann for Holy Names Academy; and a bronze portrait medallion of *Mother Cabrini* by Lillian Wehn for Columbus Hospital.[37]

Yet at other times in the city's history, the record has reflected numerous active female sculptors exhibiting their work. For example, the National Art Week exhibition held at the Seattle Art Museum in the fall of 1940 identified eleven out of a total of eighteen sculptors as female, including Johanson.

Questions concerning the role women sculptors have played in contributing public sculpture to Seattle remain. Were only a few public sculptures ever produced because there was a varying number of practicing women sculptors in the city? Or does the limited number speak more about a profession in the arts that has been traditionally dominated by a society that has favored male sculptors? Does the Harding memorial's deterioration and de-installment in the late 1970s speak more to public perception of the man himself, or to the devaluation of public sculpture by female artists? There are no easy answers, but the historical record does offer a perspective that at least recognizes Carr for her contribution of local sculpture to the city.

That Carr was an accomplished sculptor is without doubt. She looked to further continue her training in the arts and did not remain in Seattle after completing the Harding memorial. In 1926, Carr travelled to Paris to study art at the Académie de la Grande Chaumière under Antoine Bourdelle and later at the École des Animaliere with Eduard Navallier. By 1927, she had joined the sculptor José de Creeft in Spain. At the time, Creeft was undertaking his monumental commission involving over 200 direct carvings in stone for Roberto Ramonje's Forteleza in Majorca. Over the eighteen months it took de Creeft to compete these direct stone carvings of column capitals and fountains adorned with a wide variety of animals, Carr assisted him as his studio assistant. The two sculptors were married at St. Paul's Church, Covent Garden, in London on March 15, 1928.

During this period Carr de Creeft continued to exhibit work both abroad and back in the United States, with exhibitions that included the Salon de la Société Nationale des Beaux-Arts and the Salon d'Automne in Paris (1927); and at the Northwestern Artists exhibition in Seattle (1929); and at the Stockbridge, Massachusetts Art Exhibition (1930).[38]

Throughout the 1930s, Alice Carr de Creeft spent time with her husband living in New York, France and Majorca, Spain. She had a son, William, born in Paris in 1932, and a daughter, Nina, a year later in 1933. When the Spanish Civil War erupted under Franco in 1936, Alice Carr de Creeft and the two children were forced to leave the country and go back to the United States without José. They arrived in New York aboard the British battleship *HMS Repulse*.

When the couple was once again reunited, they lived for several weeks with Dugard Carr, the sculptor's younger brother, at his home in Gibbstown, New Jersey.[39] They relocated to California in 1937, with José eventually returning to New York to pursue his own work and solo exhibitions. The couple divorced in 1938.

Alice Carr de Creeft remained in Santa Barbara and continued working on sculpture with a realistic portrayal of animals and in particular, thoroughbred racehorses. Her bronze sculpture of *Secretariat* was accomplished from the life model of the horse and later accepted into the collection of the Smithsonian Institution. During the 1970s, she taught sculpture at the Santa Barbara Art Institute.

Aside from the two memorials produced for Seattle between 1923 and 1925, Carr created no other public sculptures for the city. Aside from the original contract with the Elks, no record of correspondence has been found between the sculptor and any of the principle groups that originally sponsored or otherwise supported the Harding memorial.

Both *The Fountain* at the Woodland Park Rose Garden and the lone bronze Boy Scout statue at the main office for the Boy Scouts, Chief Seattle Council, remain her lasting artistic legacy to Seattle.

11

James FitzGerald
(1910–1973)

Compared to other Seattle sculptors who focused on a figurative or realistic approach to their subjects, James FitzGerald was more of a modernist in his technique and creative output. Like August Werner, who had a background in music, FitzGerald wasn't trained as a sculptor, either: he started out his career as a painter, and was also a student of architecture. However, these pursuits would later help FitzGerald form the basis for his work in public sculpture.

To understand his evolution as a sculptor requires a look back to the Great Depression years, which were formative for the artist in more ways than one.

FitzGerald was born and raised in Seattle. Initially, the artist held an interest in architecture, and at the age of 19, this led him to undertake a five-year course of study at the University of Washington. His studies earned him a Bachelor degree in Architecture in 1934. FitzGerald completed his academic studies at the height of the Great Depression, which he later recalled as "bad times for artists anyway."[1]

FitzGerald remained on the move during much of the decade, embracing a passion for the arts while focusing on painting for his creative expression. His experiences during this time were broad and encompassing. After leaving the University of Washington, he worked for the next two years at the Art Center School in Los Angeles. Continuing south, he hitched a ride on the back of a manure truck headed to Mexico and there experienced the work of Diego Rivera and studied first-hand the famous muralist's work. It was during the summers of 1935 and 1936 that he studied fresco mural painting under Jose Clemente Orozco.

Upon returning to the states, he next studied under Thomas Hart Benton at the Kansas City Art Institute and taught painting, water color and drawing there for two years. Miro FitzGerald recalls her father telling tales "of going skinny dipping with Thomas, Rita Benton and E.E. Cummings."[2] During this time, he also worked at the Colorado Springs Fine Art Center in Wyoming, teaching water color technique, and formed close working associations with the painters Boardman Robinson and Henry Varnum Poore.

In addition to continuing his studies of art and teaching, FitzGerald sought out commissions and used this early work to help refine his own style and vision through art. He was selected (along with fellow painter Vic Steinbrauch) by the U.S. Treasury Department Art Program (TDAP) to document the West. In one such lithograph drawing, *Harvey Canyon from Snyder Lookout* completed in 1934, FitzGerald shows a tonal view of rolling hills and valleys, with textured layers of shadow that speak to future forms he would attempt in bronze. The artist confirmed this outlook as well, in his recollection of the work done under TDAP:

> Vic was sent to do scenes of Washington and I was sent to Idaho. We had letters that enabled us to live in Forest Service stations and C.C.C. [Civilian Conservation Corps] camps, etc. I spent all summer hiking in northern Idaho from one mountain fire lookout to another. This summer was valuable to me and I imagine these early studies of nature have some bearing on the abstractions of our western landscape I am doing today in bronze.[3]

After assisting Robinson in the summer of 1938 with a series of murals for the Department of Justice, FitzGerald moved again to the East Coast when he was awarded a Carnegie Foundation Fellowship to attend the Yale Graduate School. At Yale, he studied architecture, philosophy, and Flemish painting. The following year FitzGerald was living in New York at 46 West 8th Street, working with a group of fellow artists as part of the New York Works Progress Administration (WPA) which counted Jackson Pollock among their number. Brief as it was, the time spent in New York formed a lasting impression of how public art programs were a benefit to artists: "And so I had one visualization of what I thought the art projects of America were like, from seeing the New York artists. They were real artists, painters and sculptors, working in their studios, and they made personal things."[4]

By the fall of 1939, FitzGerald had come full circle. He returned to Seattle, and started teaching as an associate instructor in painting for the University of Washington. It was at the Art Department of the University that the artist met Margaret Tomkins, an assistant professor who taught drawing, painting and history of art. The two married just a year later.

As timing would have it, the year of FitzGerald's arrival back to the state coincided with a Public Works Association (PWA) funded project already underway: the construction of a new, twin-bore tunnel under the Mount Baker ridge. These tunnels would effectively connect the city with a new floating pontoon bridge span across Lake Washington. It also marked the artist's first effort to create a public sculpture.

The Mount Baker ridge lies 260 feet above the west shore of Lake Washington, and in the words of PWA engineer Harold Judd, represented "the greatest natural obstacle in the route of the west approach to the Lake Washington Floating Bridge."[5] In all, eleven "units" were assigned different parts of the construction project by the Washington Toll Bridge Authority, with the project's managing body including the Washington State Director of Highways, Lacey R. Murrow; engineer-in-charge, R.M. Murray; and L.R. Durkee for the Public Works Administration.

The construction of the twin tunnels under the ridge was assigned to Unit 2, and had been in progress since the project began on December 30, 1938. One of the Unit architects, Lloyd Lovegren, had been tasked with designing the east entrance façade of the tunnels. To his credit, Lovegren envisioned a series of three, monumental vertical panels in concrete, which would be placed on the south, central and north sides of the façade as bas-reliefs.

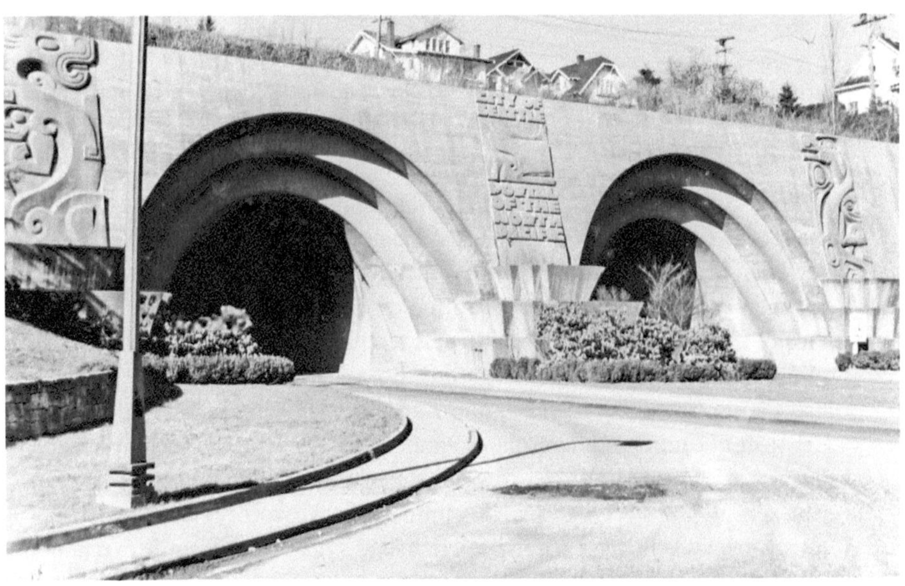

Lake Washington floating bridge tunnel entrance with reliefs **by James FitzGerald and Lloyd Lovegren. Photograph 1960. Werner Lenggenhager, Photographer. Seattle Public Library.**

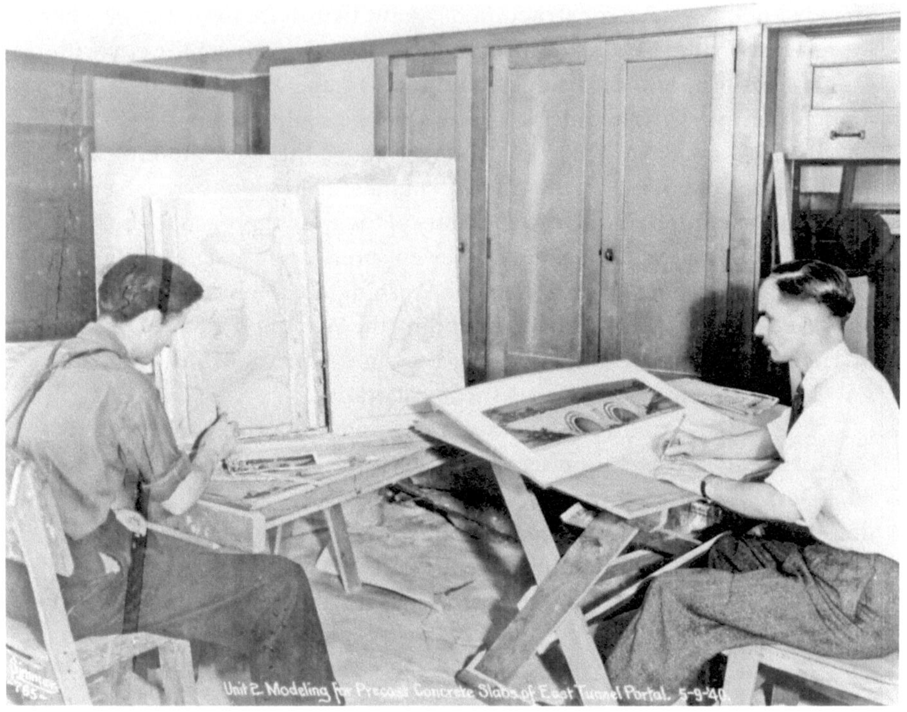

Artists Design the Mt. Baker Ridge Tunnel portals, May 9, 1940. James FitzGerald (left) and Lloyd Lovegren. May 9, 1940. Alfred Simmer, Photographer. Washington State Archives.

In a drawing by Lovegren originally dated July 25, 1939, the initial concept for these reliefs called for each panel to measure eleven feet wide by twenty-five feet high. However, a notation of revision indicating "precast concrete details added" was added on January 26, 1940, lending credence to the timing of FitzGerald's role as the designer for both the south and north panel designs. For the south portal, a Chinese dragon was pictured facing to the right, the tail curled into a corkscrew shape, while a swirl of smoke emerged from the dragon's nose. As a finishing compliment, the vertical addition of the words "The Orient" was added with the dragon in the center. On the north panel, a bald eagle sat atop a Native American totem pole, with the base comprised of a bear's head with tongue extruded. Text also was added to this panel to identify it as symbolic of another major travel destination for the Pacific Northwest: "Alaska."

The third panel in the tunnel façade design, which showed a ship under sail with the text "City of Seattle—Portal of the North Pacific," may be attributed solely to Lovegren, for several reasons. In a biographical memoir of her husband, Margaret Tomkins noted that "the north and south reliefs on the Lake Washington Floating Bridge were cast from scale models designed by FitzGerald."[6] In a photograph taken by Alfred Simmer, both Lovegren and FitzGerald are shown working in a studio: FitzGerald is sketching the south panel design on paper, while Lovegren consults his artist rendering of the 1939 architecture drawing of the east portal. In the final version, the central panel retained its full text, with the ship design adapted into a different motif altogether, showing the head and body of a whale.

A FitzGerald portfolio containing black and white photographs of sculptural works by the artist also offered views of both the completed south and north portals in concrete, with Margaret shown standing in the foreground with a smile (a photograph of the third central panel noticeably absent).

An examination of both the July 1939 architectural drawing and later artist rendering done by Lovegren, illustrates that changes were made to both the south and north panels by FitzGerald. Under his hand, the forms of the Chinese dragon and the Alaska totem underwent an evolution in design. With the south panel, the dragon went from a traditional representation to one more abstract in appearance. The curls from the tail and smoke from the mouth became merged with the dragon's body, the whole comprised of an interlocking series of loops, swirls and circles. The north panel underwent an even more elaborate adaptation. The head of the eagle now formed the left side of the panel, beneath the neck of a rearing animal's form: perhaps a bear, but left to the viewer to decide. The right side of the north panel showed a crouching, smiling figure, his right arm wrapped around knees. As with the south panel, the interplay of swirls, lines and circles emphasized the abstraction of the whole as a totem pole, yet simultaneously invoked patterns seen in traditional NorthWest Coastal art. In both north and south panels, FitzGerald removed any text as part of the final design.

The final versions of all three panels were modeled first in clay, and then cast into concrete by another local sculptor, James Wehn. In terms of size, the only change was in the final width of each panel: an extra foot had been added, making for an even twelve-foot span for each one. By May 18, 1940, both the center and north panels were set and grouted into place by the Bates and Rogers Construction Company, with the third south panel in the process of being casted into concrete.[7] Just two months later, the tunnel's portal façade was completed, with the public opening of the tunnel and bridge taking place on July 2, 1940.

While the Lake Washington floating bridge construction did receive a Works Progress Administration (WPA) grant for $3,794,400 to offset costs for part of the work done by Unit 2, the Mount Baker Tunnel reliefs were never officially considered a part of the local WPA's Art Program in Seattle. FitzGerald confirmed this in a 1965 interview, when asked by Dorothy Bestor if the WPA Art Project produced any important murals or commissioned sculpture works:

> Not to my knowledge. I have heard it said that the three large sculptured reliefs on the first floating bridge tunnel entrance were a product of the project. But that is not true. I was paid by the Washington State Highway Department as a field foreman to make the three, one-inch-to-the-foot models and Lloyd Lovegreen and I molded the full size works in clay out in Ballard.[8]

While significant as his first public sculpture, the reliefs done for the *Portal of the North Pacific* were equally important in illustrating how the artist preferred to continue his career in a direction oriented towards painting as a preferred medium. He produced only one other major sculpture relief in the early 1940s: a six-foot-by-four-foot "sgraffito" panel for the Catholic Seaman's Church in Seattle. The technique involved layering different colors of concrete, then carving the whole while the concrete was yet hardened. Like the tunnel reliefs, the Church panel design illustrated how even at this early stage, FitzGerald had a preference for creating abstract forms over strictly representational depictions in sculpture.

FitzGerald established a studio in Seattle in 1940, but eventually relocated to Spokane to direct the WPA Art Program's new Spokane Art Center in 1941. He returned to Seattle in the following year, to head the Boeing Company's Production and Illustration Department. In this role, the artist used his drawing skills to make simple sketches showing different parts of the B-17 bomber aircraft and how these should be assembled. Some sketches provided cutaway perspectives to show the interior designs of parts, while others showed assemblies of parts "exploded" to illustrate how the pieces all fit together. Throughout the war and the nine years that followed its conclusion, FitzGerald continued to paint, using both egg tempera and oils for his media.

The period between 1954 and 1959 provided FitzGerald with both new inspiration and direction for a renewed approach to sculpture as a more permanent medium. Natural forms continued to predominate in his work, but now eschewed direct representation in favor of abstraction. These forms were also tied to the landscape of the Pacific Northwest, "the topography, windswept coastline," where FitzGerald and wife Margaret had established separate studios for their work on the north end of Lopez

Island in the San Juan Islands.[9] Of these forms in sculpture, one group of new public art commissions found a recurrent theme in the use of water to enhance his vertical formed designs. The first of these fountains were done for Washington State University and Western Washington University in 1954 and 1959, respectively.

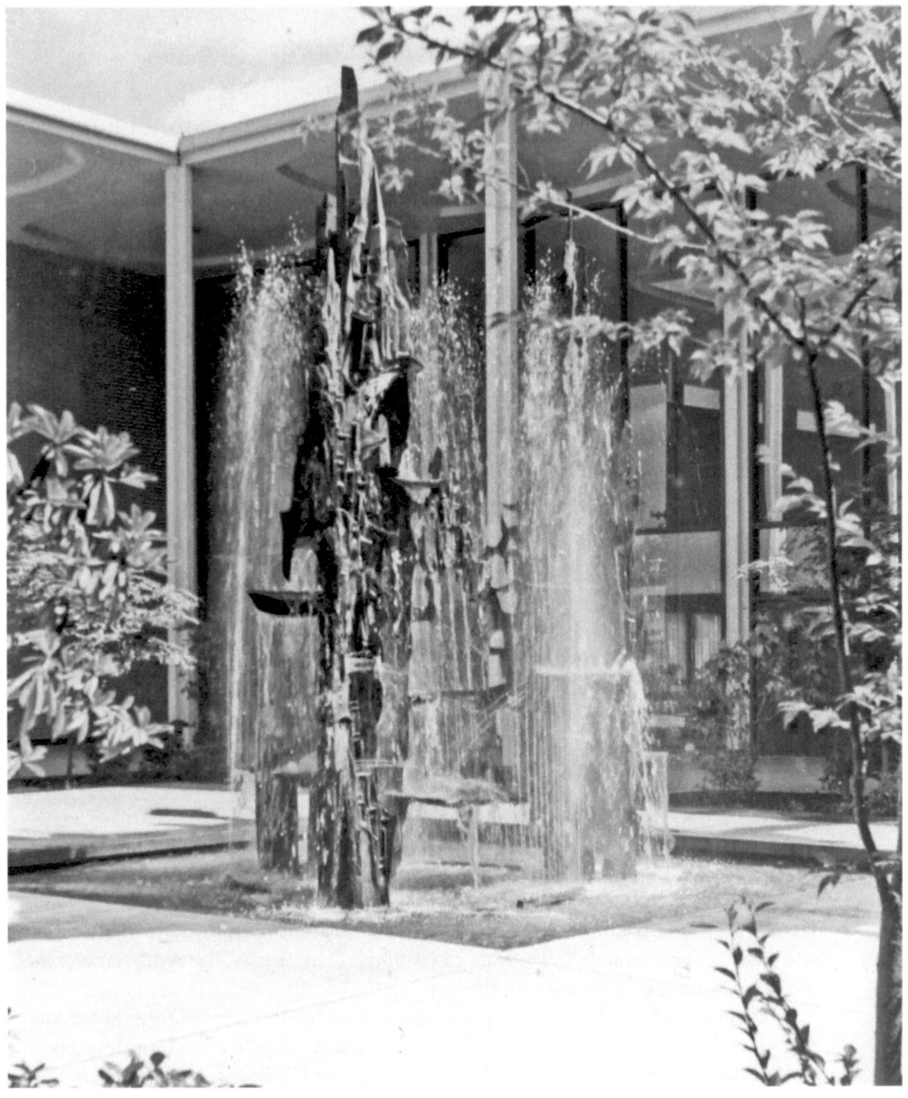

Fountain of the Northwest by James Fitzgerald. 1962. Werner Lenggenhager, Photographer. Seattle Public Library.

Concurrent with these fountains was another key sculpture which FitzGerald was bringing to completion from 1958 to 1959. Called *Rock Totem*, its design reflected a desire to meld forms found in the nature to FitzGerald's own creative interpretation, which remained grounded in abstraction. At a glance, the sculpture appeared as a series of angular blocks stacked and interconnected to form a vertical column, with a terminal height of twelve feet.

Ironically, it was the early successes of his first two fountains cast in bronze, combined with another event that steered FitzGerald towards sculpture as a preferred medium. On July 13, 1959, a fire broke out at the studio of FitzGerald and his wife located on lower Tenth Avenue, burning the structure to the ground. The artist cut his right hand attempting to break down the door, to make sure his two daughters, Miro and Gala (ages twelve and eight, respectively) were not inside. While none of the family lost their lives, the loss of their artwork was substantial. In addition to the glass panels from a new commission for the Seattle Library, the fire destroyed "99% of the paintings up to that date by FitzGerald and Tomkins."[10] FitzGerald noted the loss of one sculpture work in particular as devastating to him: "the most valuable thing I lost was a wax and wood model for a 12-foot bronze sculpture called 'Rock Totem.' I have been working on it all my life, in one way of speaking."[11] Miro FitzGerald recalled the importance of this work as well, in how it "symbolized a rebirth I believe to my dad, an ascension upwards from the traumatic loss they had suffered…"[12]

The fire's lasting effect was in convincing FitzGerald that sculpture, and specifically, work cast in bronze, would prevail against any future repetitions of disaster. The loss of the first *Rock Totem* model also spurred the sculptor to renew his efforts in the medium with greater purpose, which had a lasting effect on his portfolio of public sculpture commissions for both the city of Seattle and across the nation.

As an insight into both process and technique, Tomkins highlighted key points to the sculptor's approach to his rediscovered medium:

FitzGerald's creative response to the observation of nature in form, texture, color, and motion structured his paintings and sculpture. In bronze, the synthesis of varied cast shapes and textures with dynamic water energy characterizes FitzGerald's notable large scale sculpture. The method employed: hand formed individual patterns cast in a sand mold. The original idea for the sculpture was not developed through drawings, but by making small scaled sculpture in wax which was cast by the lost wax method. This model indicated a general conception from which the sculpture later developed in its own way in relation to scale and inter-related forms.[13]

One other public art commission in 1958 would soon lead to others for the artist. Following a recommendation made by Northwest painter Kenneth Callahan to architect Paul Thiry, FitzGerald was counted amongst those artists selected to include work in the new State Library building Thiry was designing for the Capital campus in Olympia. The inclusion of such artwork was the end result of Thiry's "economical design" which provided for "savings that became available for enhancements."[14] FitzGerald's contribution was a magnificent mosaic done in a tesserae style using colored ground marble, cement and latex. It was placed as a partition wall at the first floor's entry. The interior color scheme of the furnishings was also attributed to FitzGerald's mural, from the coverings used on the davenports to the reading room tabletops. The artist received $6,716.66 for the completed mosaic, which went on public view with the dedication of the Joel M. Pritchard Building on January 23, 1959.

In addition to the appeal of having a new public artwork on view in Olympia, the mosaic reflected two other vital details about FitzGerald. First, the import of the mosaic's design continued his preference for abstract natural forms in sculpture. According to the 1959 State Library Building Dedication informed by the artist, the forms were intended to suggest Washington's native forests with "'linear and textual patterns of water, fields, and foliage.'"[15] Along with water as an inter-

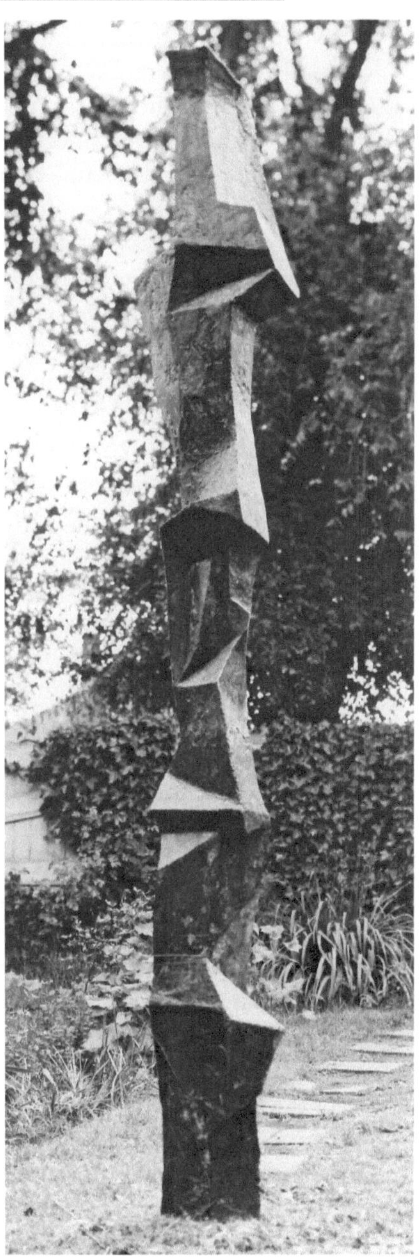

Rock Totem (First Version) by James Fitzgerald. 1959. Art Hupy, Photographer. Courtesy Miro FitzGerald.

active force, the theme of forests were a perpetual form found repeatedly in many of FitzGerald's later public sculpture fountains.

FitzGerald's inclusion as an artist on the project also helped to solidify his relationship with architect Paul Thiry. The sculptor had already worked on one other previous public sculpture commission several years earlier: a bronze fountain (FitzGerald's first) for the Women's Dormitory designed by Thiry for the Washington State University in Pullman, Washington. The connection between the two men would lead them to collaborate on one of the most ambitious civic projects yet in Seattle, for the "Century 21" World's Fair Exposition of 1962.

After years of discussion at various levels of city government, an initiative was begun in 1954 under Seattle Mayor Allen Pomeroy, who appointed a committee to examine the creation of a new civic center. The arts in all of its forms were envisioned as an important part of such a center, and it was by no coincidence that just a year later the City Council passed Ordinance No. 84162 which created the first Municipal Arts Commission on May 31, 1955. Pomeroy backed the new Arts Commission effort as well, approving it on June 7, 1955.

By March 1956, a site had been selected for the future World's Fair, with the goal of having it continue to serve as a civic center after the fair's conclusion. The public endorsed the idea, and approved a $7.5 million bond issue on November 6, 1956, for the project to proceed. The site would encompass seventy-four acres in a thirteen square block layout in the Lower Queen Anne neighborhood. Architect Paul Thiry was selected as the primary architect for the project, and together with Clayton Young coordinated the design and supervision of all buildings created for the site.

Following Thiry's lead, FitzGerald made a contribution to the '62 World's Fair in the form of sculpture. Two of these were designed as pieces for public exhibition during the run of the World's Fair from its opening on April 21, 1962, through October 21, 1962. The first of these was an abstract, small bronze sculpture titled *Song of Wind* (1962). In the time since his studio had burned to the ground, the sculptor had also recreated three new versions of *Rock Totem*. Two of the sculptures were cast into bronze in 1960 and 1961, with a third study done in wax. FitzGerald was invited to include the wax version of *Rock Totem* as part of the "Art Since 1950, American" exhibition curated by Sam Hunter for display in the Fine Art Pavilion Building.

While the *Rock Totem* and *Song of Wind* were both only offered for temporary display, FitzGerald coordinated with Thiry to create a more permanent public sculpture as part of the Exposition's site plan. In part this action reflected FitzGerald's own opinionated views about how public sculpture had thus far been incorporated into certain sculptural features on the '62 Fair grounds. The sculptor noted his dissatisfaction with one area in particular and its lack of a sculptor's sensibility:

> The City of Seattle is confronted with a real problem in trying to determine just what is to be done with the large International Fountain in the Seattle Civic Center. The winning design that was selected by the jury is in my estimation a failure. The winning design naturally resulted in an architectural solution created on a drafting table, a design object for others to construct. No real piece of sculpture could ever be made in that manner as the hand of the creative artist must directly work the material to achieve a significant work of sculpture. The proposed Japanese treatment for future landscape development using large rectangular blocks of glass around the pool is the result of immature and trivial thinking. It is as several European sculptors told me, "a stupid fountain."[16]

FitzGerald's solution offered a modernist design for another fountain in the courtyard of the new Playhouse Building to be constructed in the northwest corner of the Seattle Civic Center. The design was similar in appearance to his earlier fountain done for the Western Washington University campus, but larger in overall scale with four separately cast pieces in bronze welded together to form a primordial forest rising out of a central concrete pool. Water and lighting sources completed the effect for a viewer. Just as totem figures had served as a basis for his earlier reliefs and the *Rock Totem* pieces, FitzGerald adapted representational forms of wood and forests to conceptualize these as distorted abstractions. The sculpture's height, at over twenty feet tall, helped to emphasize the impression of vertical forms found in nature.

FitzGerald clearly identified the importance of the conceptual design as part of the creative process, saying "the preliminary design is most critical and time consuming. I required two and one half months to make and study the models used on the Seattle Civic Center, 'Fountain of the Northwest.'"[17] The sculptor then took these intricate wax patterns and cast molded them in French sand, which served as a material that duplicated the exact textures of the wax patterns.

For the casting of his sculpture molds into bronze for *Fountain of the Northwest*, FitzGerald used the services of Leon Morel, a longtime foundry owner in the area. Using the lost wax method of investment casting, Morel was able to cast all four pieces into bronze for FitzGerald to later weld together back in the studio. Margaret Tomkins described how this arrangement eventually convinced the sculptor to start his own foundry later in 1964:

When we got back in '62, the Playhouse fountain was not cast at our foundry; We didn't have our own foundry at that time—there was an old fellow that used to live out toward Kenmore [Leon Morel], a really skilled caster in lost wax—and so Jim used to take the investment materials out there, but transporting lost wax investment materials that distance is pretty damaging. So eventually we built our own foundry.[18]

FitzGerald had completed his design work for *Fountain of the Northwest,* at the same time construction was finished on the Playhouse Theater in 1961. The fountain was formally dedicated on March 21, 1962, one month before the official opening of the World's Fair to the public. It was a vindication of the sculptor's efforts to offer a non-representational, yet creative public sculpture in bronze, to the visionary landscape being formed on the Center's grounds. The achievement was all the more distinctive in its tacit acknowledgement of the Seattle City Mayor Clinton's stated position in 1960, which favored new public sculptures that incorporated fountains into their design.

FitzGerald's technical approach to combining his bronze cast elements with water were also novel and an important consideration in the final design of the sculpture as a functioning fountain. As these bronze pieces were welded together, special channels were contained within the bronze to convey water through the assembled whole. Rather than rely on an internal pipe system, the water became diffused as a result of the sculpture's shape and created its own patterns spraying out into the surrounding pool.

The historical significance of *Fountain of the Northwest* in the Playhouse courtyard comes from its being one of eleven total fountains FitzGerald created over the span of his career. Five more were completed for Seattle alone, and collectively they help to underscore the ascendance of "modern art" over more traditional and representational historical monuments, statues and portraits as acceptable public art. Yet it was the monolithic design for *Rock Totem* which continued to impact the sculptor's life for years after its exhibition at the '62 World's Fair in Seattle.

Most biographies about FitzGerald and indexes of his work to date do not mention *Rock Totem* as a specified sculpture of either note or accomplishment. However, it represented a formative piece of work for the artist in more than one respect. The process of its conceptual design aided FitzGerald to transition from representational forms found in nature viewed firsthand during his early travels around the country as a young painter. Out of the abstracted forms of Native American totems from his first attempts at these in relief form for the Mount Baker tunnel project,

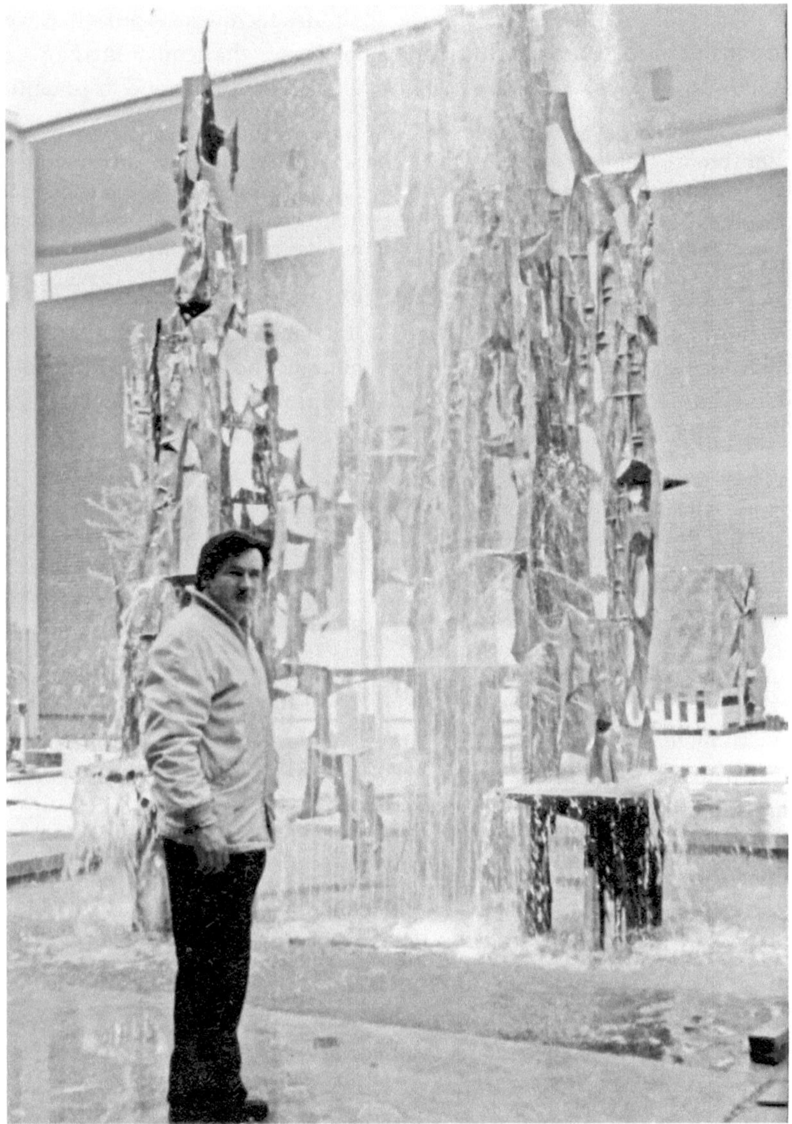

Playhouse Fountain and James FitzGerald. **Photograph ca. 1962. Art Hupy, Photographer. Courtesy Miro FitzGerald.**

he took away the concept of the "totem" as a vertical construct but left behind the notion of predesigned scale or interpretation. The later sculptures of the 1950s were the end result of this evolution, with *Rock Totem* one of the very first to give form to the approach.

This outlook was reflected in the sculptor's technical approach as well. Tomkins described how her husband's notion of what constituted a "scale model" was imperative to his new attitude about sculpture and its potential:

> FitzGerald always made a scale model in wax and then cast in lost-wax process into bronze. This model gave a general conceptual idea which was then interpreted in various ways compatable [*sic*] with the full scale and aesthetic direction of the sculpture. There were no scale drawings from which measurements were taken (common to most other's sculptures), but the form evolved as the sculpture grew.[19]

Despite being destroyed in the 1959 studio fire, the concept for the first *Rock Totem* lived on in the mind of FitzGerald. Its recreation in 1960 helped the sculptor to realize a re-invented self as an artist dedicated to the medium of sculpture. The steps he employed to create each version of *Rock Totem* were likewise an evolution in forms:

> These pieces were laboriously coated in the plaster mold process to create a "lost wax" refined image. It required an elaborate inner stick/wood bracing support system to steady it and sustain weight ... the sections even required a chain lift to move them before any casting in bronze. The Totem sections were each about 3–4' in height and I believe in the final stage bronze welded together and carefully fit in order to achieve their significant height.[20]

That he had three versions of the design created speaks to the importance FitzGerald placed on this work as part of his evolution as an artist. However, an incident which occurred during the final month of the '62 World's Fair involving *Rock Totem* underscored the work as both a talisman and a harbinger for FitzGerald.

A student working towards his Master of Arts degree in sculpture named Robert Hopkins had visited the Fair, and seen *Rock Totem* on public display. Two months later, Hopkins received a commission to undertake a new sculpture for the rear entry of the new Washington Federal Savings and Loan Association's Ballard branch bank. The commission had been granted in large part after the project's architects, McClelland and Osterman of Seattle, had received a recommendation from the eminent sculptor George Tsutakawa, who was one of Hopkins' professors in sculpture at the University of Washington. Hopkins completed his eight-foot sculpture in bronze, called *Transcending*, while "sculpting by day and working nights in a 'Colonel Sanders Kentucky Fried Chicken' spot."[21]

Not long after its installation at the bank, FitzGerald learned about the sculpture after seeing a picture of it in a local newspaper. The similarity of the Hopkins sculpture to that of *Rock Totem* was nearly identical, except for minor deviations in the angles of vertical column and for the fact that Hopkins' artwork was slightly shorter.

FitzGerald's reaction was immediate. After reviewing the bank's sculpture in person, according to court records he then "went to the office of the bank's architects [and] reported that 'Transcending' was a copy of his 'Rock Totem.'"[22] A lawsuit for copyright infringement soon followed by FitzGerald against both the bank and Hopkins, for $50,000 in damages and a removal of the offending sculpture from public view. Hopkins' reply was both nonchalant and unapologetic at the same time: his position was that his work was authentic, in spite of having seen FitzGerald's piece on view two months prior to his award of the bank commission. He initiated his own counter-suit for $25,000 "based upon alleged libel and slander" and furthermore commiserated to the public, "'I'm not mad at FitzGerald, or anything, but if he was sore and if he'd been a good Irishman, he'd have punched me in the nose'—instead of resorting to litigation."[23]

Over the next three years of court battles, FitzGerald's attorney, Irving Clark, Jr., could not prove that *Rock Totem* was a design deliberately copied by the younger sculptor. The courts noted that vertical sculpture forms as well as Native American totems had been around for hundreds of years, and were available for both sculptors to review and draw inspiration from to create their own artworks. Hopkins was legally exonerated from any wrongdoing, with local newspapers portraying him as a figure akin to David vs. Goliath. Arts Editor Maxine Cushing Gray opined on the legal case result and its impact on the art world, saying "to have ruled otherwise would have opened a Pandora's box of restraints that have no place in a free society, Great or otherwise."[24] Others were less moved. Dr. Richard Fuller, the President and Director of the Seattle Art Museum at the time, observed, "People shouldn't have got so hot and bothered over this thing."[25]

For FitzGerald, the contested ownership of the design was a matter of principle, and perhaps a reflection of his own beliefs after having studied the philosophy of Zen, Socrates, Descartes and other philosophers throughout his life. That he was passionate about these beliefs was evident in the sharing of these lessons with his children, with the assertion to them "we only get to walk around this big ball of mud once."[26]

To add insult to injury, the final judgment of the Washington State Supreme Court also found that FitzGerald was accountable for remarks he made to bank employees and in a written letter offered up as evidence at proceedings, which called Hopkins "a thief … [whose] desire for money has guided his hand in his path of plagiarism…."[27] With no direct proof available to show Hopkins had deliberately copied *Rock Totem*, and with the subsequent judgment that Hopkins had violated no copyright of the work, such words were deemed unfounded in the legal review and in the end cost

FitzGerald $15,000 in the judgment against him. In the days that followed, Miro described the aftermath of the court's decision: "the house felt somber, like a morgue when I came home from school. I knew we had lost."[28]

The legal precedent that the case involving *Rock Totem* helped to establish was a dubious legacy for the sculpture, and yet did not herald the end of it as a design of importance for FitzGerald. One bronze casting of the sculpture done in 1961 was eventually acquired for the private collection of Jon and Mary Shirley, later donated to the City of Bellevue and accepted for that city's public art collection on October 21, 2002. The fourteen-foot-tall sculpture was installed in 2008 at the corner of 108th Avenue Northeast and Northeast 12th Street in Bellevue, where it still resides today.

The legal reviews surrounding the work also coincided with a final period in the sculptor's life where he made a full transition away from sculpture based on forms represented in nature, to those wholly abstract in conception and which incorporated found objects such as children's toy parts. These were a reflection of the late 1960s, as the Vietnam War raged overseas and at home, as FitzGerald found himself drawn to conflict as a new theme in both his new emerging work and worldview:

> Sculpture must speak the language of plastic form, a language deeply seated in our emotions and not governed or motivated by our mental process. Today our lives are smothered in gross materializations and our emotional inner reality is neglected and starved. Young people today are keenly aware of our dilemma and are taking every means to free them-

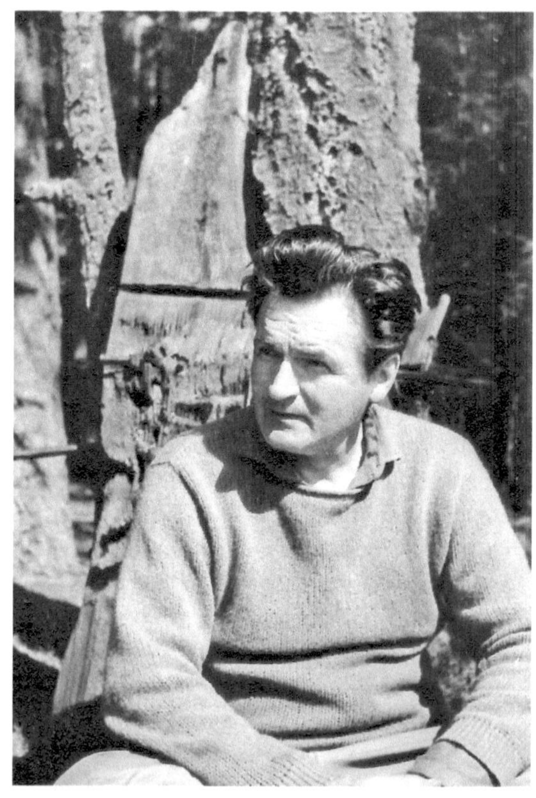

James FitzGerald, Lopez Island. **Art Hupy, Photographer (1964). Courtesy Miro FitzGerald.**

selves of our mad destruction of our fellow man and are trying to move completely away from the materialistic "garbage culture" we have assembled and wish to pass on to our children.[29]

FitzGerald's new bronzes in this abstract vein were featured in exhibitions held at the Gordon Woodside Gallery in Seattle and at Everett General Hospital in 1968. The following year, he was at the Catherine Vivan Gallery with a one-man exhibition in New York. His last fountain design which was cast in bronze at his Seattle foundry was done for the Civic Center Waterfront Park in Kirkland, Washington, in 1970.

James FitzGerald died of bone cancer at the age of sixty-three in 1973. Before his death, he designed one last fountain for the Seattle waterfront park, but the casting for that sculpture was finished by Margaret. It shows a collection of cubical structures, again composed in a vertical design like other fountains before it. She closed down the foundry shortly after it was completed and relocated to a studio on Lopez Island.

From the reliefs on the Mount Baker tunnel entrance, throughout the evolution of his transformative *Rock Totem*, to the several bronze forest fountains scattered around the city, FitzGerald marked his life as a sculptor with a progression of work from representational to abstract in their revelation as public sculptures. They are historical in that aspect, and reflect the man, the environment of the Pacific Northwest, and his time well spent on this mud ball.

12

August H. Werner
(1893–1980)

When at your home, when you were devoting your wonderful talent to modeling a bust of me I asked you why you were doing it. You promptly replied "Because I like you." Those words, August, are written upon the red leafed tablets of my heart in indelible ink, never to be erased.[1]
—Frank Lazier, December 24, 1947

By some standards, August Werner did not "make a living" as a professional sculptor. This was certainly the case in terms of being paid for his work in the medium, of which he could claim less than a dozen completed sculptures in his lifetime. His achievements in sculpture were part of a broader passion he maintained throughout his life for the arts, which also notably included abilities and accomplishments as a baritone singer, a chorus director, a composer and writer, as an instructor in voice and master of many languages. It was in this respect that his desire to paint, draw and sculpt served to reflect a multi-faceted personality: both broad in its creative outreach yet also narrow in focus, especially when the creative process involved others. His legacy in sculpture for Seattle was a long-time coming.

From his beginnings as a young man in Bergen, Norway, Werner's interests were diverse. For a time he studied agriculture, earning a Bachelor of Science degree from the University at Stend—but that was not the answer. Neither, it turns out, was a calling to join the ministry, although Werner remained devote throughout his life, believing "his talents were God-given."[2] His studies in architecture aimed at providing some practical outlet for his creativity, but this too did not last.

Out of these wanderings, two constants emerged that gave Werner direction. The first was a standard of music found in Norwegian grade schools which encouraged group singing by students, which ultimately lead him to a profession that gave literal voice to his passion. He was also captivated by Nordic explorers of the era—Nansen; and the polar explorer Amundsen. As much as singing would later prove to be his lifelong vocation, Norse exploration remained a subject of study and design throughout his life. This was true especially at an early age, as Werner recalled: "I was crazy for ships. What drawing I did was of ships."[3]

Werner found an opportunity to live his own maritime adventure in 1915, when he passed a poster on the Bergen waterfront advertising for crews to work on the Norwegian/American Line (N.A.L.). He signed on soon after with two other friends as pantrymen, for transatlantic crossings that could take up to three weeks at a time.

Perhaps the danger afforded by repeat maritime travel across the Atlantic encouraged Werner to take his final voyage as a passenger on the N.A.L. ocean liner SS *Bergensfjord* back to New York on February 14, 1916. The crossing took 11 days out of Bergen, and marks the last such crossing he would make until 1924. Werner settled in Bay Ridge, a Norwegian community in Brooklyn, New York, and begun a new life as an immigrant to the United States.

His new beginning in America also marked the beginning of his singing career in earnest. Werner was a baritone, or basso soloist, and in one of his first public performances in New York sang as part of a war-themed quartet in the Rivoli Theatre. It awakened in him a realization of his passion and talent for music. Werner sang for churches, local concert halls and civic clubs, at equal ease performing in both English and Norwegian languages owing to his earlier schooling in Norway.

It was during one of his rehearsals for an upcoming soloist performance that the singer met Gertrude Gunston, an accomplished singer and piano accompanist in her own right. Werner's regular accompanist had become sick, and so he called twice on her asking for assistance. After that first rehearsal at her home, Werner called upon her the following evening. They were married two years later, on December 17, 1920.

Just three years later, Werner found himself recording records for the Victor label, singing songs in his native Norwegian with titles such as "Overmaade fuld af naade," "Den første sang," and "Sang til Bergen." Between 1919 and 1927, he produced over 50 solo vocal performances in his native tongue and another seven motion picture soundtracks in English.

Werner had also sought to further train his voice by enrolling in studies at the Master School of Music in Brooklyn under Mme. Melanie

Guttman-Rice, who prepared him for his debut recital in New York's Town Hall on March 6, 1929. The instructor was not unfamiliar to Werner, since Rice had also trained his wife Gertrude in voice. The role was the first of many for the singer turned opera-performer. His career as a professional singer was further bolstered for three years on Broadway, performing as a solo baritone at the Rivoli, Rialto and Criterion Theatres under the musical direction of Dr. Hugo Riesenfeld.

The 1920s were good to the Werners, but ultimately, proved better for August Werner. As his repertoire grew, so did his invitations to sing and perform, and by extension, his accolades and opportunities for further advancement. He spent a good deal of time traveling: twice to Norway and back again, in 1924 and 1926, to perform with choruses from New York. The 1926 trip with the United New York Singers featured him as a soloist, and toured Europe for several months. His fame as a singer reached the ears of those highest in Norwegian royal society as well. In the same year, he honored a request from the Norwegian government to represent Norway in concert at the Sesquicentennial International Exposition held in Philadelphia. He toured again with the United New York Singers across the United States in 1928.

Werner was a dashing figure, combining passion, ability and poise. While Gertrude continued her work with the Norwegian Seaman's Church back in Brooklyn, August was expanding to a tenor role from *Aida* to an audience of 40,000 and reading his review the following week in the *New Yorker* magazine. Local performances by the couple where Gertrude would accompany him on the piano or flute became less frequent, as his star of fame ascended. Owing to an attitude of Norwegian pragmatism or perhaps just a realist, Gertrude voiced no public regrets about Werner's chosen path as this affected her own: "'there wasn't room in a family for two artists striving for recognition, but now that my husband has attained success, I have begun to think of my own musical career.'"[4]

As his public exposure grew, so did the demand for his talent. Fans would write to him, entreating him to perform for a seasonal concert series or with special requests for songs by Scandinavian composers, such as Edvard Grieg, C.L. Sjöberg, and Hakon Børresen.[5] The Mozart Club of New York hosted him as a featured soloist for four consecutive seasons, as did the Schola Cantorum ("singers' school") in New York City under the direction of composer Kurt Schindler for three seasons.

A series of performances between 1929 and 1931 would lead to Werner's discovery of the Pacific Northwest, both as a new home and a source of inspiration for his work. On November 5, 1929, "direct from New York," Werner sang with the Norwegian Male Chorus at the Eagles Hall on Seventh Avenue in Seattle. The concert was his first ever performance on the West Coast. In a congratulatory Western Union telegram, his friend A. Halvorsen wrote "wishing you success tonight" while in the company of a "good stag party" for a mutual acquaintance's birthday.[6] Additional performances followed, with the majority offering rave reviews. One of these by the *Santa Cruz Morning Sentinel* highlighted "his wonderful breath control ... musicians present remarked upon this phrase of his splendid work."[7]

Some West Coast venues, however, were not so promising, though not for any lack of Werner's skill as a singer. One performance in Stanwood, Washington, on November 10, 1929, netted the singer just $65. Next, an intermediary in Los Angeles tried to secure him a concert with the Grays Harbor Symphony Orchestra in Aberdeen, but no contract was forthcoming "due to the present business depression."[8] Another reply from a representative of the Bellingham Male Chorus refuted Werner's offer of $125 to come sing at a future date, to just $50 and a portion of tickets sold, owing to the difficulties of filling a concert hall where only solo performers were offered as an attraction.

During a respite from touring the Northwest, he was invited to lend his voice in the baccalaureate commencement at the University of Washington in June 1930. The event would serve as an introduction to a larger opportunity with the University of Washington only one year later, and the time spent in Seattle only further reinforced the singer's appreciation for the city's Norwegian-American community.

On March 15, 1931, he was invited to a repeat performance at the University as the featured baritone for the Music Department's final program of the winter quarter. The soloist spent the next several months in negotiations with the school's administration over his qualifications and starting salary. Werner had asked for a base salary of $4,000 a year, which Vice-President David Thomson viewed as challenge for the University to meet as an expectation. He outlined his concerns to Werner while the singer was staying at the Spring Apartment Hotel in Seattle:

As you know, Voice, like Piano, etc., has hitherto been handled on the fee system and the budget recently adopted makes no provision for the straight salary plan. In what I am saying there is no suggestion that the figure you named as the salary for yourself should be changed. Our difficulty is that the fee for each individual set as it is at present at $25 a quarter the returns from the number of students whom you would fairly be caring for would not be $4000 a year, and we have no inclination to suggest that you take care of a larger number.[9]

In the final deliberations between Thomson and University President Spencer, Werner prevailed in his salary stipulation. He was appointed as a full Professor of Music teaching "Voice" at the University of Washington on August 22, 1931. A month later the new professor settled in the University District of Seattle, and was joined over a year later by Gertrude, who had remained in Brooklyn with her younger brother to continue her own pursuits and interests as a musician.

With his new appointment to the University, Werner found his time in more demand than ever before. He became more selective in his choice of concert performances offsite from the University. In 1934, he turned down subsequent invitations to perform as a soloist with the Pacific Coast Norwegian Singer's Association at the 27th Sängerfest in Vancouver, British Columbia, Canada (he would later lead the group as Director in 1960); a solo from "Valkyries" for the Vancouver Symphony Orchestra; another Sängerfest concert in Fargo, North Dakota, with the Orpheus Male Chorus; and a concert organized by the Norwegian Glee Club of Portland in 1935. His reply to the Vancouver Symphony Orchestra's offer highlighted the toll of overwork: "I have had more than my share of work and my voice and most of all my self [*sic*] needs rest."[10]

As had proven the case with the University of Washington, financial commitments also continued to weigh in heavily as far as Werner's availability. The Fargo event in particular seemed to pressure Werner to attend, with its offer of only $250 for his anticipated performance scheduled for June 21–23. The organizers of the Sängerfest petitioned the Luther College Musical Union and others acquaintances of Werner's "in the east" to try to persuade the singer to change his mind about attending the concert. In a diplomatic reply letter, Werner outlined his rationale to one such petitioner:

> Letters from Fargo stated at first the limited amount of funds and also that one soloist was already engaged and others available. Not being in the habit of bargaining with my country men [*sic*] any more about pay for my services I at that time gave reasons for not feeling I could come ... $250 would not cover my own expenses such as traveling from Seattle to Fargo and back again, hotels, Pullman fare, meals, and the loss of earnings at the summer school while away.[11]

As hinted at by the Fargo letter, Werner first and foremost presented a worldview of himself as an accomplished professional singer. This view of himself as one of the finest baritones of the era was echoed by eminent Norwegian critics of his time. It is to Werner's credit that he sought out this high self-standard not only in himself but in others, when it came to music. As both an instructor in voice and as a choral director, he expected the highest caliber of performance in others: "'He didn't have to say a word—just a look was enough to tell a singer he was off key ... he demanded perfection ... and he could be really mean with his students.'"[12]

A key to understanding Werner's efforts in sculpture was that the man considered his work in that medium to be the natural extension of the greatness he had already achieved in the musical arts. Werner also made a conscious choice to not limit himself to just one art form, even when he found that these competed for his attention. It was a practice he carried on as an artist throughout his life. As a playwright in 1938, he created and staged a three-act play in commemoration of the 300th anniversary of the Delaware settlement in Sweden. He made paintings of fantastic trolls and Norwegian floral designs and scrollwork on furniture, one of which was a betrothal gift. Owing to a lifelong interest in Viking ships and maritime history, Werner made oil on canvas paintings of these subjects to decorate his home. During the late 1920s and into the 1930s, Werner experimented with studio photography, and had produced a number of prints as studio portraits of fellow opera performers, musicians, and Gertrude. Yet all of these artistic pursuits took a second seat to his music. His time spent in the studio for sculpture as a medium was no different. During his performance in a public run of Beethoven's *Fidelio* in 1954, the completion of a bust of the same composer in that year offered a sad admission on this point: "'I haven't had much time to work on my sculpture or to touch my painting this spring.'"[13]

Unlike his musical ability, which had benefited from years of training and practice, the sculpture Werner created was born from the man's passion for his portrait subjects and relied primarily on what innate ability he possessed. Werner was never formally trained as a sculptor, and as with his other pursuits in the media arts, practiced his modeling of portrait busts in clay, plastina and plaster using his home as a studio. Werner's views on the arts were all-inclusive, and this philosophy was reflected in his attempts at media art:

> It is misleading to speak of versatility in art ... all art is one. When you hear a great musical work, you see the composer in three dimensions. That is sculpture. And you see the color of his flesh, his eyes, his hair. That is a canvas, a painting, portraiture. And you think of his times, his surrounding culture, even his idiosyncrasies. That is history.[14]

With this approach, Werner's first public sculpture was a bas-relief plaque inscribed "Leiv Eiriksson" for a new monument installed at Leif Erikson Square for the sculptor's old neighborhood of Bay Ridge, in Brooklyn, New York. The bronze plaque shows the figure Erikson in profile, wearing a horned helmet, holding aloft a spear in one hand and shield in the other. A Viking longboat appears under sail in the background, while a Christian cross appears at the center, top, of the plaque, and flanked on either side by dragons. The monument was designed as a replica of a Viking runestone in Tune, Norway. The monument was notable for having been dedicated June 6, 1939, by the Crown Prince Olav of Norway and served to only further strengthen Werner's reputation as a Norwegian-born artist in America. The design proved to be so popular that a second copy of the plaque was installed at the Norway Hall in Seattle that same year.

Figure studies and portraits were to represent the majority of Werner's completed work in sculpture. The earliest bust was a model of the Finnish composer, Jean Sibelius, in 1942. Originally a commissioned work for John Sundsten, Concert Master of the Seattle Symphony (1943–1945) Werner later conveyed that his motivation for making both the Sibelius bust and another of Beethoven were due to his devotion to each composer and their music.[15] Both of these busts were monumental in size, and cast into plaster. Werner gave the Sibelius bust to the University of Aub in Finland in 1954, after a Finnish professor visited the University of Washington that year and complimented the sculptor on the quality of the portrait. It was a high note of praise for Werner, and echoed an early sentiment expressed by one of Sibelius' sons-in-law in California, who had called it "'the best ever done.'"[16] Copies of a third bust of Norwegian composer and pianist Edvard Grieg done in 1945 reveal the same realism vein and attention to detail, and were later accepted for display by both the Norwegian embassy in Washington, D.C., and the campus at Pacific Lutheran University in Tacoma, Washington.

From the early 1940s to the mid–1950s proved to be Werner's most active period as a sculptor. As with the composer busts, the portrait subjects were all closely associated with Werner on a personal level. He produced one bust of Dr. Stanley Chappel, who had joined the University of Washington staff as Director of the School of Music in 1948 and collaborated with Werner on many joint productions for the Seattle Opera Guild. Other busts were made posthumously of both the University's Vice President David Thomson and the former Director of the Scandinavian Languages and Literature Department, Edwin Vickner. Both men Werner worked closely with at the University for many years.

This period of increased activity for Werner served him well in terms of the timing for his most ambitious undertaking in sculpture: a monumental statue of Leif Erikson intended for the City of Seattle. However, it would be an undertaking different in many respects from his other works, and notably not in collaboration with those who shared a similar background in music or academia.

The date of April 29, 1957, marked the formation of the Leif Erikson League (L.E.L.) of Seattle as an official, non-profit organization. Its members ranged from thirteen to seventeen different lodges, clubs and other civic groups with a focus on Scandinavian heritage, arts and culture in the Seattle area. Predominantly, these were Norwegian-American immigrants and their families, but also included Icelandic and Swedish representation.

For years, dating back the Alaska-Pacific-Yukon (A-Y-P) Exposition of 1909, these local citizens had informally celebrated annual "Leif Erikson" festivals in the city, with October 9 as the designated official Leif Erikson Day beginning in 1941.[17] Erikson's proposed discovery of America (Vinland) around the year 1000 AD figured prominently in the minds of citizens with a shared ethnic heritage, and remained a consistent source of inspiration and achievement personalized in the historical figure of Leif Erikson as an explorer.

The formation of the L.E.L. in 1957 established a specific charter and goals, one of which called for "a fund for the establishment of a memorial to Leif Erikson; and for that purpose, receive gifts, devises, and bequests and other donations, which may be made to the League from time to time."[18] The statement would help begin the process of crystalizing support in the local community, while also providing a focus for the group members' efforts to both develop a plan for a physical memorial and fund it going forward.

By the time Leif Erikson Day was celebrated on October 9 of that year, the "memorial" was further refined as a concept when the President of the League, Trygve "Ted" Nakkerud, announced a committee was being formed "to plan and work for the erection of a suitable statue of Leif Erikson."[19]

Werner was no stranger to either the local Scandinavian community in Seattle or the subject of Leif Erikson. As far back as 1936, Werner led the Norwegian Male Chorus during its choral performance at the Civic Auditorium in celebration of Leif Erikson Day. He had also produced one bas-relief sculpture that featured the Viking as part of a public memorial with the same goal of highlighting Erikson's discovery of the New World.

It was a subject he knew well, having studied Norse ship design and the exploration history of Vikings in literature. Werner was well read on the subject, and made pages of notes and sketches of ships with insights gleaned from the writings of contemporary authors, such as Alexander Bugge's *Seafaring and Shipping during the Viking Ages* (1908) and N. Nicolaysen's *The Viking Ship Discovered at Gokstad in Norway* (1882). One series of notations described his observations concerning the ships used by Erikson and other Viking seafarers:

> Centers of civilization go westward until they meet the great obstacles–"Böygen"—Only the warships had many rowers and consequently a low freeboard easy for entering-for fighting. The merchant ships were higher, had more freeboard and were undoubtedly better equipped in board since room usually occupied by many warriors and their weapons, provisions.[20]

In another series titled "On Sailing," Werner listed calculations for distances travelled and time spent by Erikson to go from Norway to America and then to Greenland. The journey from Iceland to Greenland he calculated at a distance of 330 miles, or the equivalent of four days of sailing.[21] Another set of handwritten notes on the back of a torn up University of Washington's School of Music concert program offered details about the *Long Serpent*, a Viking boat built by the Norse King Olaf, reputed to be 117 feet long and which could carry over 600 men.

These studies translated into physical work as well, as seen in a wood carving of a miniature figurehead, for placement on the prow of a scale model Viking ship. Werner constructed the model based on the real Viking ship discovered in the fjord shore at Gokstad, in southwestern Norway.

Werner was passionate on the subject and took pride in the identity of the Norsemen. More than that, he held contempt for those that doubted the veracity of Erikson as the first "European" to discover the New World:

> It is a whole lot easier to merely state he was not here, and have no proof of the statement, or being unable to give one single scientific or historical fact to back up such a statement—just foist the whole thing away with one fell swope ... it is lots easier to do that, then it is to follow the saga and then work out the possible route he [Erikson] took.[22]

In spite of his expertise on the subject of Erikson, it would not be until early 1959 that Werner would become formally involved in the League's project to create a new Leif Erikson statue.

The first record of the League bringing the project to the attention of the City of Seattle was a report submitted by Municipal Art Commission (MAC) member John S. Detlie on June 12, 1958. Detlie reported that the "Norwegian community" had indicated its interest in erecting a statue to Leif Erikson as a gift to the city. A brief discussion amongst the members followed, with a recurrent suggestion that this offer might somehow incorporate a fountain as part of a design.

A year after the formation of the League, a self-appointed "Committee of Placement," wrote a letter to Seattle Mayor Gordon Clinton on September 5, 1958, which outlined in more definitive terms the League's plans to erect a statue to Leif Erikson, preferably during the Century 21 Exposition of 1962. The Chairman of the committee, Thorbjorn "Tom" Grønning, concluded the letter by asking for the Mayor's help in securing a "suitable location for this statue."[23] The letter was assigned as a new petition with the Comptroller's Office under File No. 235441, and was forwarded to the Parks and Public Grounds Committee for review.

Several items stand out in the initial petition submitted by the League and the review process that followed. The timing of the letter to Mayor Clinton was only seventeen days after a report from the City Engineer to the Parks and Public Grounds Committee was formally adopted by the City Council on the subject of statues and monuments on all City-owned property. File No. 235222 proclaimed that the Parks Department had jurisdiction on the maintenance of all statues and monuments on all City owned property and that notice to this effect be given to the City Engineer, Superintendent of Buildings, Board of Park Commissioners, Board of Public Works, and the Municipal Art Commission.

The Chairman of the Parks and Public Grounds Committee, Mrs. Harlan Edwards, sent the League's petition along for further review and recommendations to Ewen Dingwall with the Civic Center Advisory Commission and also to Robert Durham, Chairman of the Municipal Art Commission. In the correspondence that followed, the Civic Center was named as the location of choice for the placement of the Leif Erikson statue, while no mention was made of the sculptor selected to undertake the work.[24]

For the Civic Center's involvement, aside from the suggestion of a meeting between the coordinating architect, Clayton Young, and Grønning, nothing ever came of the League's vision to include the statue on the grounds of the new center as part of the upcoming World's Fair. The MAC members had reviewed the Civic Center plans back in December 1957, and made a recommendation that funds be allowed for the inclusion of appropriate artworks but had made no provisions for the assignment of specific sculptures (including statuary) in the plan design.

The petition came under the scrutiny of the Municipal Art Commission, which since the passing of City Council Ordinance No. 84162 in 1955, was charged by the city to act in an advisory capacity in connection with the artistic and cultural development of the city. A second Ordinance (No. 86692) passed in 1957 further clarified the Commission's role with respect to public art: that its fifteen members had the advisory responsibility concerning the purchase or the donation of artworks to the City, and furthermore that each painting, sculpture or fountain—and its location—had to be approved by the Commission. The commission's members were well aware of this mandate, as discussion in their July 11, 1957, meeting clearly reflected: "It was agreed that plans of various projects in initial stages as well as in the finalized state should be brought to the Art Commission for perusal and approval."[25]

A cordial letter from Durham to the Leif Erikson League was sent soon after the petition had circulated amongst the city's representatives. It proposed three other sites in addition to the Civic Center where the statue might be placed: a view park near the Pike Place Market, an unnamed city center park, and a third site at Golden Gardens Park near the Shilshole Bay breakwater. It also called out the lack of a named sculptor for the statue, citing quality concerns for any artwork being "donated" to the city.[26]

After several months, a combination of factors had effectively stalled the project in its tracks. The Parks Board went on public record in the newspapers stating it had a policy in place against placing new statues in a public park. Nor were the City Council's Parks and Public Grounds Committee offering any solutions to the League's petition. The Municipal Art Commission, which on the merits of its advisory mandate seemed to be in the best position of authority to assist and move the project forward, deferred making a recommendation on the grounds that is "could not make policy decisions for the Council nor any department of city government."[27]

The opposition from the Art Commission members appears to be rooted in value judgements of what was considered acceptable as new public art, even when freely offered to the city. A lack of basic detail in how the statue would appear, and who would be creating it, no doubt hindered the review of the first League petition and in turn, securing any support for it amongst the Art Commission members. At the Parks level, their reluctance to support the Erikson statue was a matter of policy borne out of both limitation (new memorial statues could be placed only in public squares and street intersections) and an established authority to exercise "censorship over any statuary, monuments or works of art presented to the city."[28]

Aside from further discussion of possible sites, a meeting held in January 1959, between Robert Durham and League members produced no results. A second petition was sent by the League to Mayor Clinton on February 13, 1959. It differed only in offering a statue of Erikson for placement in an unnamed city park. The Board of Park Commissioners replied with a letter to the City Council, to the effect that not only was placement of a new statue in a city park not possible, but that groups like the Leif Erikson League should be instead encouraged to offer "living memorials" to the city as expressions of tribute.[29] The degree to which the term "living memorials" was clarified for the benefit of the League's members is an open question. However, the new petition under File No. 236587 was again referred to the Municipal Art Commission for review and recommendations. As before with the first petitions' review, the Art Commission would not offer a formal recommendation to accept the statue for the city, but did attempt to show its support for the League by voting approval on a motion that the League proceed with creating a design of the statue. At their meeting on March 13, Detlie went on record that the Commission should encourage the League to create the sculpture in as fine a fashion as can be created, and that the Commission would in turn stand ready to recommend a suitable location.

The League membership decided to hold a contest at the Norway Center to select a sculptor to undertake the design of the statue. August Werner was not among those who submitted a design for consideration, but regardless, became the sculptor in charge. Years later, the League's President and chief fundraiser for the statue, Ted Nakkerud, recalled Werner as being adamant in his desire to undertake the design.[30] Werner's position on the matter was that it was the League who asked him to create the statue.[31] The outcome was one born of both necessity and mutual agreement. By March 1959, Werner was appearing in the local press in connection with the project as the confirmed sculptor for the statue.

Another local sculptor weighed in on the debate the following month. James Wehn, the sculptor who had modeled the [*Chief Seattle*] fountain statue and a host of other sculptures in bronze around the city, was asked by a reporter to comment on the Mayor's preference for living memorials over new statues for city parks. Wehn's reply was supportive, and pointed out that art by its very nature is difficult—if not impossible—to quantify: "'Saying we have too many statues is like saying we have a surplus of poetry … or too many books, or paintings. Perhaps we shall be judged by our sculptures.'"[32] A longtime figure in the Seattle arts community, Wehn was no stranger to the intricacies of city government when it came to having a design approved. It was not until 1936 that his medallion with the profile portrait of Chief Seattle had been approved by the City Council and adopted as the official city seal.

Wehn was also familiar with the Municipal Art Commission, having served on it as one of the founding members in 1955. Once his tenure ended August 1, 1957, he elected not to participate further with the group. He turned over his Chairmanship of the Painting, Sculpture & Crafts Committee to another sculptor on the Commission, Everett DuPen.

While Werner and the League were in agreement that he was up to the task, it required an uneasy alliance between the sculptor and Ted Nakkerud. Despite a desire towards a common goal, personality clashes between these two men and a third, architect John Engan, would later offer new challenges to seeing the statue through to completion.

While discussions with the Municipal Art Commission were on temporary hold, Werner spent the year developing his design for the statue with League members. Minutes from meetings of the League reflect internal discussions about how the figure of Erikson should be portrayed. Werner conceptualized the Viking as a scout wearing leggings, a conical helmet, a sheathed sword on a belt, and a Christian cross worn around the neck. One of Werner's sketches of the monumental statue contained details telling in their omission as well: a shield was left out, as a casting cost-saving measure; the right hand, empty in the sketch, would later hold an ax added to the design; and the helmet lacked horns, unlike the figure of Erikson seen in the 1939 plaque.

Throughout the process of the statue's design review by elements of city government, the League membership, under the direction of Nakkerud, continued efforts at fundraising to support the project. Donations of money and offers of materials were generously given, and in respect to many public sculpture projects, this was one challenge that while difficult, was not insurmountable as a concern. Funds collected by the League from bazaars and festivals, pledges of cash from local Norwegian-American businesses, even loans taken out by League committee members went to support the cause. The statue also found voice as well through the locally published Norwegian language newspaper *Washington Posten*: "et framstöd for Norskdommen" and "We have had this vision for 60 years."[33]

It was a vision that had so far been refused endorsement by both the Municipal Art Commission and the Parks Department. The League however was persistent. At the January 14, 1960, meeting of the Art Commission members, Chairman Schulman reported that a meeting was being planned between Nakkerud, Mayor Clinton, and a representative of the Art Commission to discuss terms for an agreement regarding the donation of a statue to the city. A second meeting between Durham of the Commission and the Mayor yielded little in the way of progress. The Mayor's focus was on the upcoming Century 21 Exposition with all eyes turned towards Seattle, and wanted "beautification projects that would promote fountains as well as sculpture."[34]

The following month finally saw movement with the Art Commission review. At the meeting on March 10, 1960, Nakkerud produced the sketch by Werner for review to the assorted members. The Commission still asserted the same noncommittal message it had continued to offer the League for the past two years. The acceptability of the statue was still called into question, and had to be determined before any decision or offer could be made as to its placement. Furthermore, the sketches alone were not enough to determine the quality of the statue design. Commissioner Frank McCaffrey suggested that the League needed to have a three-dimensional model of the statue design made. Motions were made by the group in favor of this approach, and also to have Chairman Robert Schulman consult with both the City Council and the League's legal counsel on options for tax exemption status of the project's funds.

While a promising development, the next phase of the Leif Erikson statue proved to be a challenge for both Werner and the League. As with previous sculptures, Werner worked on the model for the statue in his home, in this instance constructing a four-foot model first in clay, then plaster over a period of several months. Lacking a live model for his portrait subject, Werner drew upon the familiar for his inspiration. He took the face of his own father, Christian Werner, and used it for the likeness of Leif Erikson in the figure drawings and subsequent models for the statue. Like his natural ability in sculpture, the representation of the model was as unconscious as it was immediate: "all of a sudden there was father's face."[35] The model of the Viking was adapted from the sketch, with two differences. Where before the right leg had been shown placed forward, now the figure stood with legs straddling the base. Also, the figure now held an ax in the right hand, which previously had been empty.

Like many of the other statue committee members of the League, their president, Nakkerud, felt a vested interest in the project. He and a second League member, John Engan, agreed to provide assistance with the construction of the model on Werner's dining room table. The sculptor's first wife, Gertrude, had passed away in 1958, so the prospect of some company was perhaps one factor which persuaded Werner to accept their offer of support.

The statue was unlike any sculpture Werner had undertaken previously. It was his first, full figure model, and his acceptance of assistance in its construction was a reflection of the sculptor's lack of formal training in the medium. As much as Nakkerud and Engan wished to ensure the

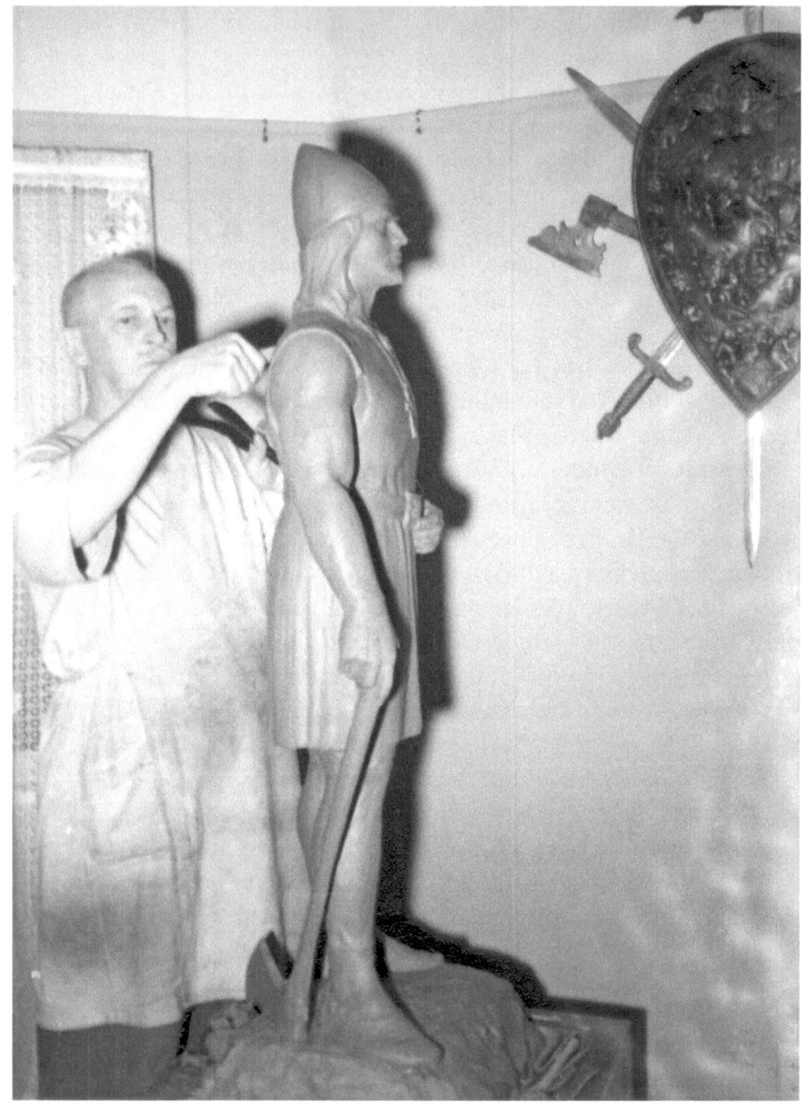

August Werner sculpting clay maquette of Leif Erikson statue, Seattle. Ca. 1961. Photographer unknown. August Werner Photograph Collection, Special Collections, University of Washington Libraries.

project benefited from their participation, their presence also helped Werner with the model's construction. Werner also still lacked a formal studio, preferring to model busts and other works out of a spare bedroom at his home residence in North Seattle. However, the time spent in

Werner's home proved productive, with the three men often working all day and into the early hours of the following morning.

By early October 1960, the model was completed in plaster. It was assembled in three parts: the legs and waist, torso with arms, and finally, the head adorned with a helmet. As a measure of stability, Engan had suggested that additional supports be placed to brace the model as the plaster cured, but Werner disagreed. Part of the reasoning was that the sculptor had contacted a reporter from the *Seattle Times* to come see the model the next day, and any supports visible might convey an impression the work was not yet complete.

Nakkerud and Engan departed for the night. As soon as he arrived home, Nakkerud told his wife, "if anyone calls, don't wake me before 7:00 am."[36]

The architect's reservations were well founded. Werner made calls to both men early the next morning to report "my boy Leif is in a thousand pieces."[37] An already tense relationship between the three men was further exacerbated by the comment, with Engan finally deciding he had enough and would no longer work with Werner. Nakkerud returned to the sculptor's house, and he and Werner repaired the damaged model using a combination of metal rods, more plaster and toothpicks.

The repairs were successful, and both the model and Werner's earlier sketches were offered on display at the October 9 Leif Erikson Day Festival held at the Norway Center auditorium in Seattle. Information included mention that a large portion of the statue's funding was secured, and that the model would soon be traveling to a foundry in Norway for casting into bronze.

On October 30, the League held a meeting at Werner's studio to formally approve the model, and to designate both Werner and statue committee member Edvard Mahlum to secure services for the enlargement and casting of the statue into bronze. An architect by profession, Mahlum was a logical choice to replace Engan. Still to be determined as well, was the city's acceptance of the model as an artwork of suitable quality. The determination of this lay in the control of the Municipal Art Commission membership, with their final recommendation to the city on both the question of quality and also placement.

By early November, the Art Commission members had visited Werner's home to view the model for the proposed statue. But if the League was hoping this would help bring the matter to a conclusion and a final endorsement by the city, they were mistaken. At the MAC meeting on November 17, Chairman Schulman initiated the discussion by asking the assembled members if the statue was "appropriate for the City to accept from an aesthetic point of view."[38]

As Nakkerud looked on, a heated debate ensued between the members. Dr. J. H. Lehmann asserted the model should instead be submitted to a panel of professional sculptors for their review and evaluation, calling into direct question Werner's capabilities as a sculptor, while also opening the door for further prolonged debate. Both McCaffrey and O.E. Holmdahl objected to Lehmann's suggestion, and Holmdahl was vocal in his opposition saying the commission "had no right to expose the work to other sculptors, and besides they all have their own likes and dislikes and would find things wrong with any sculpture that was not their own."[39] Also in favor of the sculpture were members Blanchet and Conway.

The lone sculptor on the review panel, Everett DuPen, expressed direct reservations about the quality of the model. DuPen was also of the opinion that the sculptor chosen to do the statue should also be the one to determine its location (an opinion not shared by the Parks Board). Member James Hussey agreed with DuPen, and added that it was the commission's mandate to uphold the highest standards of art and make recommendations to this effect for the city. Lehman echoed this sentiment, and further raised the prospect of the city being deluged with offers of inferior works of art in the name of goodwill.

It was Schulman who finally offered a suggestion that addressed the question of placement for the statue, and lay to rest deliberations as to the issue of quality in the work so that the commission might make a united determination. Schulman informed the group that he had recently met with Howard Burke, Manager for the Port of Seattle, and that Burke had offered to place the 16-foot statue at either the Salmon Bay Terminal or the Shilshole Boat Moorage.[40] Either of these options would also serve to fulfill a belief shared by several members of the Art Commission, that the Viking statue would best find appropriate placement at a site facing the water. Nakkerud indicated that of the two sites offered, the League would prefer the Shilshole location. As further incentive to spur a decision, Nakkerud also reported that the League had only $4,000 remaining for the total project cost of $40,000. In quick order, McCaffrey was asked by the Chairman if he would amend an earlier motion made for the commission to approve the statue, with the added stipulation that the statue would be accepted by the Port on behalf of the city and placed in Shilshole. McCaffrey agreed, and the motion passed unanimously.

On February 23, 1962, the Port of Seattle's Capital Improvements Committee sent a final recommendation to the Port's General Manager,

Howard Burke, that the League's placement of the statue at the marina should be approved. At this point a formality, the recommendation was passed unanimously at a Port Commission meeting four days later, on February 27, 1962.

As an interesting side note, in the months leading up to the November 17, 1960, meeting of the Art Commission, the Port of Seattle had been discussing for months with the Park Board another project involving the completion of a breakwater at the north entrance to the Shilshole Bay Marina. Since part of the breakwater was on land controlled by Parks, the Port negotiated a deal where Parks would pay $20,000 in compensation

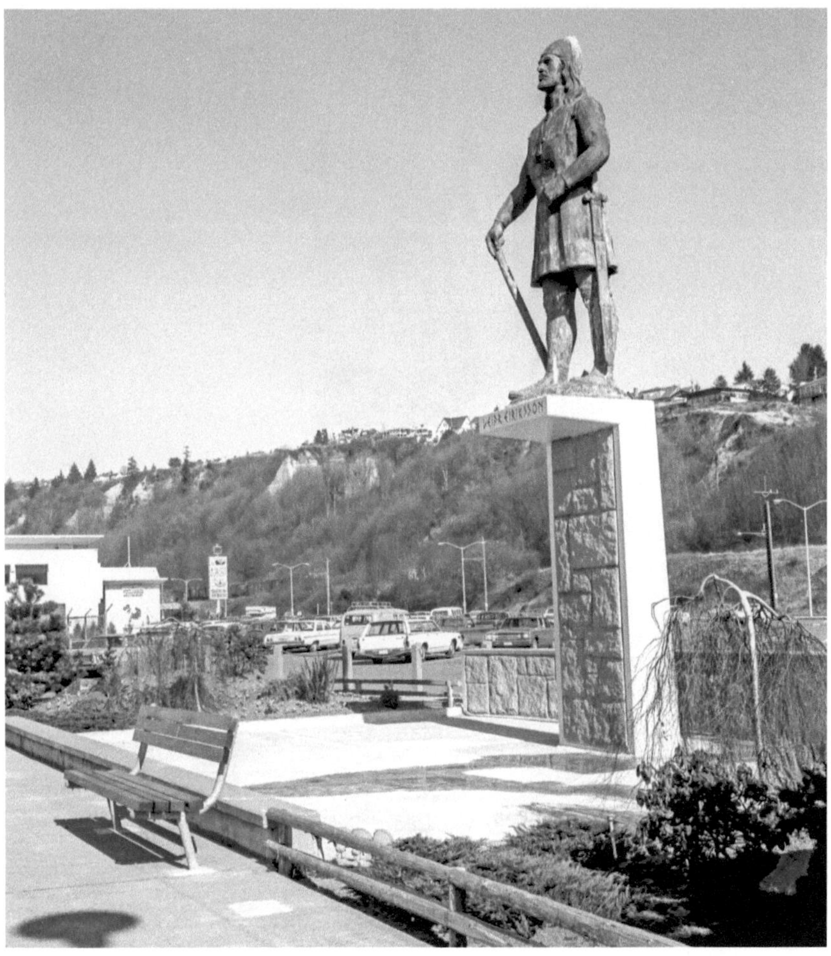

Leif Erikson **by August Werner. 1962. Courtesy Port of Seattle.**

to the Port for its share of the project. The final invoice was sent to George Fahey, President of the Board of Parks Commissioners on November 23, just six days after the agreement proposed by the Port for the statue was ratified by the Art Commission.[41] It would be easy to view the Port as doing the Parks Department a favor by helping out with the placement of the Leif Erikson statue, in order to make the $20,000 bill owing to the Port all the more palatable to the Parks Department.

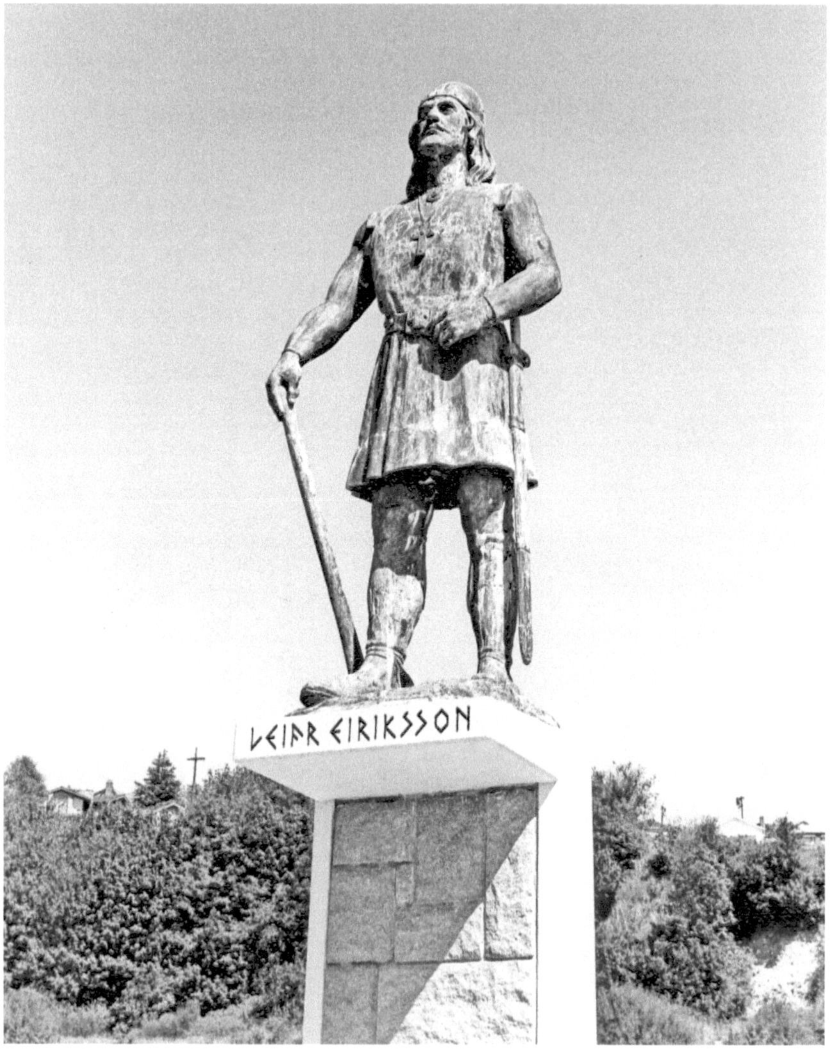

Leif Erikson by August Werner. 1962. Courtesy Port of Seattle.

Once the location of the statue was determined and the city in agreement to accept it as a new public artwork, there remained the challenge of enlarging the four-foot maquette to monumental proportions for final casting in bronze. Werner and Mahlum had been charged with this task by the League, with the expectation by Nakkerud and other League members that the final work would take place at a foundry in Norway.

While assistance was available to provide the statue's fourteen-foot-high base of Norwegian blue granite through Nakkerud's contact, Askim Stenhuggeri in Oslo, no cost-effective source for the casting was identified overseas. A similar appeal made by Nakkerud to the Sculpture House Company foundry in New York placed the cost of the enlargement alone at $3,875, with the sixteen-foot-high plaster version ready in six months, but the agreement went unsigned.[42] Another $9,700 was anticipated for the bronze casting to be done in Norway. In the final analysis, the logistics and costs for both New York and Norway were prohibitive.

Werner provided a solution through his contacts with the University of Washington, and was able to suggest two artists in Berkeley, California, who could undertake both the enlargement and casting in bronze using the lost-wax method. The choice ultimately resulted in yet more controversy over the statue and increased animosity between Nakkerud and Werner.

One of the artists in California, a Greek sculptor named Spero Anargyros, spent several months to create the enlargement in plaster to a four-to-one proportional size. It was completed in time for the Leif Erikson Day Festival in Seattle, which had become one of the annual progress reports on the statue for the League membership, and the Norwegian and Icelandic communities. That year's program for October 8, 1961, featured a photograph of August Werner posing with arms crossed in front of the monumental Viking, with the smaller model to one side.

In that same year, Nakkerud received a phone call from Werner's other artist contact in California, Franco Vianello, requesting more funds. Vianello had misjudged the amount of bronze needed for the enlargement's proportions, which had increased the casting cost from $10,000 to $15,000. When asked later about the cost overrun, Nakkerud would not confirm how much over the $40,000 that had been collected the project was needed for completion, saying only that it had been "taken care of."[43]

With notification of the final cast for the statue delayed, Nakkerud made a visit down to Berkeley to assess the project firsthand. He was greeted by the sight of "a U.W. female faculty member sunbathing at the foot of the statue wearing only a pair of white tennis shoes and Franco

[Vianello] combing the beaches for bronze propellers that might have washed up from ships."[44] Both Werner's lack of oversight and inexperience as a sculptor with the lost wax process were most likely contributing factors to this latest setback. With Nakkerud's arrival and assistance on the funding front, the bronze casting finally proceeded and produced a heroic-scale statue measuring fourteen-and-a-half feet tall by six feet wide and four-and-a-half feet from front to back.

Due to a lack of bronze used in the final casting, the hip section of the statue's Viking figure was later determined to be only a half-inch in thickness. As a solution, cement was pumped into the hollow cast, thereby enabling it to be strengthened for support prior to installation. The casting oversight was ironic, given Werner's earlier experience with his scale model which had also collapsed from lack of proper support. With the addition of the cement, the statue was now deemed solid enough for public display.

Nakkerud arranged for the final transportation of the four-ton statue by truck back to Seattle on May 10, 1962. Even this task was not without its complications. At the Oregon border, the truck ran afoul of Teamsters Union members who objected to the transport not being done by Union drivers. With his background in labor relations, Nakkerud again interceded, and the truck was allowed to go on its way north.

Throughout February 1962, Ed Mahlum continued to coordinate the final details of the statue's installation at Shilshole Marina with both the Art Commission and the Port of Seattle. A plan for the statue, base and site development outlined by Mahlum's architectural firm was sent to Kenneth King, Planning Director for the Port of Seattle on February 9, 1962. It showed a breakdown of costs for the concrete walls and footings, use of a crane to install the statue, and work to lay the granite being shipped from Norway. All told, the estimated construction time was five weeks, and set to begin May 14, 1962. The plan also called for the public unveiling of the statue to take place at 3:00 pm on June 17, 1962, to coincide with "Icelandic National Day" and the Century 21 Exposition in Seattle.

A follow-up memorandum from the Capital Improvements Committee for the Port of Seattle to Howard Burke, General Manager for the Port, recommended approval of the statue installation plan on February 23, 1962, with the stipulation that the Port of Seattle would maintain the statue and surrounding grounds going forward. The Committee highlighted that the "art and cultural value" of the statue would enhance the marina to the general public.[45] The recommendation was passed unanimously at a Port Commission meeting four days later, on February 27, 1962.

Both Mahlum and the Port of Seattle managed the final installation

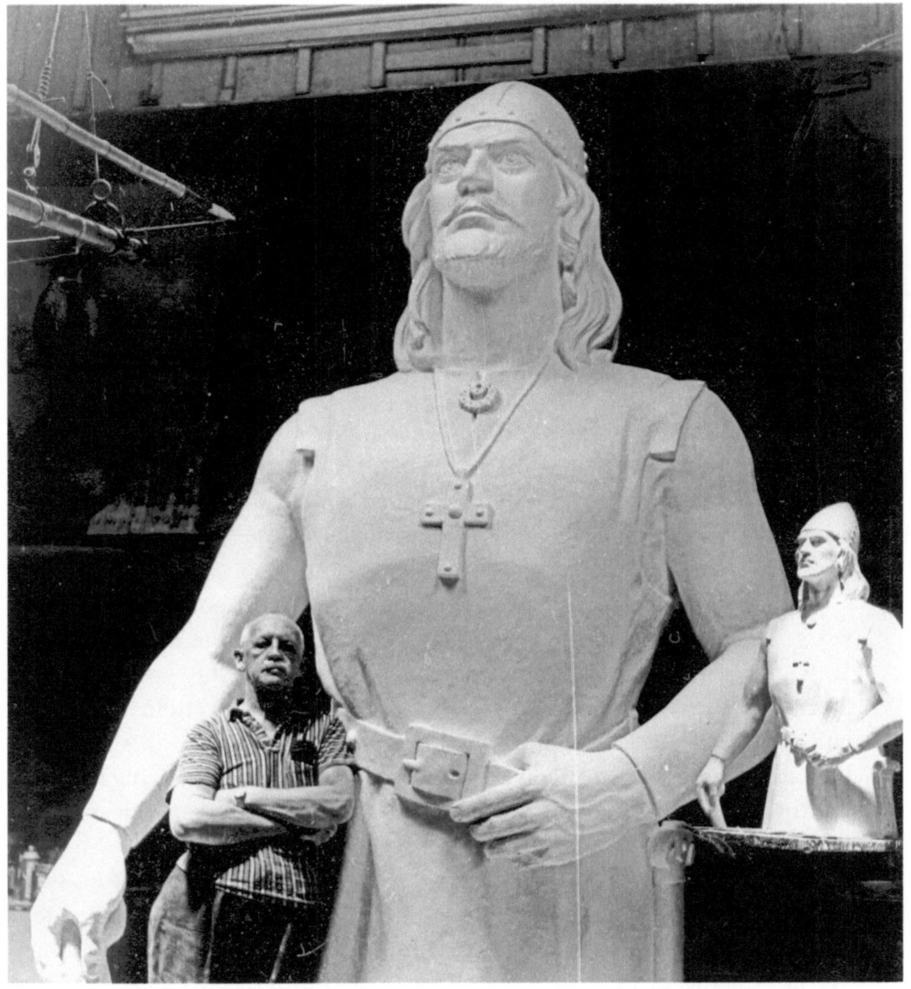

Sculptor August Werner posing with maquette and cast mold of Leif Erikson statue. Photograph 1961. Photographer unknown. August Werner Collection, Nordic Heritage Museum.

of the Leif Erikson statue onto a plinth base that was sixteen feet tall and decorated with Norwegian blue granite shipped from Oslo. The site was chosen for its setting south of the Port's new $1,000,000 administration building at the marina, with the statue facing the water, as agreed to by the League. In a show of support for the project, the Port paid the $2,000 cost to add a square reflecting pond surrounding the base, complete with park benches and a masonry wall.

Werner's involvement as the project's sculptor became very limited after February 1962. The League under Nakkerud's direction took charge of publicity and planning for the unveiling ceremony held on June 17 that year, with dignitaries from Norway and Iceland attending as well as Governor Albert Rosellini and Mayor Gordon Clinton. Of the eight local Seattle citizen's awarded St. Olav's medal on the day of the unveiling by the Norwegian Ambassador to the United States, Paul Koth, both Nakkerud and Mahlum were so honored but Werner was not. For the unveiling program Werner was allowed to direct the Norwegian Male Chorus in its opening rendition of the National Anthem, and was briefly introduced as the sculptor, while Mahlum shared introductions as the architect and Nakkerud presented the statue to the city. In a final omission, Werner's name was left off the base of the statue as the sculptor credited for its design. Not until 2007, after the statue had been re-installed at Shilshole's Central Plaza and the names of 2,351 Scandinavian immigrants added to fourteen runestones placed around the statue, was Werner's name finally added to the statue's base.[46]

That Nakkerud disliked Werner during the Leif Erikson statue project years is clearly evident. And yet, a postcard featuring the new statue at Shilshole sent to the retired University of Washington professor by Nakkerud a year following the public dedication offered a note of consolation: "Dear friend: I think I know what you will say about this card ... the next shall be better!"[47] Nakkerud may be credited to his having helped see the project through to its completion, but was also a tireless self-promoter and much like Werner in this respect.

In April 1977, Nakkerud petitioned Captain Winslow Buxton, the Superintendent of the Shilshole Bay Marina, that his name be added to the dedication plaque for the statue, while making no mention of adding Werner's name as well. In July that year, Buxton wrote back to Asborn Nordheim, Vice President of the Leif Erikson League, that Nakkerud's name had been added. In the years that have followed since its installation, the League has continued to serve as a community body dedicated to the preservation of the statue as a public monument. In this respect, an agreement reached in 1985 between the Port and the League reflects a joint stewardship interest in allowing the statue to weather naturally over time.

For Werner, the Leif Erikson statue represents his most signatory artwork in many respects. It was the last major sculpture project he undertook in his lifetime. Its completion marked a new phase in his personal life, with marriage to his second wife, Agnes Enge, on April 12, 1962, and subsequent adoption of a stepson, Kleve.

The Leif Erikson statue served as one of the last historical figurative sculptures to find placement as a public sculpture both owned by the City of Seattle and placed on city-controlled property. After 1962, Modern art sculpture became the preferred standard for acceptable public art within the city. A few notable exceptions since Werner's time have included the Sadako Sasaki Peace Child statue in Seattle's Peace Park (1990); a 16-foot bronze statue of Vladimir Lenin by Emil Venkov placed in the Freemont neighborhood of Seattle (1995); a bronze sculpture of the musician Jimi Hendrix placed in Capitol Hill neighborhood (1997); and a statue of Sri Chinmoy installed on Lake Union (2010).

The successful installation of the Leif Erikson statue at Shilshole did not mark the end of the statue design, and Werner's legacy, for other venues on the international scene. Since 1962, three, ten-foot copies of Werner's original Leif Erikson statue design were cast in bronze and installed in Trondheim, Norway (1997), Brattahlid (Qassiarsuk), Greenland (2000) and L'Anse aux Meadows, Newfoundland (2013). These other versions of the Werner statue were near copies, and had only the cross worn on the figure's neck and his footwear changed from Werner's original design.

Werner received notable recognition for his many other lifetime achievements and contributions to the Norwegian-American community and for promoting Scandinavian culture and the arts. As a tribute to his assistance with the Leif Erikson League, on May 1, 1967, he became a life member of Sons of Norway Lodge no. 1 in Seattle. For his contributions to Scandinavian music, culture and the fine arts, Werner was later decorated with medals awarded by King Olav V of Norway and King Gustav VI Adolf of Sweden. He also received the "Honorary Distinguished Citizen" award from John A. Cherberg, the Lieutenant Governor of Washington State, in 1979.

Werner died on August 10, 1980, at the age of 87. His monumental statue to Erikson still looks out over the water to this day.

Abbreviations

Sources frequently cited have been identified by the following abbreviations:

AVLP Alonzo Victor Lewis Papers. Accession no. GA1959.94. Special Collections. Washington State Historical Society, Tacoma, WA.

ASWP Allen S. Weller Papers. Series no. 12/1/20. University of Illinois Archives, Urbana–Champaign, IL.

AWP August Werner Papers. Accession nos. 82.120; 82.120wc. Special Collections Archives. Nordic Heritage Museum, Seattle, WA.

HAGC "Artist" File for John C. Ely. Henry Art Gallery Collection, Seattle, WA.

JAWP James A. Wehn Papers. Accession no. GA1973.52. Special Collections. Washington State Historical Society, Tacoma, WA.

LTP Lorado Taft Papers, 1857–1953. Series no. 26/20/16. University of Illinois Archives, Urbana–Champaign, IL.

PSHF Port of Seattle History Files-Shilshole Bay Marina. Series no. PS667-29-0-48. Puget Sound Regional Branch, Washington State Archives, Bellevue, WA.

SC-SPL Special Collections. Seattle Public Library (Central Branch), Seattle, WA.

SC-UWL Special Collections. University of Washington Libraries, Seattle, WA.

SC-WSHS Special Collections. Washington State Historical Society, Tacoma, WA.

SCA-NHM Special Collections Archives. Nordic Heritage Museum, Seattle, WA.

SMA Seattle Municipal Archives, Seattle, WA.

UDCA United Daughters of the Confederacy Archives, Richmond, VA.

WSA Division of Archives & Records Management. Washington State Archives, Olympia, WA.

Chapter Notes

Chapter 1

1. "Society" section, *Seattle Daily Times*, 2 April 1905, 4.

2. "Not Ready with Design," *Seattle Daily Times*, 9 May 1905, 5.

3. [LTP] Edmond S. Meany to Lorado Taft, 11 April 1905, 2.

4. Harry B. Bauer, "The George Washington Statue—U. of W.'s Patriotic Shrine," *Seattle Times*, 21 May 1960, 3.

5. "Taft Picks Site for Statue," *Seattle Daily Times*, 2 November 1905, 5.

6. *Ibid.*

7. [LTP] "Lorado Taft on 'Art in America,'" *Seattle Post-Intelligencer*, 2 November 1905, 16.

8. "Statue of George Washington to be Erected at U. of W. and Sculptor Lorado Taft," *Seattle Daily Times*, 25 February 1907, 1.

9. [LTP] Elinor Ingersoll Thorne to Dr. Henry Suzzallo, 5 February 1919, 2. As of October 2015, the plaster cast model of Taft's design resides in an alcove overlooking the balcony of the Marion Palace Theater, in Marion, Ohio.

10. [LTP] Charles R. Alloway, *Our Country's Father*, reprinted in telephone cable, *Chicago Tribune* to Lorado Taft, 31 January 1910.

11. Alansa Bates, ed., "UW Hails 75th Anniversary of A-Y-P Exposition," *Washington Alumnus Digest* (1984): 2.

12. Bauer.

13. [SCA-NHM] M.M. Godman et al., "Washington Statue," *Report of the Alaska-Yukon-Pacific Exposition Commission of the State of Washington* (Seattle: The Pacific Press, Inc., 1909), 135.

14. There are several sources that cite the official unveiling of the George Washington statue having occurred on Flag Day, June 14, 1909 (including the D.A.R. dedication plaque on the base of the statue). However, in a letter to University President Henry Suzzallo from Elinor Ingersoll Thorne, one of the original members of the Rainier Chapter's Statue Committee, she had cited the date of the unveiling as June 1, 1909, "at the opening of the Alaska, Yukon, Pacific Exposition." Thorne wrote her letter ten years after the dedication ceremony, which may explain the date discrepancy. See: [LTP] Thorne to Suzzallo, 2. Also: Bauer, 3; Stein and Becker, 60.

15. Alan J. Stein, Paula Becker and the HistoryLink Staff, *Washington's First World's Fair—Alaska-Yukon-Pacific Exposition, A Timeline History* (Seattle: History Ink, 2009), 135.

16. Frank Lynch, "Too Many Statues? It's News to Him," *Seattle Post-Intelligencer*, 1 April 1959, 9.

17. "Plea for Beauty," *Seattle Daily Times*, 17 March 1920, 3.

18. "G. Washington on Pedestal; That Pleases Sculptor Taft," *Seattle Daily Times*, 14 November 1934, 1.

19. "George Washington's Feet Too Big for Ten-Foot Base," *Seattle Daily Times*, 12 October 1930, 11.

20. [ASWP] Lorado Taft to R.W. Lahr, 1 October 1935.

21. "Washington Goes for W.P.A. 'Ride,'" *Seattle Daily Times*, 9 August 1938, 5.

Chapter 2

1. [SC-UWL] Thomas Burke to Edmund [*sic*] S. Meany, 28 December 1906, Edmond S. Meany Papers, 1877–1935.

2. [SC-SPL] Seattle Chamber of Commerce, "Regular Meeting of the Board of

Trustees, Seattle, Wash.," 31 October 1906, *Record of the Minutes of the Meetings of Seattle Chamber of Commerce* (Seattle: [The Chamber], 1906), 283.

3. [SC-SPL] Seattle Chamber of Commerce, "Regular Meeting of the Board of Trustees, Seattle, Wash.," 7 November 1906, *Record of the Minutes of the Meetings of Seattle Chamber of Commerce* (Seattle: [The Chamber], 1906), 289.

4. [SC-SPL] Roland W. Cotterill, comp., *Report of the Board of Park Commissioners—Seventh Annual Report* (Seattle: Lowman & Hanford, 1910), 10–11.

5. [SC-UWL] M.F. Backus to William H. Seward, 14 December 1906, Edmond S. Meany Papers.

6. Burke to Meany.

7. "Seward Statue Contract Let," *Seattle Daily Times*, 17 June 1907, 2.

8. Lorado Taft, *The History of American Sculpture* (New York: The MacMillan Company, 1924), 540.

9. "Proposes to put Statue of Seward in Pioneer Place," *Seattle Post-Intelligencer*, 8 October 1909, 1.

10. Cotterill, 39.

11. [SMA] City of Seattle, *The Charter of the City of Seattle* (Seattle: Lowman & Hanford, 1911), 77–78.

12. *Ibid.*, 78–79.

13. "Memorial to Former Governor Unveiled," *Seattle Daily Times*, 23 July 1913, 19.

14. *Ibid.*

15. [SMA] Hans A. Thompson to Alf Collins, 20 October 1971, Department of Parks and Recreation, Parks Superintendent Subject Files, 1936–1993.

Chapter 3

1. Taft, *The History of American Sculpture*, 570.

2. Mary T. Henry, research by Olaf Kvamme, "Frolich, Finn Haakon (1868–1947), Sculptor," 20 November 2008, http://www.historylink.org/index.cfm?DisplayPage=output.cfm&file_id=8849); originally from: Margaret Guilford-Kardell, comp., "Sea Dog and Sea Wolf at Play in the Valley of the Moon," *The Californians* (January/February 1991): 14–23. The sculptor James Wehn also confirmed the arrival of Frolich to Seattle as June, 1908. See: [JAWP] James A. Wehn, *History of the Chief Seattle Statue* (unpublished manuscript, 1962): 6.

3. "Wuxtra! Wuxtra! Fun Breaks Loose in Gobs," *Seattle Daily Times*, 4 December 1910, 25.

4. "Last Act of Old University Building—the production of Exposition's Sculptural Masterpiece," *Seattle Sunday Times*, 4 October 1908, 48.

5. *Ibid.*

6. "A.-Y.-P. Statuary and Monuments," *Seattle Sunday Times*, 14 February 1909, 14.

7. *Ibid.*

8. "1909 Ledger," Roman Bronze Works Archive, 249. The ledger entry for Frolich's order on July 19, 1909, does not specify the sculpture or project that was involved in the casting.

9. "Many Praise Idea of Monument to Hill," *Seattle Sunday Times*, 7 March 1909, 22.

10. "The bust of James J. Hill...," *Seattle Sunday Times*, 21 February 1909, 6.

11. Alan J. Stein, Paula Becker, et al., *Washington's First World's Fair—Alaska-Yukon-Pacific Exposition—A Timeline History*, 91.

12. *Ibid.*, 47.

13. "Many Praise Idea of Monument to Hill."

14. "Johnson Unveils Hill Monument," *San Francisco Call*, no. 65 (August 4, 1909): 3.

15. F.M. Foulser, "The Cruise of the Viking Ship," *The Rudder*, vol. XXIII, no. 4 (April, 1910): 344.

16. James Elverson, "Latter-Day Vikings," *Seattle Sunday Times*, 13 February 1910, 59.

17. "Unveil Bust of Norse Composer," *Seattle Daily Times*, 3 September 1917, 7.

18. [SCA-NHM] M.M. Godman, et al., "Washington Statue," *Report of the Alaska-Yukon-Pacific Exposition Commission of the State of Washington*, 135.

19. Mary T. Henry, "Finn Haakon Frolich," *Nordic Heritage Museum Historical Journal*, vol. 5, no. 1 (Winter/Spring 2009): 38.

20. "Sculptor Frolich Accused by Wife of Stealing Baby," *Seattle Sunday Times*, 16 July 1911, 19.

21. Lionel Rolfe, "Notes of a Californian Bohemian—Jack London May have Slept Here," n.d. [2001] www.dabelly.com/columns/bohemian43.htm.

22. Frolich was not the only sculptor from Seattle to create a large-sized bust of Amundsen from life. The sculptor Alonzo Victor Lewis also modeled a three-foot high sculpture bust of the polar explorer, when Amundsen visited the Pacific Northwest in 1926. Amundsen signed the Lewis bust, which was

cast into gypsum and later disappeared from the artist's studio following his death in 1946. The bust was rediscovered in a First Avenue, Seattle antique shop by Robert Stevens. Two copies of the bust were cast into bronze and installed in 1976 at Kings Bay, Spitsbergen, Norway and Nome, Alaska, respectively.

Chapter 4

1. "Umbrella Man Statue Sale begins Monday," *Seattle Sunday Times*, 20 February 1910, 7.

2. [JAWP] Wehn, *History of the Chief Seattle Statue*, 5.

3. *Ibid.*

4. Sally Hayman, "Looking Back on the Creation of a Landmark ... Sculptor James Wehn Remembers How it Was," *Seattle Post-Intelligencer*, 13 May 1973, 13.

5. "The Unveiling of the Cushman Statue at the Washington State Historical Society, Tacoma, Washington, January 16, 1912," *Washington State Historical Society Publications*, vol. 2 (1907–1914): 245.

6. Don Sherwood, "Jefferson Park (Golf)," Sherwood Park History files, 1972–1977, http://clerk.seattle.gov/~F_archives/sherwood/JeffersonPkGolf.pdf.

7. Martin Pool, "Jefferson Park Golf Course, Seattle, WA," February 2015, http://thewsga.org/jefferson-park-golf-course-a-centennial-celebration/.

8. *Ibid.*

9. *Ibid.*

10. "Sherwood Gillespy Memorial Fount at City Golf Links," *Seattle Daily Times*, 6 June 1915, 40.

11. "1915 Ledger," Roman Bronze Works Archive, 356.

12. Janice Krenmayr, "A Golfer's View can be superb," *Seattle Times*, 24 March 1963, 2.

13. "Yesler Tablet on Courthouse Urged," *Seattle Daily Times*, April 19, 1915, 3.

14. [JAWP] Edmond S. Meany to James A. Wehn, 4 April 1915.

15. "The Unveiling of the Cushman Statue at the Washington State Historical Society, Tacoma, Washington, January 16, 1912," 253–254.

Chapter 5

1. William H. Lee, *Glimpses of the Alaska-Yukon-Pacific Exposition*, 1.

2. Nancy Burkhalter and David Wilma,

"Memorial Day in Washington State," May 24, 2007, http://www.historylink.org/File/7777.

3. [UDCA] Minutes of the 29th Annual Convention of the United Daughters of the Confederacy Inc. (1922), 313. The memorial at Lake View has been referred to by various names, including: the United Confederate Veterans (U.C.V.) memorial; the Confederate States of America (C.S.A.) memorial; the Confederate Veterans of America (C.V.A.) memorial; and through association of their primary sponsor, as the United Daughters of the Confederacy (U.D.C.) memorial.

4. *Granite Cutters' Journal*, vol. 45 (1921): 32.

5. Majorie Ann Reeves, *A Chapter in Pacific Northwest History* (Seattle: Tommie Press, 2006), 35.

6. [JAWP] Wehn, *History of the Chief Seattle Statue*, 6–7.

7. *Ibid.*, 14.

8. *Ibid.*, 16.

9. [JAWP] James A. Wehn, dedication for the Chief Seattle Fountain, 13 November 1912.

Chapter 6

1. Thomas Newman, "Allen George Newman, A.N.A., 1875–1940" [Thomas Newman Lecture Notes] (1995), 2. The lecture offered by Thomas Newman (son of the sculptor) was held in Deerfield Beach, Florida. The notes were obtained from Newman by Jack Conklin during an undated interview.

2. *Ibid.*, 5.

3. "Seattle to get her first military statue," *Seattle Daily Times*, 14 March 1926, 22.

4. Stanley Karnow, *In Our Image: America's Empire in the Philippines* (New York: Random House Publishing Group, 2010), 375.

5. Newman, 3; Jack Conklin, email to Fred Poyner IV, July 4, 2016.

6. Newman, 4.

7. "Tacoma's Big Bid against Seattle," *Seattle Daily Times*, 25 July 1899, 1.

8. "Assault on Manilla," *Seattle Daily Times*, 19 August 1899, 1.

9. [SMA] John Resch to the Board of Park Commissioners, 8 September 1942, Park History Files—Veterans Area, Artillery.

10. Don Sherwood, "Woodland Park," Sherwood Park History Files, 1972–1977, http://www.seattle.gov/parks/history/WoodlandPk.pdf.

11. "Seattle Honors War Heroes—Veterans Dedicate Statue," *Seattle Daily Times*, 1 June

1926, 5. While Newman's statue may be credited as the first example of public statuary that was installed in Seattle as a dedicated war memorial, cases can also be made for a similar claim by either Lorado Taft's statue of Washington of 1909 (as an earlier example of an American military leader) or John Carl Ely's bronze plaques for West Seattle High School and Queen Anne High School (commemorations to the World War I military service of Seattle students) done in 1919 and 1920, respectively.

12. Lucile MacDonald, "Spanish War Vets' Ranks are Growing Thin," *Seattle Times*, 30 June 1957, 3.

Chapter 7

1. Charles T. Conover, "Judge Thomas Burke Fought for Seattle's Future," *Seattle Times*, 9 February 1950, 60.

2. Junius Rochester, "Burke, Judge Thomas (1849–1925)," January 30, 1999, www.historylink.org/index.cfm?DisplayPage=output.cfm&file_id=2610.

3. Charles T. Conover, comp. & ed., *Thomas Burke 1849–1925: His Life in Outline* (Seattle: Acme Press, 1926), 15.

4. Taft, *The History of American Sculpture*, 437.

5. Jean Stansbury Holden, "The Sculptors MacNeil," in *The World's Work ... A History of Our Time*, vol. 14, Walter Hines Page and Arthur Wilson Page (New York: Doubleday, Page, 1907): 9418.

6. Taft, *The History of American Sculpture*, 439. While the sculpture *The Sun Vow* was first modelled in Italy in 1899, it was later cast into bronze following MacNeil's return to the United States. Copies are in the collections of the Montclair Art Museum, New Jersey (1902), the Corcoran Gallery of Art, Washington, D.C. (1905), the Buffalo Bill Historical Center, in Cody, Wyoming, and several others.

7. [SC-UWL] Thomas Burke to Edmond S. Meany, 13 December 1915, Edmond S. Meany Papers, 1877–1935.

8. Taft, *The History of American Sculpture*, 445.

9. "Burke Memorial, soon to be dedicated, viewed by artist," *Seattle Daily Times*, 27 March 1930, 5.

10. Clarence Bagley, *History of King County Washington* (Chicago: The S.J. Clarke Publishing Company, 1929), 13.

11. "Suggestions pour in for Burke Memorial," *Seattle Daily Times*, 17 January 1926, 8.

12. *Ibid.*

13. "$100,000 Statue is Planned for Burke," *Seattle Municipal News*, vol. 16, no. 19 (May 8, 1926): 3.

14. [SC-UWL] Theodore N. Haller to Mrs. E.S. Meany, 29 November 1926, Edmond S. Meany papers, 1877–1935.

15. Taft, *The History of American Sculpture*, 437.

16. "Burke Memorial, Soon to be Dedicated, Viewed by Artist," *Seattle Daily Times*, 27 March 1930, 1, 5.

17. [SMA] "Judge Burke Memorial," *Park Board Minutes, June 1925-May 1929*, vol. 9 (May 16, 1929), 399.

18. [SMA] "Judge Burke Memorial," *Park Board Minutes, May 1929-August 1933*, vol. 10 (June 6, 1929), 3.

19. "Burke Monument now en route to Volunteer Park," *Seattle Daily Times*, 20 October 1929, 11.

20. "City Pays Tribute to memory of Late Judge," *Seattle Daily Times*, 6 April 1930, 1.

21. *Ibid.*

22. Bagley, 17.

23. "Sculptor of Burke Tribute Given Honors," *Seattle Sunday Times*, 9 August 1931, 20.

Chapter 8

1. [AVLP] Mrs. Evans to Alonzo Victor Lewis, 1 November 1909, 1.

2. [AVLP] Alonzo Victor Lewis to Bess Lewis, 7 December 1915, 1.

3. *Ibid.*, 3.

4. [SC-UWL] Alonzo Victor Lewis to Edmond S. Meany, 26 April 1915, Edmond S. Meany Papers, 1877–1935, 4.

5. [AVLP] Warren Lewis to Alonzo Victor Lewis, 7 December 1913, 2.

6. [AVLP] Roman Bronze Works, Inc. to Alonzo Victor Lewis, 17 September 1918.

7. [AVLP] Agreement between Alonzo Victor Lewis and William Nielson, 25 January 1915.

8. [AVLP] Lena Lewis to Warren Lewis, 1 September 19[?], 1–2.

9. [AVLP] Warren Lewis to Alonzo Victor Lewis, 6 May 1916.

10. "Wild Westerners of 91st Division to Hold Reunion," *Seattle Daily Times*, 19 September 1926, 16.

11. [SC-UWL] Ervin Raymond Gahringer, *Diary of Ervin Raymond Gahringer—World*

War I, 91*st* Division, 347 Machine Gun Battalion, Company B* (unpublished diary, 1918), Ervin R. Gahringer Papers, 18.

12. [SC-UWL] H.Q. 91*st* Div. A.E.F., "General Orders: No. 6," 27 January 1919, 5.

13. "Shrine to Veterans Proposed Statue of Heroic Size Ready," *Seattle Daily Times,* 23 November 1924, 22.

14. "American Doughboy Bringing Home the Bacon," *Seattle Daily Times*, 10 December 1922, 90.

15. *Ibid.*; Evergreen Washelli, "The Doughboy," *Heroes & Dignitaries—A Self-Guided Tour* (Seattle: Evergreen Washelli, 2009), 8.

16. "American Doughboy Bringing Home the Bacon," 90.

17. [AVLP] Roman Bronze Works, Inc. to Alonzo Victor Lewis, 16 October 1922, 2.

18. "Shrine to Veterans Proposed—Statue of Heroic Size Ready," 22.

19. John McClelland, Jr., *Wobbly War* (Tacoma: Washington State Historical Society, 1987), 192.

20. [SC-UWL] C.W. Ardery to L.A. Williams, 13 April 1926, Steven Fowler Chadwick Papers.

21. [SC-UWL] C.W. Ardery, Letter to S.F. Chadwick, 14 April 1926, Steven Fowler Chadwick Papers.

22. [SMA] "Special Business," *Board of Park Commissioners Minutes, June 1925-May 1929*, vol. 9 (February 23, 1928), 251.

23. [SMA] Thomas J.L. Kennedy to Philip Tindall, 12 March 1928, Comptroller File no. 115105, Seattle City Clerk's Office.

24. "Statue will be erected in tribute to Seattle men who gave their lives for nation; committee named," *Seattle Daily Times*, 12 August 1928, 1.

25. "Veteran's Memorial Row taken to Mayor," *Seattle Daily Times*, 14 August 1928, 11.

26. "Memorial Statue to be placed at new auditorium," *Seattle Daily Times*, 8 November 1928, 2.

27. "Proposed war memorial statue arouses criticism," *Seattle Daily Times*, 9 November 1928, 10.

28. [SMA] E.L. Blaine to R.V. Ankeny, 1 December 1929, Comptroller File no. 115105, Seattle City Clerk's Office.

29. "1928–1930 Ledger," Roman Bronze Works Archive, 118–119.

30. [SMA] Herbert E. Kelly, letter and report to Phillip Tindall, 4 January 1932, Comptroller File no. 134181, Seattle City Clerk's Office.

31. "Jury will be art critics of 'The Doughboy,'" *Seattle Daily Times*, 18 November 1931, 8.

32. *Ibid.*

33. *Ibid.*

34. "Scores a smacking victory," *Seattle Daily Times*, 8 February 1932, 1.

35. Evergreen Washelli, 9.

36. Frederick Case, "Stone Soldiers Never Die—Memorials may be Unheeded Reminders of those who Served in Forgotten Wars," *Seattle Times*, 27 May 1985, D-1.

37. Washington State Department of Enterprise Services, "Winged Victory Monument," n.d., www.des.wa.gov/services/facilities/Capitol Campus/MemorialsArt/Pages/Victory.aspx.

38. "Alonzo Lewis will get home," *Seattle Daily Times*, 10 February 1943, 7.

39. [SMA] Walter L. Wyckoff to Frank J. Laube, 1 February 1945, Comptroller File no. 183684. Seattle City Clerk's Office.

40. "Attorneys in Lewis Trial trade 'Blows,'" *Seattle Daily Times*, 20 March 1946, 4.

Chapter 9

1. [HAGC] Seattle Fine Arts Gallery, "Memorial Exhibit" program, April 1930.

2. [JAWP] James A. Wehn, handwritten note authorizing access for John Carl Ely, 8 April 1920.

3. "648 Graduating at University Record Class in Campus History," *Seattle Daily Times*, 18 June 1922, 13.

4. [JAWP] W. Frank Purdy to James A. Wehn, 3 October 1922.

5. [HAGC] Mabel de la Mater, "Sculptor Here Follows Work in Expressionism," *Seattle Post-Intelligencer*, 26 February 1924, [n.p.].

6. *Ibid.*

7. *Ibid.*

8. [HAGC] Frances R. Grant to John Ely, 7 October 1924.

9. [HAGC] David Plummer, "Table 1," *Catalogue of John Carl Ely's Artwork as of 31 March 1994* (March 19, 1994): 8–13. To Plummer's total number of sculptures listed, I have added both the diptych World War I panel relief from West Seattle High School and the relief plaque from Queen Anne High School.

10. John Hennes, email to Fred Poyner IV, 21 April 2016.

11. [HAGC] Wanda Von Kettler, "Seattle Boy Recognized at Eastern Art Exhibit," *Seattle Star*, 12 February 1925, [n.p.].

12. David E. Plummer, "John Carl Ely Ex-

patriate Seattle Sculptor," *Artifact* (January/February 1997): 30.

Chapter 10

1. Alice Robertson Carr to "Mr. Beckworth," n.d., William Carr Collection.

2. [SC-SPL] Seattle Chamber of Commerce, "Prefontaine Place," 14 February 1906, *Record of the Minutes of the Meetings of Seattle Chamber of Commerce* (Seattle: [The Chamber], 1906), 59.

3. [SMA] "Park Board Minutes," 23 February 1922, *Board of Park Commissioners Minutes, August, 1921–December, 1925,* vol. 8 (Seattle: The Board of Park Commissioners, 1925), 64.

4. Don Sherwood, "Prefontaine Place," Sherwood Park History files, 1972–1977, www.seattle.gov/parks/history/PrefontainePl.pdf.

5. [SMA] "Park Board Minutes," 10 October 1923, *Board of Park Commissioners Minutes, August, 1921–December, 1925,* vol. 8, 182.

6. [SMA] "For Your Information—History of Woodland Park Zoological Gardens," series no. VF-0000, Vertical Files, 1883–2011, 1.

7. *Ibid.,* 2.

8. [SMA] "Park Board Minutes," 25 April 1923, *Board of Park Commissioners Minutes, August, 1921–December, 1925,* vol. 8, 145.

9. "World's Rose Lovers to Worship at Seattle Shrine," *Seattle Daily Times*, 3 June 1923, 62.

10. [SMA] "Park Board Minutes," 27 August 1924, *Board of Park Commissioners Minutes, August, 1921–December, 1925,* vol. 8, 266.

11. [SMA] Park Board Minutes," 4 March 1925, *Board of Park Commissioners Minutes, August, 1921–December, 1925,* vol. 8, 319.

12. Junius Rochester, "Prefontaine, Francis Xavier (1838–1909)," 2 December 1998, www.historylink.org/index.cfm?DisplayPage=output.cfm&file_id=3633.

13. [SMA] "For Your Information—History of Woodland Park Zoological Gardens," 3.

14. Warren G. Harding, James W. Murphy, comp., *Speeches and Addresses of Warren G. Harding, President of the United States, Delivered during the Course of His Tour from Washington, D.C., to Alaska and Return to San Francisco, June 20 to August 2, 1923* (Washington, D.C., 1923), xi.

15. [SC-WSHS] Robert T. Barry to Menne Barry, 10 July 1923, MsSC 177, 2–3.

16. [WSA] Louis F. Hart to President Warren G. Harding, 16 February 1922, Governor's Papers, vol. 3.

17. Harding and Murphy, 338–339.

18. Boy Scouts of America, "President Harding as Honorary President of the Boy Scouts of America," *Scouting* (August 1923): 2.

19. "Chronology History of Woodland Park Zoo History, 1900–1929," www.zoo.org/about/chronologicalhistory#1900–1929.

20. "President Harding," *Elks Magazine* (September 1923): 5.

21. "Wallace Backs Fund," *Seattle Daily Times*, 30 August 1923, 3.

22. [JAWP] Lillian Hocking, Letter to "Sec'y of Elk Lodge No. 92," 21 August 1923.

23. [SMA] "Park Board Minutes," 26 November 1924, *Board of Park Commissioners Minutes, August, 1921–December, 1925,* vol. 8, 293.

24. Carr to Beckworth.

25. [SMA] Jacob Umlauff to Board of Park Commissioners, 10 May 1939, Parks History Files.

26. [SMA] Anna A. Coffin to the Chamber of Commerce, 21 February 1939, Parks History Files.

27. [SMA] Theo Johnson to the Board of Park Commissioners, 12 June 1939, Parks History Files.

28. [SMA] "Recommendations for Design Development of Zoo," *Final Report of the Citizen's Advisory Committee for the Seattle Zoo* (July 1971), A-II.

29. Byron Johnsrud, "Cannons, anyone? Unzoolike Objects must go," *Seattle Times*, 14 November 1971, A-23.

30. [SMA] Wes Uhlman, "Part IV—Project Narrative," *Local Public Works Program Application Supplement* (October 13, 1976), 8.

31. [SMA] "African Savanna Cost Estimate," *Woodland Park Zoo—African Savanna*, 30 June 1977, 12.

32. [SMA] Arthur Skolnik to City of Seattle, 1 October 1976, series no. 1611-01.

33. David Towne, phone communication to Fred Poyner IV, 12 February 2016.

34. Nina Ward (nee Carr), email to Fred Poyner IV, 27 February 2016.

35. Towne to Poyner IV.

36. The statue of Marcus Whitman by the sculptor Avard Fairbanks was originally envisioned as a sculpture that also featured Narcissa Whitman. However, upon being informed by the Architect of the Capitol that only single figure statues could be offered to the collection, only the figure of Marcus Whitman was retained for the Fairbanks design.

37. [SC-UWL] Maxine Cushing Gray, comp., *The Argus Art Reference Map of Seattle* (Seattle: The Argus Publishing Co., 1956).

38. According to Alice's daughter, "only her work before her marriage would be signed Alice Robertson Carr. Any work after her marriage would be signed Alice Carr de Creeft." See: Nina Ward (nee Carr), email to Fred Poyner IV, 31 March 2016.

39. Nina Ward (nee Carr), email to Fred Poyner IV, 26 February 2016.

Chapter 11

1. Dorothy Bestor, interview with James and Margaret Fitzgerald, 27 October 1965, 15, www.aaa.si.edu/collections/interviews/oral-history-interview-james-herbert-fitzgerald-and-margaret-tomkins-12432.

2. Miro FitzGerald, email to Fred Poyner IV, 28 March 2016. Miro was the second of three children of James FitzGerald and Margaret Tomkins, with an older brother, Jared, and younger sister, Gala.

3. Bestor, 2.

4. *Ibid.*

5. [WSA] Harold V. Judd, "Twin Bore Tunnels," *Bridges of 1940 Built by the Washington Toll Bridge Authority*, Washington State Department of Transportation History Files: 1905–2000.

6. [SC-UWL] Margaret Tomkins to Jo Nilsson, 25 August 1977, 3, James FitzGerald and Margaret Tomkins Papers.

7. [WSA] "Progress Report—Issue no. 78," 18 May 1940, Washington State Department of Transportation History Files: 1905–2000.

8. Bestor, 17. A review of the *Index to Reference Cards for Works Projects Administration Project Files, 1939–42*, also does not include any listing of the Lake Washington Floating Bridge or Mount Baker Tunnel construction as an official project of the WPA. See: Publication number T937, n.d., National Archives and Records Administration, Seattle, Washington.

9. Miro FitzGerald, email to Fred Poyner IV, 28 March 2016.

10. Tomkins to Nilsson, 2.

11. [SC-UWL] Barry Farrell, "Artist's Spirit Burns Bright after Fire Ruins Treasures," *Seattle Post-Intelligencer*, 19 July 1959, 31.

12. Miro FitzGerald, email to Fred Poyner IV, 21 March 2016.

13. [SC-UWL] Margaret Tomkins, "James FitzGerald," 24 August 1978, 2, James FitzGerald and Margaret Tomkins Papers.

14. Artifacts Consulting, Inc., *Washington State Library Historical Structures Report* (Olympia: Washington State Department of General Administration, 2002), 54.

15. *Ibid.*, 57.

16. [SC-UWL] James FitzGerald, "Notebook-Loose Pages-1961" (1961), 1, 5, James FitzGerald and Margaret Tomkins Papers.

17. [SC-UWL] James FitzGerald to Paule M. Anglim, 21 January 1963, James FitzGerald and Margaret Tomkins Papers.

18. Bruce Guenther, interview with Margaret Tomkins, 6 June 1984, 3, www.aaa.si.edu/collections/interviews/oral-history-interview-margaret-tomkins-12308.

19. Tomkins to Nilsson, 1.

20. FitzGerald to Poyner IV, 21 March 2016.

21. "Critic in Court," *Newsweek* (February 14, 1969): 74.

22. "JAMES H. FITZGERALD et al., Appellants, v. ROBERT HOPKINS et al., Respondents," No. 38535. The Supreme Court of Washington, 30 March 1967, 3, casetext.com/case/fitzgerald-v-hopkins.

23. *Ibid.*, 4; "Critic in Court."

24. Maxine Cushing Gray, "Judge Leads an Art Case into Fresh Air of Free Expression," *Argus* (January 15, 1965): 6.

25. "Critic in Court."

26. Miro FitzGerald, email to Fred Poyner IV, 28 March 2016.

27. "JAMES H. FITZGERALD et al., Appellants, v. ROBERT HOPKINS et al., Respondents," 3.

28. FitzGerald to Poyner IV, 21 March 2016.

29. [SC-UWL] James FitzGerald, "Notebook—FitzGerald," n.d., 10, James FitzGerald and Margaret Tomkins Papers.

Chapter 12

1. [AWP] Frank B. Lazier to August Werner, 24 December 1947.

2. Ann Cole, "August Werner: A man rich in many talents," 11 May 1981, *Seattle Times*, 4.

3. Bob H. Hansen, "August Werner," *Seattle Times*, 16 December 1973, 9.

4. Margaret Mara, "Wife Strives for Musical Career After Husband Wins Recognition," *Brooklyn Daily Eagle*, January 27, 1932, 41.

5. [SC-UWL] Albeu Lindane to August

Werner, 24 February 1929, August Werner Papers.

6. [SC-UWL] A. Halvorsen, telegram to August Werner, 5 November 1929, August Werner Papers.

7. [SC-UWL] "August Werner," *Santa Cruz Morning Sentinel*, 10 October 1930 [n.p.], August Werner Papers.

8. [AWP] A.D. Giles to Ramona Little, 3 February 1931.

9. [AWP] David Thomson to August Werner, 2 July 1931.

10. [AWP] August Werner to "De Ridder," n.d. [1934].

11. [AWP] August Werner to Christian Olsen, n.d.

12. Cole, 4.

13. Louis R. Guzzo, "Meet August Werner, Man of Many Arts," 18 May 1954, *Seattle Times*, 25.

14. Alvaro C. Shoemaker, "'All Art is One'—August Werner, Master of All," *Scandinavian American*, vol. 1, no. 3 (March, 1945): 2.

15. Guzzo, 25.

16. *Ibid.*

17. "House Joint Resolution No. 15," *Session Laws of the State of Washington—27th Session* (Olympia: State Printing Plant, 1941), 953.

18. [PSHF] Marie Sherwin, *A Short History of the "Leif Erikson League, Incorporated, of the Seattle Area"* (Seattle: Leif Erikson League, Inc., 1968), 1.

19. Christine Leander, "The Saga of Seattle's Leif Erikson Statue," *Nordic Heritage Museum Historical Journal* vol. 1, no. 1 (Spring/Summer 2005): 58.

20. [AWP] August Werner, "For Leif Erikson Tale," n.d. [ca. 1960].

21. [AWP] August Werner, "On Sailing," n.d.

22. Werner, "For Leif Erikson Tale."

23. [SMA] T. Grønning to Gordon Clinton, 5 September 1958, Comptroller File no. 235441.

24. [SMA] Mrs. Harlan Edwards to Ewen Dingwall, 9 September 1958, Comptroller File no. 235441; [SMA] Mrs. Harlan Edwards, Letter to Robert Durham, 9 September 1958, Comptroller File no. 235441.

25. [SMA] "Minutes of the Municipal Art Commission," 11 July 1957, 1, Department of Community Development Municipal Art Commission, Commission Minutes, 1955–1969.

26. [SMA] Robert L. Durham to Leif Erikson League, 15 September 1958, Comptroller File no. 235441.

27. Louis R. Guzzo, "Site Remains Problem in Erikson-Statue Plan," 13 March 1959, *Seattle Times*, 49.

28. [SMA] "Amendment to Section 3 of Article XI of the City Charter," 9 March 1948, City Charter Amendment, 1948–1962.

29. [SMA] Paul V. Brown to Mrs. Harlan H. Edwards, 6 March 1959, Comptroller File no. 236587. The reference to "living memorials" here may also be identified with the efforts of the Century 21 Exposition committee appointed by Seattle Mayor Allen Pomeroy in 1954, which used the phrase in a planning document to describe the Civic Memorial Center site's facilities as constituting "a living memorial to our war dead." See also: [SMA] "Elements of a Civic Memorial Center," n.d., Civic Memorial Center Collection.

30. [SC-NHM] Trygve Nakkerud, "Trygve Nakkerud Interview" to Leif Eie, 1986.

31. Bob H. Hansen, "August Werner," *Seattle Times*, 16 December 1973, 8.

32. Frank Lynch, "Too Many Statues? It's News to Him," Seattle Scene, *Seattle Post-Intelligencer*, 1 April 1959, 9.

33. Sherwin, 1.

34. [SMA] "Minutes of the Municipal Art Commission," 11 February 1960, 2, Department of Community Development Municipal Art Commission, Commission Minutes, 1955–1969.

35. Hansen, 8.

36. Nakkerud to Eie.

37. Leander, 54.

38. [SMA] "Minutes of the Municipal Art Commission," 17 November 1960, 2, Department of Community Development Municipal Art Commission, Commission Minutes, 1955–1969.

39. Louis R. Guzzo, "After Stormy Voyage League Sights Land at Last!" *Seattle Times*, 18 November 1960, 17.

40. [SMA] "Minutes of the Municipal Art Commission," 17 November 1960, 3, Department of Community Development Municipal Art Commission, Commission Minutes, 1955–1969.

41. [PSHF] J. Eldon Opheim to George E. Fahey, 23 November 1960.

42. [SC-UWL] Alex J. Ettl to Trygve Nakkerud, 16 February 1961, August Werner Papers.

43. Nakkerud to Eie.

44. Leander, 55–56.

45. [PSHF] Capital Improvements Committee to Howard Burke, 23 February 1962.

46. "We Came in His Wake," n.d., www.leiferikson.org/2351names.htm. The statue's relocation at Shilshole Marina took over two years to complete. The Port of Seattle and the Leif Erikson International Foundation finalized an agreement which outlined the planning and scope of the statue move on October 20, 2006. See: "Memorandum of Agreement Regarding Leif Eriksson Statue and Memorial Wall," October 20, 2006 (Port of Seattle, electronic communication to Fred Poyner IV, MOA signed.pdf, Port of Seattle_15–475, March 29, 2016).

47. [SC-UWL] Trygve Nakkerud, postcard to August Werner, 3 May 1963, August Werner Papers.

Bibliography

Archives

Alaska-Yukon-Pacific Exposition Collection, 1906–1910. Collection no. 2006.3. Special Collections. Museum of History & Industry (MOHAI), Seattle, WA.

Alaska-Yukon-Pacific Exposition postcard collection, 1908–1909. PH 0777. Special Collections. University of Washington Libraries, Seattle, WA.

Art Inventories Catalog. Smithsonian American Art Museum. Smithsonian Institution Research Information System (SIRIS) website. URL: siris-artinventories.si.edu.

"Artist" File for John C. Ely. Henry Art Gallery Collection. Seattle, WA (cited as HAGC)

Burke, Caroline McGilvra Papers, 1876–1932. Manuscript Collection no. 4697. Special Collections. University of Washington Libraries, Seattle, WA.

Burke, Thomas Papers, 1875–1925. Accession no. 1483–002. Manuscript Collection no. 1483. Special Collections. University of Washington Libraries, Seattle, WA.

Chadwick, Stephen Fowler Papers. Accession no. 0014–001 (part 1). Manuscript Collection no. 0014. Special Collections. University of Washington Libraries, Seattle, WA.

City of Bellevue City Council. Summary Minutes of Regular Session. October 21, 2002. City of Bellevue Archives, Bellevue, WA.

Death Records Series. Washington State Death Records Collection. Washington State Digital Archives, Olympia, WA.

Department of Community Development Municipal Art Commission. Commission Minutes, 1955–1969. Series no. 1652–01. Seattle Municipal Archives, Seattle, WA.

Department of Parks and Recreation. Parks Superintendent Subject Files, 1936–1993. Series no. 5802–01. Seattle Municipal Archives, Seattle, WA.

Division of Archives & Records Management. Washington State Archives, Olympia, WA (cited as WSA).

FitzGerald, James and Margaret Tomkins Papers. Accession no. 2848–002. Special Collections. University of Washington Libraries, Seattle, WA.

Frolich, Finn. Correspondence to Charmian London. JL 6337–6348. Jack London Papers. The Huntington Library, San Marino, CA.

Gahringer, Ervin R. Papers. Accession no. 5399–001. Special Collections. University of Washington Libraries, Seattle, WA.

Hart, Louis F., Papers. Collection no. AR2_J. Division of Archives & Records Management. Washington State Archives, Olympia, WA.

Jones, Wesley L. Papers. Ms 0157. Special Collections. University of Washington Libraries, Seattle, WA.

Lewis, Alonzo Victor Papers. Accession no. GA1959.94. Special Collections. Washington State Historical Society, Tacoma, WA (cited as AVLP).

London, Charmian. Correspondence to Finn Frolich. JL 9852–9855. Jack London Papers. The Huntington Library, San Marino, CA.

McGilvra, John J. Papers, 1861–1926. Accession no. 4806–001. Special Collections. University of Washington Libraries, Seattle, WA.

Meany, Edmond S. Papers, 1877–1935. Accession no. 0106–001. Manuscript Collection no. 0106. Special Collections. University of Washington Libraries, Seattle, WA.

Microfilm Collection. Seattle Public Library, Seattle, WA.

Minutes of the 29th Annual Convention of the United Daughters of the Confederacy

Inc. 1922. United Daughters of the Confederacy Archives, Richmond, VA.

Nowell, Frank H. Alaska Yukon Pacific Exposition Photographs. PH Coll. 727. Special Collections. University of Washington Libraries, Seattle, WA.

Office of the City Clerk. City Charters, 1869–2006. Series no. 1801–01. Seattle Municipal Archives, Seattle, WA.

Olmsted Brothers. Correspondence. Olmsted Brothers Agreement with Board of Park Commissioners, 1904–1904. Series no. 5801–01. Seattle Municipal Archives, Seattle, WA.

Olmsted Brothers. Olmsted Brothers Records, 1903–1915. Accession no. 0170–001. Special Collections. University of Washington Libraries, Seattle, WA.

Park Board Minutes, August, 1921-December, 1925, vol. 8. Series no. 5800–01. Seattle Municipal Archives, Seattle, WA.

Park Board Minutes, June 1925-May 1929, vol. 9. Series no. 5800–01. Seattle Municipal Archives, Seattle, WA.

Park Board Minutes, May 1929-August 1933, vol. 10. Series no. 5800–01. Seattle Municipal Archives, Seattle, WA.

Park History Files—Veterans Area, Artillery. Series no. 5801–01. Seattle Municipal Archives, Seattle, WA.

Passenger Search Catalog. The Statue of Liberty—Ellis Island Foundation, Inc. website. URL: libertyellisfoundation.org/passenger.

Port of Seattle-History Files-Shilshole Bay Marina. Series no. PS667–29–0¬48. Puget Sound Regional Branch. Washington State Archives, Bellevue, WA (cited as PSHF).

Prints on General Subjects, 1851–2000. Series no. AR280–1¬–1. Photograph Collection. Division of Archives & Records Management. Washington State Archives, Olympia, WA.

Prints and Photographs Division. Library of Congress, Washington, D.C.

Roman Bronze Works, Inc. Roman Bronze Works Archive, 1902–1977. Amon Carter Museum of American Art Archives, Fort Worth, TX.

Seattle Municipal Archives, Seattle, WA (cited as SMA).

Sherwood, Don. Don Sherwood Parks History Collection. Series no. 5801–01. Seattle Municipal Archives, Seattle, WA.

Special Collections. Seattle Public Library (Central Branch), Seattle, Washington (cited as SC-SPL).

Special Collections. Washington State Historical Society, Tacoma, Washington (cited as SC-WSHS).

Special Collections Archives. Nordic Heritage Museum, Seattle, WA (cited as SCA-NHM).

Special Collections. University of Washington Libraries, Seattle, WA (cited as SC-UWL).

Taft, Lorado Papers, 1857–1953. Series no. 26/20/16. University of Illinois Archives, Urbana-Champaign, IL (cited as LTP).

United Daughters of the Confederacy Archives, Richmond, VA (cited as UDCA).

United States Army Division 91st Records. Accession no. 4929–001. Ms 4929. Special Collections. University of Washington Libraries, Seattle, WA.

Vertical Files, 1883–2011. Series no. VF-0000. Seattle Municipal Archives, Seattle, WA.

Wehn, James A. Papers. Accession no. GA1973.52. Special Collections. Washington State Historical Society. Tacoma, WA (cited as JAWP).

Wehn, James A. Papers. Series no. 2353–001. Special Collections. University of Washington Libraries, Seattle, WA.

Weller, Allen S. Papers. Series no. 12/1/20. University of Illinois Archives, Urbana-Champaign, IL (cited as ASWP).

Werner, August Papers. Accession nos. 82.120; 82.120wc. Special Collections Archives. Nordic Heritage Museum, Seattle, WA (cited as AWP).

Werner, August Papers. Accession no. 2923–001. Record group 19.15.2923. Special Collections. University of Washington Libraries, Seattle, WA.

Werner, August Photograph Collection. PH Coll. 708. Special Collections. University of Washington Libraries, Seattle, WA.

Books

Alaska-Yukon-Pacific Exposition. *Official Guide to the Alaska-Yukon-Pacific Exposition: Seattle, Washington, June 1 to October 16, 1909.* [Seattle]: Alaska-Yukon-Pacific Exposition Pub. Co., 1909.

Artifacts Consulting, Inc. *Washington State Library Historical Structures Report.* Olympia, WA: Washington State Department of General Administration. 2002.

Artifacts Consulting, Inc., HistoryLink.org. *Seattle Center Historic Landmark Study.* Seattle: City of Seattle, Seattle Center Redevelopment Department. March, 2013.

Bagley, Clarence. *History of King County, Washington*. Vols. 1 and 2. Chicago: The S.J. Clarke Publishing Co., 1929.

Bagley, Clarence. *History of Seattle from the earliest settlement to the present time*. Chicago: The S.J. Clarke Pub. Co., 1916.

Bagley, Clarence. *Indian Myths of the Northwest*. Seattle: Lowman and Hanford Co., 1930.

Campos, Jules. *The Sculpture of José Campos*. New York: Kennedy Graphics, Inc. / Da Capo Press, Inc., 1972.

Castor, Dick. *Native American Presence in the Federal Way Area*. Federal Way: Historical Society of Federal Way, 2010.

Chaplin, Ralph, Industrial Workers of the World. *The Centralia Conspiracy*. [Washington], [1920].

City of Seattle. *The Charter of the City of Seattle*. Seattle: Lowman & Hanford Co. 1911. [SMA].

Conover, Charles T., comp. & ed., *Thomas Burke 1849-1925: His Life in Outline*. Seattle: Acme Press, 1926.

Cotterill, Roland W., comp. *Report of the Board of Park Commissioners—Seventh Annual Report*. Seattle: Lowman & Hanford, 1910. [SC-SPL].

Dimmick, Lauretta, and Donna J. Hassler. *American Sculpture in the Metropolitan Museum of Art: A catalogue of works by artists born between 1865 and 1885*. New York: Metropolitan Museum of Art, 1999.

Eaton, R.W. *Seattle and Environs, 1852-1924*, vol. III. Chicago; Seattle: Pioneer Historical Publishing Co., 1924.

Evergreen Washelli. *Heroes & Dignitaries—A Self-Guided Tour*. Seattle: Evergreen Washelli. 2009.

Falk, Peter H. *Who was who in American art: compiled from the original thirty-four volumes of American art annual—Who's who in art, biographies of American artists active from 1898-1947*. Madison, Conn: Sound View Press. 1985.

Gibb, William K., Gloria D. Campbell and Robert Mortenson. *The Fiery Furnace: A History of the Foundry Industry in King County and the Puget Sound Region*. Kirkland, WA: Sundial Press LLC, 2011.

Godman, M.M., G.E. Dickson, L.P. Hornberger, R.W. Condon, L.H. Burnett, J.W. Slayden. *Report of the Alaska-Yukon-Pacific Exposition Commission of the State of Washington*. Seattle: The Pacific Press, Inc., 1909.

Harding, Warren G., James W. Murphy, comp. *Speeches and Addresses of Warren G. Harding, President of the United States, Delivered during the Course of His Tour from Washington, D.C., to Alaska and Return to San Francisco, June 20 to August 2, 1923*. Washington, D.C., 1923.

Holden, Jean Stansbury. "The Sculptors MacNeil," in *The World's Work ... A History of Our Time*, vol. 14, Walter Hines Page and Arthur Wilson Page. Doubleday, Page, 1907. 9401-9419.

Holstine, Craig and Richard Hobbs. *Spanning Washington: Historic Highway Bridges of the Evergreen State*. Pullman, WA: Washington State Press, 2005.

Index to Reference Cards for Works Projects Administration Project Files, 1939-42. n.d. Publication number T937. National Archives and Records Administration. Seattle, Washington.

Karnow, Stanley. *In Our Image: America's Empire in the Philippines*. New York: Random House Publishing Group, 2010.

Kelly, Cindy, and Edwin H. Remsberg. *Outdoor Sculpture in Baltimore: A Historical Guide to Public Art in the Monumental City*. Baltimore: Johns Hopkins University Press, 2011.

Kroll Map Company, Inc. *Atlas of Seattle*. Seattle: [Kroll], [1972].

Lampman, Ben Hur. *The Centralia Tragedy and Trial*. [Centralia, Wash.]: Grant Hodge Post No. 17, 1920.

Lee, William H. *Glimpses of the Alaska-Yukon-Pacific Exposition*. Chicago: Laird & Lee, 1909.

McClelland, Jr., John. *Wobbly War*. Tacoma: Washington State Historical Society, 1987.

Meany, Edmond S. *History of the State of Washington*. New York: The Macmillan Co., 1950 (original printing 1909).

Morgan, Ann Lee. *The Oxford Dictionary of American Art and Artists*. Oxford: Oxford University Press, 2007.

Official Illustrated Catalogue, Fine Arts Exhibit, United States of America, Paris Exposition of 1900. Boston: Noyes, Platt & Company, 1900.

Park Board Minutes, August, 1921-December, 1925, vol. 8. Seattle: The Board of Park Commissioners. 1925. [SMA].

Park Board Minutes, May 1929-August 1933, vol. 10. Seattle: The Board of Park Commissioners. 1933. [SMA].

Polk, R. L. *Seattle City Directory, 1906*. Seattle: R. L. Polk & Co., 1906.

Polk, R. L. *Seattle City Directory, 1909*. Seattle: R. L. Polk & Co., 1909.

Polk, R. L. *Seattle City Directory, 1910*. Seattle: R. L. Polk & Co., 1910.

Polk, R. L. *Tacoma City Directory, 1915*. Tacoma: R. L. Polk & Co., 1915.

Polk, R. L. *Seattle City Directory, 1922*. Seattle: R. L. Polk & Co., 1922.

Polk, R. L. *Seattle City Directory, 1923*. Seattle: R. L. Polk & Co., 1923.

Poyner IV, Fred. *The First Sculptor of Seattle: The Life and Art of James A. Wehn*. North Charleston, SC: CreateSpace Independent Publishing Platform, 2014.

Pritzker, Barry M. *Native Americans*. Vol. 1. Santa Barbara, CA: ABC-CLIO, Inc., 1998.

Reeves, Majorie Ann. *A Chapter in Pacific Northwest History: United Daughters of the Confederacy, Robert E. Lee Chapter #885, Seattle, Washington*. Seattle: Tommie Press, 2006.

Rubinstein, Charlotte Streifer. *American Women Sculptors*. Boston: G.K. Hall & Co., 1990.

Seattle Chamber of Commerce. *Record of the Minutes of the Meetings of Seattle Chamber of Commerce*. Seattle: [The Chamber]. 1906. [SC-SPL].

Session Laws of the State of Washington—27th Session. Olympia: State Printing Plant, 1941.

Snowden, Clinton A. *History of Washington*, vol. 4. New York: The Century House, 1909.

Stein, Alan J., Paula Becker & The HistoryLink Staff, *Washington's First World's Fair—Alaska-Yukon-Pacific Exposition, A Timeline History*. Seattle: History Ink, 2009.

Taft, Lorado. *The History of American Sculpture*. New York: The MacMillan Company, 1924.

Weller, Allen Stuart; Robert G. La France, Henry Adams with Stephen P. Thomas, eds. *Lorado Taft—The Chicago Years*. Urbana-Champaign: The University of Illinois Press and Krannert Art Museum, The University of Illinois Library, and The Spurlock Museum. 2014.

Washington State Historical Society. *Washington State Historical Society Publications*, vol. 2. Tacoma: [Washington] State Historical Society. [1907–1914] 1915.

Periodicals

Alaska-Yukon Magazine. "Spirit of the Pacific" (October, 1908): 45.

"Amendment to Section 3 of Article XI of the City Charter." March 9, 1948. Series no. 1801–01. City Charter Amendment, 1948–1962. [SMA].

Ballard Tribune. "Leif Erikson Statue is Dedicated Sunday on Ballard Waterfront." June 20, 1962.

Barrett, Eldon. "Memorial Day." *Seattle Times*. May 27, 1978.

Bates, Alansa, ed. "UW Hails 75th Anniversary of A-Y-P Exposition." *Washington Alumnus Digest*. (1984): 1–3.

Bauer, Harry B. "The George Washington Statue—U. of W.'s Patriotic Shrine." *Seattle Times*. May 21, 1960.

Boy Scouts of America. "Nation-Wide Boy Scout Memorial to President Harding," *Scouting* (August, 1923): 1.

Boy Scouts of America. "President Harding as Honorary President of the Boy Scouts of America," *Scouting* (August, 1923): 2.

Case, Frederick. "Stone Soldiers Never Die—Memorials may be Unheeded Reminders of those who Served in Forgotten Wars." *Seattle Times*. May 27, 1985.

Cole, Ann. "August Werner: A man rich in many talents." *Seattle Times*. May 11, 1981.

Conover, Charles T. "Judge Thomas Burke Fought for Seattle's Future." *Seattle Times*. February 9, 1950.

Conover, Charles T. "U. of W. Statue Waited for Proper Pedestal." *Seattle Times*. August 5, 1954.

Craft, John Richard. "Bronzes by Alice Carr de Creeft," (biographical pamphlet). n.d. Nina Ward Collection.

Crowder, Joan. "Sculptor of Animals dies at daughter's home." *Santa Barbara Independent*. August 15, 1996.

"Dixie Day, Alaska Yukon Pacific Exposition, August 24, 1909" (program). No. 979.7432 Alaska Yukon Pacific Exposition. Special Collections Pamphlet File. [SC-UWL].

Boeing Magazine. "Born 450 Years Too Soon" (October 1943): 12–14.

Elks Magazine. "Goldfield Lodge Observes 'Boy Day'—Hundreds of Youngsters Entertained" (July, 1923): 44.

Elks Magazine. "Harding Memorial in Woodland Park Nearing Completion" (February, 1925): 39.

Elks Magazine. "President Harding" (September, 1923): 5.

Elks Magazine. "Salt Lake City Lodge Carries Through 'Boy Day' Program" (August, 1923): 50.

Elverson, James. "Latter-Day Vikings." *Seattle Sunday Times*. February 13, 1910.

Farr, Sheila. "Seattle's public art has shaped view of city." *Seattle Times*. August 1, 2004.

Farrell, Barry. "Artist's Spirit Burns Bright after Fire Ruins Treasures." *Seattle Post-Intelligencer*. July 19, 1959. Accession no. 2848–002. James FitzGerald and Margaret Tomkins Papers. Folder Clippings: House Fires and its Subsequent.... Box 1. [SC-UWL].

Final Report of the Citizen's Advisory Committee for the Seattle Zoo. July, 1971. Document 2028. Published Documents Collection, 1801–92. [SMA].

Foulser, F.M. "The Cruise of the Viking Ship." *The Rudder*, vol. XXIII, no. 4. April, 1910. 344–345.

Gilje, Svein. "Explorer's bust raised to life." *Seattle Times*. August 6, 1976.

Gilmore, Susan. "Downtown park, statue honor man who stood up to a mob," *Seattle Times*. February 9, 2011.

Granite Cutters' Journal, vol. 45 (1921): 32.

Gray, Maxine Cushing, comp. *The Argus Art Reference Map of Seattle*. Seattle: The Argus Publishing Co. 1956. Accession no. 0737–001. Allied Arts of Seattle Records, 1954–1966. Folder 37. Box 1. [SC-UWL].

Gray, Maxine Cushing. "Judge Leads an Art Case into Fresh Air of Free Expression." *Argus* (January 15, 1965): 6.

Guilford-Kardell, Margaret, comp. "Sea Dog and Sea Wolf at Play in the Valley of the Moon." *The Californians* (January/February 1991): 14–23.

Guzzo, Louis R. "After Stormy Voyage League Sights Land at Last!" *Seattle Times*. November 18, 1960.

Guzzo, Louis R. "Meet August Werner, Man of Many Arts." *Seattle Times*. May 18, 1954.

Guzzo, Louis R. "Site Remains Problem in Erikson-Statue Plan." *Seattle Times*. March 13, 1959.

Hansen, Bob H. "August Werner." *Seattle Times*, December 16, 1973.

Hayman, Sally. "Looking Back on the Creation of a Landmark ... Sculptor James Wehn Remembers How it Was." *Seattle Post-Intelligencer*. May 13, 1973.

Henry, Mary T. "Finn Haakon Frolich." *Nordic Heritage Museum Historical Journal*, vol. 5, no. 1 (Winter/Spring 2009): 26–44.

Johnson, Michael Bruce. "Harding's unusual Scouting legacy." Letters section, *Scouting Magazine*. March-April 2001. scouting mahazine.org/issues/0103/d-lett.html.

Johnsrud, Byron. "Cannons, anyone? Unzo-olike Objects must go." *Seattle Times*. November 14, 1971.

Judd, Harold V., Lacey V. Murrow. "Twin Bore Tunnels." *Bridges of 1940 Built by the Washington Toll Bridge Authority*. Washington State Department of Transportation, History Files, 1905–2000, Accession No. 02-A-469. Folder Bridges of 1940: Lacey V. Murrow Bridge. Box no. B-1. [WSA].

Kettler, Wanda Von. "Seattle Boy Recognized at Eastern Art Exhibit." *Seattle Star*. February 12, 1925. [HAGC].

Krenmayr, Janice. "A Golfer's View can be superb." *Seattle Times*. March 24, 1963.

Krenmayr, Janice. "Woodland Park Zoo." *Seattle Times*. March 11, 1962.

Kvamme, Olaf, trans. "Sivert Engelsen Sagstad," *Washington Posten*. September 24, 1909. [SCA-NHM].

Kvamme, Olaf. "Viking Ship of the Alaska-Yukon-Pacific Exposition," *Nordic Heritage Museum Historical Journal*, vol. 5, no. 1 (Winter/Spring 2009): 4–45. [SCA-NHM].

Leander, Christine. "The Saga of Seattle's Leif Erikson Statue." *Nordic Heritage Museum Historical Journal*, vol. 1, no. 1 (Spring/Summer 2005): 53–63.

Lynch, Frank. "Too Many Statues? It's News to Him." *Seattle Post-Intelligencer*. April 1, 1959.

MacDonald, Lucile. "Spanish War Vets' Ranks are Growing Thin." *Seattle Times*. June 30, 1957.

Mara, Margaret. "Wife Strives for Musical Career After Husband Wins Recognition." *Brooklyn Daily Eagle*. January 27, 1932.

Mater, Mabel de la. "Sculptor Here Follows Work in Expressionism." *Seattle Post-Intelligencer*. February 26, 1924. [HAGC].

National Music League. "August Werner—Baritone" (music program/pamphlet). New York: National Music League, Inc. [1930]. [AWP].

Newsweek. "Critic in Court" (February 14, 1969): 74.

Olmsted, John C. "Natural Features of the Fair." *Alaska-Yukon Magazine*, vol. II, no. 5 (November, 1906).

Plummer, David E. "John Carl Ely Expatriate Seattle Sculptor." *Artifact* (January/February 1997): 29–30.

Port of Seattle. *Shilshole Bay Marina Welcomes his Highness, King Olav V, of Norway....* May 1, 1969. Folder Leif Erickson Statue 1962–1984 (folder 2 of 3). Box 517599708. [PSHF].

"Progress Report—Issue no. 78." May 18, 1940. Accession No. 02-A-469. Washington State Department of Transportation History Files: 1905–2000. [WSA].

San Francisco Call. "Johnson Unveils Hill Monument." August 4, 1909.

Santa Cruz Morning Sentinel. "August Werner." October 10, 1930. August Werner Papers. Folder 1. Box 1. [SC-UWL].

Seattle Daily Times. "361st Infantry Makes Record for Gallantry." November 21, 1918.

Seattle Daily Times. "648 Graduating at University Record Class in Campus History." June 18, 1922.

Seattle Sunday Times. "A.-Y.-P. Statuary and Monuments." February 14, 1909.

Seattle Daily Times. "Alonzo Lewis will get home." February 10, 1943.

Seattle Daily Times. "American Doughboy Bringing Home the Bacon." December 10, 1922.

Seattle Daily Times. "Assault on Manilla." August 19, 1899.

Seattle Daily Times. "Attorneys in Lewis Trial trade 'Blows.'" March 20, 1946.

Seattle Daily Times. "Base for Statue of Washington to be Approved." December 23, 1931.

Seattle Sunday Times. "Burke Memorial Dedication is set for April 5." March 30, 1930.

Seattle Daily Times. "Burke Memorial, Soon to be Dedicated, Viewed by Artist." March 27, 1930.

Seattle Daily Times. "Burke Memorial Statue to be Unveiled Saturday." April 2, 1930.

Seattle Daily Times. "Burke Monument now en route to Volunteer Park." October 20, 1929.

Seattle Daily Times. "Burke Shaft is Dedicated." April 6, 1930.

Seattle Daily Times. "Bust of Amundsen Finished, Made by Seattle Sculptor." June 13, 1926.

Seattle Daily Times. "Chief Seattle is Shown in Clay." October 17, 1907.

Seattle Daily Times. "Churches Pay Tribute." August 6, 1923.

Seattle Daily Times. "City Pays Tribute to memory of Late Judge." April 6, 1930.

Seattle Daily Times. "Elks Harding Memorial for Woodland Park Begun." January 11, 1925.

Seattle Daily Times. "For the Soldiers." August 18, 1899.

Seattle Daily Times. "G. Washington on Pedestal; That Pleases Sculptor Taft." November 14, 1934.

Seattle Daily Times. "George Washington will rise above mud of 'U' campus." September 30, 1935.

Seattle Daily Times. "George Washington's Feet Too Big for Ten-Foot Base." October 12, 1930.

Seattle Daily Times. "Harding Memorial Plan again Delayed—Capital is Amazed at Association Resolution." October 7, 1930.

Seattle Daily Times. "Harding Memorial to be Dedicated Next Sunday." March 22, 1925.

Seattle Daily Times. "Harding Memorial Unveiled—Presented to City by Elks." March 30, 1925.

Seattle Daily Times. "Hiker statue will stand at Woodland." January 24, 1926.

Seattle Daily Times. "John Carl Ely, 30, Seattle Sculptor, Is Drowned in East." August 5, 1929.

Seattle Daily Times. "Jury will be art critics of 'The Doughboy.'" November 18, 1931.

Seattle Daily Times. "Local Painting Exhibit Declared Worthy of Any Place in Whole Nation." February 16, 1916.

Seattle Daily Times. "Lorado Taft, Noted Sculptor, Dies in Chicago Studio Home." October 30, 1936.

Seattle Daily Times. "Many Officers of 91st Division Lost." November 28, 1918.

Seattle Daily Times. "Memorial to Former Governor Unveiled." July 23, 1913.

Seattle Daily Times. "Memorial Statue to be placed at new auditorium." November 8, 1928.

Seattle Daily Times. "Mrs. Burke Gives Dinner in Honor of Hermon A. MacNeil." September 23, 1927.

Seattle Daily Times. "Not Ready with Design." May 9, 1905.

Seattle Daily Times. "Noted Sculptor coming to Speak at University." March 11, 1920.

Seattle Daily Times. "Observe Anniversary of Alaska Purchase." October 19, 1925.

Seattle Daily Times. "Plea for Beauty." March 17, 1920.

Seattle Daily Times. "Proposed war memorial statue arouses criticism." November 9, 1928.

Seattle Daily Times. "Pupils Contribute for Washington Monument." February 22, 1909.

Seattle Daily Times. "Sailing put off." August 24, 1899.

Seattle Daily Times. "Scores a smacking victory." February 8, 1932.

Seattle Daily Times. "Sculptor Explains Burke Statue Aims." October 5, 1927.

Seattle Daily Times. "Sculptor L. Taft to Locate Statue." October 18, 1905, 2.

Seattle Daily Times. "Seattle Honors War Heroes—Veterans Dedicate Statue." June 1, 1926.

Seattle Daily Times. "Seattle to get her first military statue." March 14, 1926.

Seattle Daily Times. "Seward Statue Contract Let." June 17, 1907.

Seattle Daily Times. "Sherwood Gillespy Memorial Fount at City Golf Links." June 6, 1915.

Seattle Daily Times. "Shrine to Veterans Proposed Statue of Heroic Size Ready." November 23, 1924.

Seattle Daily Times. "Society" section. April 2, 1905.

Seattle Daily Times. "Sons Cherish Medallion of Mr. and Mrs. Schoenfeld." March 15, 1911.

Seattle Daily Times. "Spanish War Veterans to hold entertainment." October 27, 1926.

Seattle Daily Times. "Statue of George Washington to be Erected at U. of W. and Sculptor Lorado Taft." February 25, 1907.

Seattle Daily Times. "Statue will be erected in tribute to Seattle men who gave their lives for nation; committee named." August 12, 1928.

Seattle Daily Times. "Suggestions pour in for Burke Memorial." January 17, 1926.

Seattle Daily Times. "Tacoma's Big Bid against Seattle." July 25, 1899.

Seattle Daily Times. "Taft Picks Site for Statue." November 2, 1905.

Seattle Daily Times. "U.S. Artist takes post in Rome." December 27, 1919.

Seattle Daily Times. "U.S. Troops in Cavite." August 12, 1898.

Seattle Daily Times. "Unveil Bust of Norse Composer." September 3, 1917.

Seattle Daily Times. "Veterans Here for Big Reunion." September 24, 1921.

Seattle Daily Times. "Veteran's Memorial Row taken to Mayor." August 14, 1928.

Seattle Daily Times. "Veterans' Statue Opposition Ends." August 16, 1928.

Seattle Daily Times. "Veterans of 3 Wars Honor Men in Gray." May 24, 1926.

Seattle Daily Times. "Wallace Backs Fund." August 30, 1923.

Seattle Daily Times. "Washington Goes for W.P.A. 'Ride.'" August 9, 1938.

Seattle Daily Times. "Washington Statue Unveiled." June 14, 1909.

Seattle Daily Times. "Washington's Statue to Rise." March 19, 1938.

Seattle Daily Times. "Watchman, Padlock, Lights Protect 'Doughboy' Statue." April 13, 1932.

Seattle Daily Times. "Wild Westerners of 91st Division to Hold Reunion." September 19, 1926.

Seattle Daily Times. "World's Rose Lovers to Worship at Seattle Shrine." June 3, 1923.

Seattle Daily Times. "Wuxtra! Wuxtra! Fun Breaks Loose in Gobs." December 4, 1910.

Seattle Daily Times. "Yesler Tablet on Courthouse Urged." April 19, 1915.

Seattle Municipal News. "$100,000 Statue is Planned for Burke." May 8, 1926. 3.

Seattle Municipal News. "News Notes—Memorial to Judge Burke Dedicated Friday Afternoon." August 11, 1928. 1.

Seattle Post-Intelligencer. "Confederate Monument Rites Today." May 23, 1926.

Seattle Post-Intelligencer. "Design for the Alaska-Yukon-Pacific Grounds, by Mr. John C. Olmsted, Famous Landscape Gardener." November 18, 1906.

Seattle Post-Intelligencer. "Gives its Annual Report to Club." November 18, 1906.

Seattle Post-Intelligencer. "John C. Olmsted Visits the Fair: Landscape Architect says Natural Beauties are the Best Features." May 29, 1909.

Seattle Post-Intelligencer. "Lorado Taft on 'Art in America.'" November 2, 1905. [LTP].

Seattle Post-Intelligencer. "Lost Letters Replaced on Statue of Seward." May 10, 1952.

Seattle Post-Intelligencer. Max P. Nielsen obituary listing. March 8, 1917.

Seattle Post-Intelligencer. "Proposes to put Statue of Seward in Pioneer Place." October 8, 1909.

Seattle Post-Intelligencer. "Statue of Buyer of Golden North unveiled at Fair." September 11, 1909.

Seattle Sunday Times. "The bust of James J. Hill…" February 21, 1909.

Seattle Sunday Times. "Exhibit of Northwest Artists High Spot of Year." October 2, 1938.

Seattle Sunday Times. "Inspiring Symbol." April 6, 1930.

Seattle Sunday Times. "Judgements for Sale." August 28, 1910.

Seattle Sunday Times. "Last Act of Old University Building—the production of Exposition's Sculptural Masterpiece." October 4, 1908.

Seattle Sunday Times. "Likeness of Cushman by Seattle Sculptor." July 25, 1909.

Seattle Sunday Times. "Lorado Taft to Talk in Seattle on Tuesday." December 8, 1935.

Seattle Sunday Times. "Many Praise Idea of Monument to Hill." March 7, 1909.

Seattle Sunday Times. "Men of 91st to Meet." April 24, 1921.

Seattle Sunday Times. "Oh, it was a most jolly affair; all the statues and totems were there." May 22, 1932.

Seattle Sunday Times. "Prizes awarded in Art Exhibit." October 31, 1915.*Seattle Times.* "A Guide to the World's Fairgrounds…" April 13, 1962.

Seattle Sunday Times. "Sculptor of Burke Tribute Given Honors." August 9, 1931.

Seattle Sunday Times. "Sculptor Frolich Accused by Wife of Stealing Baby." July 16, 1911.

Seattle Sunday Times. "Select Sculptor for Seward Statue." March 10, 1907.

Seattle Sunday Times. "Umbrella Man Statue Sale begins Monday." February 20, 1910.

Seattle Sunday Times. "University Plans a Lecture Course." September 24, 1905.

Seattle Times. "Judge Hears Sculptor's $50,000 Suit." September 28, 1964.

Seattle Times. "N.W. Sculptor Appeals in Slander Case." February 10, 1965.

Seattle Times. "Suit Resumes on Charges by Sculptors," January 4, 1965.

Sherwin, Marie. *A Short History of the "Leif Erikson League, Incorporated, of the Seattle Area.* Seattle: Leif Erikson League, Inc., 1968. Folder Leif Erickson Statue 1962–1984 (folder 2 of 3). Box 517599708. [PSHF].

Shoemaker, Alvaro C. "'All Art is One'—August Werner, Master of All." *Scandinavian American*, vol. 1, no. 3 (March, 1945): 1–2.

Uhlman, Wes. "Part IV—Project Narrative," *Local Public Works Program Application Supplement.* October 13, 1976. Series no. 1611–01. Woodland Park Zoo African Savanna, Application, 1976. Folder 15. Box 3. [SMA].

Unpublished Material, Personal Communications and Web Content

Alloway, Charles R. *Our Country's Father.* Reprinted in a telephone cable from the *Tribune* newspaper (Chicago) to Lorado Taft. January 31, 1910. [LTP].

"African Savanna Cost Estimate," *Woodland Park Zoo—African Savanna*, June 30, 1977. Series no. 1611–01. Woodland Park Zoo African Savanna, Application, 1976. Folder 15. Box 3. [SMA].

"Agreement between Alonzo Victor Lewis and William Nielson," January 25, 1915. Folder 14. Box 2. [AVLP].

Ardery, C.W. Letter to L.A. Williams. April 13, 1926. Accession no. 0014–001. Steven Fowler Chadwick Papers. Folder 2. Box 5. [SC-UWL]

Ardery, C.W. Letter to S.F. Chadwick, April 14, 1926. Accession no. 0014–001. Steven Fowler Chadwick Papers. Folder 2. Box 5. [SC-UWL].

Backus, M.F. Letter to William H. Seward. December 14, 1906. Series no. 0106–001. Edmond S. Meany Papers. Folder 8. Box 6073. [SC-UWL].

Barry, Robert T. Letter to Menne Barry, July 10, 1923. MsSC 177. Accession no. 2004. 100.1.33. 1–4. [SC-WSHS].

Beeb and Gould Architects. "Plan of the Campus for the University of Washington; General Plan adopted by the Board of Regents, December, 1915." [Rev.] March, 1945.

Bestor, Dorothy. Interview with James and Margaret Fitzgerald. 27 October 1965. Archives of American Art. Smithsonian Institution website, URL: www.aaa.si.edu/collections/interviews/oral-history-interview-james-herbert-fitzgerald-and-margaret-tomkins-12432.

Blaine, E.L. Letter to R.V. Ankeny, December 1, 1929. Comptroller File no. 115105. Seattle City Clerk's Office. [SMA].

"Board of Regents of the University of Washington agreement with Architects and Engineers Howard & Galloway, to act as supervising architects for the Alaska Yukon Pacific Exposition, May 21, 1907." Regents records. Accession no. 05–039. Box 128. [SC-UWL].

Brown, Edwin J. Letter to Louis F. Hart. July 9, 1923. Governor's Papers, vol. 3. Folder Federal Dept., President—Louis F. Hart. Box Gov. Hart/2J-15. [WSA].

Brown, Edwin J. Letter to Louis F. Hart. July 19, 1923. Governor's Papers, vol. 3. Folder Federal Dept., President—Louis F. Hart. Box Gov. Hart/2J-15. [WSA].

Brown, Paul V. Letter to Mrs. Harlan H. Edwards. March 6, 1959. Series no. 1802–01. Comptroller File no. 236587. [SMA].

Buchanan, Charles M. Letter to Edmond S. Meany. January 9, 1906. Series 0106–001. Edmond S. Meany Papers. Folder 21. Box 21. [SC-UWL].

Burke, Thomas. Letter to Edmond S. Meany.

December 13, 1915. Series no. 0106–001. Edmond S. Meany Papers. Folder 43. Box 71. [SC-UWL].

Burke, Thomas. Letter to Edmund [*sic*] S. Meany. December 28, 1906. Series no. 0106–001. Edmond S. Meany Papers. Folder 9. Box 22. [SC-UWL].

Burkhalter, Nancy, and David Wilma. "Memorial Day in Washington State," May 24, 2007. HistoryLink.org website, URL: www.historylink.org/File/7777.

Capital Improvements Committee. Letter to Howard Burke. February 23, 1962. Folder Leif Erickson Statue 1962–1984. Box 517599708. [PSHF].

Carr, Alice Robertson. Letter to Mr. Beckworth. n.d. William Carr Collection.

"Chronology History of Woodland Park Zoo History, 1900–1929," Woodland Park Zoo website, URL: www.zoo.org/about/chronologicalhistory#1900–1929.

"Contract," June 28, 1978. Series no. 1611–01. Woodland Park Zoo African Savanna, Application, 1976. Folder 15. Box 3. [SMA].

Coffin, Anna A. Letter to the Chamber of Commerce, February 21, 1939. Series no 5801–01. Parks History Files. Folder 10. Box 49. [SMA].

Conklin, Jack. "Allen Newman and the Rhinebeck "Doughboy."" August 6, 2014. Wordpress.com website, URL: rhinebeck.wordpress.com/2014/08/06/the-story-behind-rhinebecks-favorite-statue-doughboy-by-jack-conklin/.

Conklin, Jack. Email to Fred Poyner IV. July 4, 2016.

Conover, C.T. Letter to Edmond S. Meany. March 29, 1930. Series no. 1016–001. Edmond S. Meany Papers. Folder 43. Box 71. [SC-UWL].

Durham, Robert L. Letter to Leif Erikson League, September 15, 1958. Series no. 1802–01. Comptroller File no. 235441. [SMA].

Ebner, Katherine. Email to Fred Poyner IV. April 12, 2016.

Edwards, Mrs. Harlan. Letter to Ewen Dingwall, September 9, 1958. Series no. 1802–01. Comptroller File no. 235441. [SMA].

Edwards, Mrs. Harlan. Letter to Robert Durham, September 9, 1958. Series no. 1802–01. Comptroller File no. 235441. [SMA].

"Elements of a Civic Memorial Center." n.d. Series no. 1650–02. Civic Memorial Center Collection. [SMA].

Elinor, Ingersoll Thorne. Letter to Dr. Henry Suzzallo. February 5, 1919. 1–2. [LTP].

Ely, Alice B. "My Personal Record," [John Carl Ely]. n.d. [HAGC].

Ettl, Alex J. Letter to Trygve Nakkerud. February 16, 1961. Accession no. 2923–1. August Werner Papers. Folder 46. Box 1. [SC-UWL].

Fiset, Louis. "World War I memorial is moved to Seattle's Evergreen-Washelli Cemetery on November 11, 1998." May 17, 2001. HistoryLik.org website, URL: www.historylink.org/File/3294.

FitzGerald, James. "Notebook—FitzGerald," n.d. Accession no. 2848–002. James FitzGerald and Margaret Tomkins Papers. Folder 1. Box 2. [SC-UWL].

FitzGerald, James. "Notebook-Loose Pages-1961." Accession no. 2848–002. James FitzGerald and Margaret Tomkins Papers. Folder Notebook-Loose Pages 1961. Box 2. [SC-UWL].

FitzGerald, James. Letter to Paule M. Anglim, January 21, 1963. Accession no. 2848–002. James FitzGerald and Margaret Tomkins Papers. Folder Correspondence-FitzGerald 1963. Box 1. [SC-UWL].

FitzGerald, Miro. Email to Fred Poyner IV, March 21, 2016.

FitzGerald, Miro. Email to Fred Poyner IV, March 28, 2016.

"For Your Information—History of Woodland Park Zoological Gardens." Series no. VF-0000. Vertical Files, 1883–2011. Folder 884. Box 3. [SMA].

Fuller, A.H. "Map of the Portion of the Campus, University of Washington, 1898" [Fuller Oval Plan]. University of Washington Special Collections website, URL: www.lib.washington.edu/specialcollections/collections/exhibits/site/images/uw15721.gif/view.

Gahringer, Ervin Raymond. *Diary of Ervin Raymond Gahringer—World War I, 91st Division, 347 Machine Gun Battalion, Company B.* (unpublished diary, 1918). Ervin R. Gahringer Papers. Accession no. 5399–001. Folder transcript. Box 1. [SC-UWL].

Giles, A.D. Letter to Ramona Little. February 3, 1931. Folder Correspondence-Werner-82.120.364ba-bz. Box 2. [AWP].

Gorman, Britni. Email to Fred Poyner IV. July 11, 2016.

Grant, Frances R. Letter to John Ely. October 7, 1924. [HAGC].

T. Grønning, Letter to Gordon Clinton, September 5, 1958. Series no. 1802–01. Comptroller File no. 235441. [SMA].

Guenther, Bruce. Oral history interview with Margaret Tomkins. 6 June 1984. Archives of American Art. Smithsonian Institution website, URL: www.aaa.si.edu/collections/interviews/oral-history-interview-margaret-tomkins-12308.

"Guide Map to Woodland Park—Showing Proposed Improvements July 1939." July 11, 1939. Series no. 8600–02. Woodland Park Zoo Brochures. Folder Maps. [SMA].

H.Q. 91st Div. A.E.F. "General Orders: No. 6." January 27, 1919. Ervin R. Gahringer Papers. Accession no. 5399–001. Folder correspondence and memorabilia. Box 1. [SC-UWL].

Haller, Theodore N. Letter to Edmond S. Meany. October 9, 1926. Series no. 0106–001. Edmond S. Meany Papers. Folder 43. Box 71. [SC-UWL].

Haller, Theodore N. Letter to Edmond S. Meany. November 30, 1926. Series no. 0106–001. Edmond S. Meany Papers. Folder 43. Box 71. [SC-UWL].

Haller, Theodore N. Letter to Mrs. E.S. Meany. November 29, 1926. Series no. 0106–001. Edmond S. Meany Papers. Folder 43. Box 71. [SC-UWL].

Halvorsen, A. Telegram to August Werner. November 5, 1929. Accession no. 2923–01. August Werner Papers. Folder 15. Box 1. [SC-UWL].

Harriman, Henry R. Letter to N.H. Harriman. December 21, 1906. Series no. 0106–001. Edmond S. Meany Papers. Folder 8. Box 6073. [SC-UWL].

Hart, Louis F. Letter to Edwin J. Brown. July 21, 1923. Governor's Papers, vol. 3. Folder Federal Dept., President—Louis F. Hart. Box Gov. Hart/2J-15. [WSA].

Hart, Louis F. Letter to President Warren G. Harding. February 16, 1922. Governor's Papers, vol. 3. Folder Federal Dept., President—Louis F. Hart. Box Gov. Hart/2J-15. [WSA].

Hart, Louis F. Telegram to President Warren G. Harding. May 14, 1923. Governor's Papers, vol. 3. Folder Federal Dept., President—Louis F. Hart. Box Gov. Hart/2J-15. [WSA].

Hassrick, Peter. Email to Fred Poyner IV. July 6, 2016.

Helland, Karen. Email to Fred Poyner IV. February 22, 2016.

Hennes, John. Email to Fred Poyner IV. April 21, 2016.

Henry, Mary T. Olaf Kvamme, rsch. "Frolich, Finn Haakon (1868–1947), Sculptor." November 20, 2008. HistoryLink.org website, URL: www.historylink.org/index.cfm?DisplayPage=output.cfm&file_id=8849.

Henry, Mary. Email to Fred Poyner IV. July 21, 2016.

Hocking, Lillian. Letter to "Sec'y of Elk Lodge No. 92," August 21, 1923. Folder 1, Biographical material. Box 1. [JAWP].

Holstein, Craig. Email to Fred Poyner IV. January 4, 2016.

Hornell, James. Letter to Jesse Brooks. December 5, 1977. Series no. 1611–01. Woodland Park Zoo African Savanna, Application, 1976. Folder 15. Box 3. [SMA].

Howard and Galloway. Letter to John W. Hartman. May 21, 1907. University of Washington Digital Collections website, URL: digitalcollections.lib.washington.edu/cdm/singleitem/collection/ptec/id/2510/rec/1. [SC-UWL].

"James FitzGerald, 1910–1973 (B. Seattle, Washington)," n.d. Accession no. 2848–002. James FitzGerald and Margaret Tomkins Papers. Folder Resumes and Artist Statements 1970. Box 2. [SC-UWL].

"JAMES H. FITZGERALD et al., Appellants, v. ROBERT HOPKINS et al., Respondents," No. 38535. The Supreme Court of Washington. March 30, 1967. Casetext.com website, URL: casetext.com/case/fitzgerald-v-hopkins.

Johnson, Michael Bruce. Email to Fred Poyner IV. February 11, 2016.

Johnson, Theo. Letter to the Board of Park Commissioners, June 12, 1939. Series no. 5801–01, Parks History Files. Folder 10. Box 49. [SMA].

Johnson, Theo. Letter to the Board of Park Commissioners, March 29, 1925. Series no. 5801–01, Parks History Files. Folder 10. Box 49. [SMA].

Kelly, Herbert E. Letter and Report to Phillip Tindall, January 4, 1932. Comptroller File no. 134181. Seattle City Clerk's Office. [SMA].

Kennedy, Thomas J.L. Letter to Philip Tindall, March 12, 1928. Comptroller File no. 115105. Seattle City Clerk's Office. [SMA].

Kerry, A.S. Letter to Mrs. Burke. December 8, 1925. Caroline McGilvra Burke Papers. Accession no. 4697–001. Box 2. [SC-UWL].

Kooiman, William. Letter to Olaf Kvamme. June 5, 2007. Nordic Heritage Museum Historical Journal Files. [SCA-NHM].

Laube, Frank J. Letter to Henry R. Berg. April

12, 1945. Comptroller File no. 183684. Seattle City Clerk's Office. [SMA].

Laubenthal, Laura. Email to Fred Poyner IV. July 11, 2016.

Lazier, Frank B. Letter to August Werner, December 24, 1947. Folder Correspondence-Werner-82.120.364la-lz. Box 2. [AWP].

Leif Erikson International Foundation. "We Came in His Wake." n.d. Leif Erikson International Foundation website, URL: www.leiferikson.org/2351names.htm.

Lewis, Alonzo Victor. *Abraham Lincoln* (unpublished manuscript). n.d. MsSC 96. Manuscript Collection. Special Collections. Museum of Northwest Art and Culture, Spokane, Washington.

Lewis, Alonzo Victor. Letter to Bess Lewis. December 7, 1915. Folder 28. Box 1. [AVLP].

Lewis, Alonzo Victor. Letter to Edmond S. Meany. April 26, 1915. Series no. 0106–001. Edmond S. Meany Papers, 1877–1935. Folder 18. Box 30. [SC-UWL].

Lewis, Alonzo Victor. Letter to Wm. F. Geiger. February 9, 1917. Folder 14. Box 2. [AVLP].

Lewis, Lena. Letter to Warren Lewis, September 1, 19[?]. Folder 26. Box 1. [AVLP].

Lewis, Warren. Letter to Alonzo Victor Lewis. December 7, 1913. Folder 24. Box 1. [AVLP].

Lewis, Warren. Letter to Alonzo Victor Lewis. May 6, 1916. Folder 22. Box 1. [AVLP].

Lindane, Albeu. Letter to August Werner. February 24, 1929. Accession no. 2923–01. August Werner Papers. Folder 15. Box 1. [SC-UWL].

Locke, John. Phone communication to Fred Poyner IV. February 10, 2015.

Lopez, Lupita. Email to Fred Poyner IV. January 21, 2016.

Lowman, J.D. Telegram to Mrs. Thomas Burke. December 5, 1925. Accession no. 4697–001. Caroline McGilvra Burke Papers. Box 2. [SC-UWL]

Martin, David. "Martin-Zambito Fine Art: Gallery Artists." 2014. Martin-Zambito Gallery website, URL: www.martin-zambito.com/gallery.

McCreery, J.H. Letter to Mrs. Thomas Burke. April 16, 1926. Accession no. 4697–001. Caroline McGilvra Burke Papers. Box 2. [SC-UWL].

McCreery, J.H. Letter to Mrs. Thomas Burke. June 2, 1927. Accession no. 4697–001. Caroline McGilvra Burke Papers. Box 2. [SC-UWL].

Meany, Edmond S. Letter to James A. Wehn. April 4, 1915. Folder 11B Meany Corr. & Memorabilia. Box 1. [JAWP].

Meany, Edmond S. Letter to Lorado Taft. April 11, 1905. 1–2. [LTP].

Meany, Edmond S. Letter to Mrs. Thomas Burke. December 5, 1925. Accession no. 4697–001. Caroline McGilvra Burke Papers. Box 2. [SC-UWL].

"Memorandum of Agreement Regarding Leif Eriksson Statue and Memorial Wall," October 20, 2006. Port of Seattle. electronic communication to Fred Poyner IV. March 29, 2016. MOA signed.pdf. Port of Seattle_15–475.

"Memorial Exhibit," *John Carl Ely, 1897–1929* (exhibition guide). April, 1930. [HAGC].

Merrick, Frank L. Letter to Edmond S. Meany. September 14, 1906. Series no. 0106–001. Edmond S. Meany Papers. Folder 2. Box 22. [SC-UWL].

Monticello Steamship Company Ledger. 1916–1927. Ms 129. California State Railroad Museum Library.

Mrs. Evans. Letter to Alonzo Victor Lewis. November 1, 1909. Folder 2. Box 1. [AVLP].

Nakkerud, Trygve. Postcard to August Werner. May 3, 1963. Accession no. 2923–01. August Werner papers. Folder 46. Box 1. [SC-UWL].

Nakkerud, Trygve. "Trygve Nakkerud Interview" to Leif Eie. 1986. Catalog no. 1997.176.103. Leif Eie Oral History Collection. [SC-NHM].

Newman, Thomas. "Allen George Newman, A.N.A., 1875–1940" (lecture notes). 1995. 1–8. Jack Conklin Collection.

"1908 Ledger." Roman Bronze Works Archive, Amon Carter Museum of American Art. Fort Worth, TX.

"1909 Ledger." Roman Bronze Works Archive, Amon Carter Museum of American Art. Fort Worth, TX.

"1915 Ledger." Roman Bronze Works Archive, Amon Carter Museum of American Art. Fort Worth, TX.

"1928–1930 Ledger," Roman Bronze Works Archive, Amon Carter Museum of American Art. Fort Worth, TX.

"Number of Cause 247743," [plaintiff: Lewis, Alonzo]. *General Index—Plaintiff, 1931–34*, vol. L-R. Microfiche roll no. 23. King County Court Records. Microfiche Collection. Superior Court, King County. Seattle, Washington. November 12, 1931.

Olmsted Brothers. *Original Report of Olmsted Brothers.* 1903. Series no. VF-0000. Vertical Files, 1883–2011. Folder 100, Box 1. [SMA].

Olmsted Brothers. "Ground plan, Alaska-Yukon-Pacific Exposition, Seattle, 1909" (map). 1909. G4284.S4:2A42 1909.O4. Pacific Northwest Collection. [SC-UWL].

Olmsted Brothers. "Olmsted Brothers' campus plan, University of Washington, 1904." 1904. University of Washington Subject Files, 1904. PH Coll. 700. [SC-UWL].

Olmsted, John C.. "Preliminary Plan for the Alaska-Yukon-Pacific Exposition of Seattle, Wash., 1909" (map). November 5, 1906.

Olmsted, John C. Letter to J.W. Thompson. November 1, 1918. [SMA].

Opheim, J. Eldon. Letter to George E. Fahey, November 23, 1960. Folder History of Shilshole Marina, 1960–1961. Box 517599707. [PSHF].

Ott, Jennifer. "Regents of the University of Washington approve John C. Olmsted's plan for the Alaska-Yukon-Pacific Exposition on May 17, 1907." February 26, 2009. HistoryLink.org website, URL: www.historylink.org/File/8939.

Pacific Department, Sanborn Map Co. "Insurance Survey of Alaska-Yukon-Pacific Exposition." March, 1909. San Francisco: Sanborn Map Co., 1909.

Plummer, David E. *Table 1. Catalogue of John Carl Ely's Artwork as of 31 March 1994.* March 19, 1994. [HAGC].

Plummer, David F. Email to Fred Poyner IV. February 25, 2013.

Plummer, David F. Email to Fred Poyner IV. January 14, 2016.

Plummer, David F. Email to Fred Poyner IV. April 7, 2016.

Pool, Martin. "Jefferson Park Golf Course, Seattle, WA." February 2015. Washington State Golf Association website, URL: thewsga.org/jefferson-park-golf-course-a-centennial-celebration/.

Port of Seattle. Electronic communication to Fred Poyner IV. Draft Agreement with LEIF 7–15–05.pdf. Port of Seattle_15–475. April 25, 2016. Port of Seattle Archives, Seattle, WA.

"Progress Report—Issue no. 78." May 18, 1940. Accession No. 02-A-469. Washington State Department of Transportation History Files, 1905–2000. [WSA].

Purdy, W. Frank. Letter to James A. Wehn. October 3, 1922. Folder 4. Box 2. [JAWP].

Remington, Frederick. *A First-Class Fighting Man* (drawing). 1899. No. 02412. Frederic Remington Catalogue Raisonné. 2014–2016. Buffalo Bill Center of the West website, URL: remington.centerofthewest.org/.

Reynolds, Clara P., et al. Letter to Phillip Tindall. January 4, 1932. Comptroller File no. 134181. Seattle City Clerk's Office. [SMA].

Resch, John. Letter to the Board of Park Commissioners. September 8, 1942. Series no. 5801–01, Park History Files—Veterans Area, Artillery. Folder 18. Box 49. [SMA].

Rochester, Junius. "Prefontaine, Francis Xavier (1838–1909)." December 2, 1998. HistoryLink.org website, URL: www.historylink.org/index.cfm?DisplayPage=output.cfm&file_id=3633.

Rochester, Junius. "Burke, Judge Thomas (1849–1925)." January 30, 1999. HistoryLink.org website, URL: www.historylink.org/index.cfm?DisplayPage=output.cfm&file_id=2610.

Rolfe, Lionel. "Notes of a Californian Bohemian—Jack London May have Slept Here." n.d. [2001]. URL: www.dabelly.com/columns/bohemian43.htm.

Roman Bronze Works, Inc. Letter to Alonzo Victor Lewis. September 17, 1918. Folder 7. Box 2. [AVLP].

Roman Bronze Works, Inc. Letter to Alonzo Victor Lewis. October 16, 1922. Series no. GA1959.94. Folder 22. Box 2. [AVLP].

Seattle City Council. "Re. Acceptance of Statue 'Doughboy.'" March 19, 1928. Resolution no. 9529. [SMA].

Seattle Fine Arts Gallery. "Memorial Exhibit" program. April, 1930. [HAGC].

Sherwood, Don. "GAR Cemetery." Sherwood Park History files. 1972–1977. Seattle Parks and Recreation website, URL: clerk.seattle.gov/~F_archives/sherwood/GAR.pdf.

Sherwood, Don. "Jefferson Park (Golf)." Sherwood Park History files. 1972–1977. Seattle Parks and Recreation website, URL: clerk.seattle.gov/~F_archives/sherwood/JeffersonPkGolf.pdf.

Sherwood, Don. "Prefontaine Place." Sherwood Park History files. 1972–1977. Seattle Parks and Recreation website. URL: www.seattle.gov/parks/history/PrefontainePl.pdf.

Sherwood, Don. "Volunteer Park." 1972–1977. Sherwood Park History files. Seattle Parks and Recreation website. URL: clerk.seattle.gov/~F_archives/sherwood/VolunteerPk.pdf.

Sherwood, Don. "Woodland Park." 1972–1977. Sherwood Park History files. Seattle Parks and Recreation website, URL: www.seattle.gov/parks/history/WoodlandPk.pdf).

Sizer, H.L. Letter to Edmond S. Meany. October 12, 1906. Series no. 0106–001. Edmond S. Meany Papers. Folder 4. Box 22. [SC-UWL].

Smith, C. Mark. Letter to Mike Wheeler. July 21, 1977. Series no. 1611–01. Woodland Park Zoo African Savanna, Application, 1976. Folder 15. Box 3. [SMA].

Skolnik, Arthur. Letter to City of Seattle, October 1, 1976. Series no. 1611–01. Woodland Park Zoo African Savanna Application, 1976. Folder 15. Box 3. [SMA].

Stein, Alan. Email to Fred Poyner IV, with map file: aypmap.jpg. Alaska-Yukon-Pacific Exposition 1909, Plan of Grounds and Buildings. August 14, 2016.

Stone Mountain Memorial Association. "Historical Overview." Stone Mountain Memorial Association website, URL: stonemountainpark.org/text/quarry4resources.001.pdf accessed: January 13, 2015.

Taft, Lorado. Letter to Edmond S. Meany. April 9, 1906. 1201020_008_George-Washington_Edmund-Meany-letter_Apr-9-1906.pdf. Found in RS 12/1/20. Allen S. Weller Papers. Series no. 12/1/20. Folder George Washington, Box 8. University of Illinois Archives. Urbana-Champaign. Illinois.

Taft, Lorado. Letter to R.W. Lahr. October 1, 1935. 1201020_049_Transcriptions-from-Lorados-letters_Washington-Statue_1935.pdf. Found in RS 12/1/20. Allen S. Weller Papers. Series no. 12/1/20. Folder Transcriptions from Lorado's Letters re: Washington Statue, ca. 1935, Box 49. University of Illinois Archives. Urbana-Champaign. Illinois.

Thiry, Paul. *Century 21 Exposition (Seattle, Wash.), proposed site plan* [architectural drawing]. Seattle: Century 21 Exposition, Inc., 1959. UW Libraries' Digital Collections website, URL: digitalcollections.lib.washington.edu/cdm/singleitem/collection/ac/id/1284/rec/40.[SC-UWL].

Thompson, Hans A. Letter to Alf Collins. October 20, 1971. Department of Parks and Recreation, Parks Superintendent Subject Files, 1936–1993. Series no. 5802–01. Folder 7. Box 21. [SMA].

Tomkins, Margaret. "James FitzGerald," August 24, 1978. Accession no. 2848–002. James FitzGerald and Margaret Tomkins Papers. Folder Correspondence 1967–1978. Box 1. [SC-UWL].

Tomkins, Margaret. Letter to Jo Nilsson. August 25, 1977. Accession no. 2848–002. James FitzGerald and Margaret Tomkins Papers. Folder Correspondence 1967–1978. Box 1. [SC-UWL].

Thomson, David. Letter to August Werner. July 2, 1931. Folder Correspondence-82.120.364ta-tz. Box 2. [AWP].

Towne, David. Phone communication to Fred Poyner IV. February 12, 2016.

Umlauff, Jacob. Letter to Board of Park Commissioners. May 10, 1939. Series no 5801–01. Parks History Files. Folder 10. Box 49. [SMA].

Ward (nee Carr), Nina. Email to Fred Poyner IV. February 26, 2016.

Ward (nee Carr), Nina. Email to Fred Poyner IV. February 27, 2016.

Ward (nee Carr), Nina. Email to Fred Poyner IV. March 31, 2016.

Washington State Department of Enterprise Services, "Winged Victory Monument," n.d. Washington State Department of Enterprise Services website, URL: www.des.wa.gov/services/facilities/CapitolCampus/MemorialsArt/Pages/Victory.aspx.

Wehn, James A. *History of the Chief Seattle Statue* (unpublished manuscript). 1962. Folder 5 Chief Seattle Statue History. Box 1. [JAWP].

Wehn, James A. Dedication for the Chief Seattle Fountain. November 13, 1912. Folder 5 Chief Seattle Statue History. Box 1. [JAWP].

Wehn, James A. Handwritten note authorizing access for John Carl Ely. April 8, 1920. Folder 6B UW Corr. Box 1. [JAWP].

Wehn, James A. Letter to Mr. and Mrs. John Ely. August 8, 1929. Folder 4. Box 2. [JAWP].

Wentworth, Michael J. Letter to David F. Plummer. March 14, 1973. [HAGC].

Werner, August. Letter to Christian Olsen. n.d. Folder Correspondence—82.120.364ja-jz. Box 2. [AWP].

Werner, August. Letter to "De Ridder." n.d. [1934]. Folder Correspondence-82.120.364a-z. Box 2. [AWP].

Werner, August. "For Leif Erikson Tale." n.d. [ca. 1960]. Folder Leif Erikson Notes-82.120.467y. Box 13. [AWP].

Werner, August. "On Sailing." n.d. Folder Leif Erikson Notes-82.120.467y. Box 13. [AWP].

Wilma, David, and Catherine Hinchliff. "Jefferson Park Municipal Golf Course (Seattle)." February 24, 2001. Historylink.org website, URL: www.historylink.org/File/3015.

Woods, Ralph. Letter to Alonzo Victor Lewis. March 3, 1917. Folder 26. Box 2. [AVLP].

"W.P.A. Washington Art Project—Self Portraits through the Ages—Current Exhibition." April 1941. James FitzGerald and Margaret Tomkins Papers. Accession no. 2848–002. Folder WPA WA Art Project, Spokane Art Center, 1941, box 1.

"W.P.A. Shows the Way to Work and Security," (poster). 1939. No. 2011.0.186. Washington State Historical Society Collection Catalog website, URL: collections.washingtonhistory.org/details.aspx?id=44334.

Wyckoff, Walter L. Letter to Frank J. Laube.

February 1, 1945. Comptroller File no. 183684. Seattle City Clerk's Office. [SMA].

Yandell, C.B. Letter to Committee on Seward Monument. November 13, 1906. Series no. 0106–001. Edmond S. Meany Papers. Folder 5. Box 22. [SC-UWL].

Yandell, C.B. Letter to Committee on Seward Monument. November 22, 1906. Series no. 0106–001. Edmond S. Meany Papers. Folder 6. Box 22. [SC-UWL].

Index